PATERNOSTER THEOLOGICAL MONOGRAPHS

Pedagogy as Theological Praxis

Martin Luther and Herman Bavinck as Sources for Engagement with Classical Education and the Liberal Arts Tradition

PATERNOSTER THEOLOGICAL MONOGRAPHS

Pedagogy as Theological Praxis

Martin Luther and Herman Bavinck as Sources for Engagement with Classical Education and the Liberal Arts Tradition

Timothy Shaun Price

Copyright © Timothy Shaun Price 2018

First Published 2018 by Paternoster

Paternoster is an imprint of Authentic Media
PO Box 6326, Bletchley, Milton Keynes MK1 9GG

authenticmedia.co.uk

The right of Timothy Shaun Price to be identified as the author of this Work has been asserted by him in accordance with the Copyright, Designs
and Patents Act 1988.

All rights reserved. No part of this publication man be reproduced, stored in a retrieval system, or transmitted, in any form or by any means, electronic, mechanical, photocopying, recording, or otherwise, without the prior permission of the publisher of a license permitting restricted copying. In the UK such licenses are issued by the Copyright Licensing Agency, Barnards Inn, 86 Fetter Ln, London EC4A 1EN

British Library Cataloguing in Publication Data
A catalogue record for this book is available from the British Library

ISBN 978-1-78893-0604

Printed and bound Lighting Source

PATERNOSTER THEOLOGICAL MONOGRAPHS

Series Preface

In the west the churches may be declining, but theology—serious, academic (mostly doctoral level) and mainstream orthodox in evaluative commitment—shows no sign of withering on the vine. This series of *Paternoster Theological Monographs* extends the expertise of the Press especially to first-time authors whose work stands broadly with the parameters created by fidelity to Scripture and has satisfied the critical scrutiny of respected assessors in the academy. Such theology may come in several distinct intellectual disciplines—Historical, dogmatic, pastoral, apologetic, missional, aesthetic and no doubt others also. The series will be particularly hospitable to promising constructive theology within an evangelical frame, for it is of this that the church's need seems to be greatest. Quality writing will be published across the confessions—Anabaptist, Episcopalian, Reformed, Arminian, and Orthodox—across the ages—patristic, medieval, reformation, modern, and counter-modern—and across the continents. The aim of the series is theology written in the twofold conviction that the church needs theology and theology needs the church—which in reality means theology done for the glory of God.

Series Editors

Trevor A. Hart, Head of School and Principal of St Mary's College School of Divinity, University of St Andrews, Scotland, UK

Anthony N.S. Lane, Professor of Historical Theology and Director of Research, London School of Theology, UK

Anthony C. Thiselton, Emeritus Professor of Christian Theology, University of Nottingham, Research Professor in Christian Theology, University College Chester; and Canon Theologian of Leicester Cathedral and Southwell Minister, UK

Kevin J. Vanhoozer, Research Professor of Systematic Theology, Trinity Evangelical Divinity School, Deerfield, Illinois, USA

Pedagogy as Theological Praxis

"The study of antiquity is therefore not only of formal and practical value: for the development of thinking, understanding Greek and Latin terms in our scholarship, understanding citations and allusions in our literature, and so forth. Its lasting value also lies in the fact that the foundations of modern culture were laid in antiquity. The roots of all our arts and learning—and also, though in a lesser degree, the sciences that study nature—are to be found in the soil of antiquity."

Herman Bavinck, in "Classical Education"

"And let us be sure of this: we will not long preserve the gospel without the languages. The languages are the sheath in which this sword of the Spirit is contained; they are the casket in which this jewel is enshrined; they are the vessel in which this wine is held; they are the larder in which this food is stored; and, as the gospel itself points out, they are the baskets in which are kept these loaves and fishes and fragments."

Martin Luther, in
"To the Councilmen of All Cities in Germany that they Establish and Maintain Christian Schools"

Contents

Series Preface	v
Contents	vii
Abbreviations	x
Acknowledgements	xi
Summary of Salient Points	xiii
Introduction	1
Setting the Context	4
The Trivium	7
The Quadrivium	10
Liberal Arts Education and the Western Tradition	11
Truth, Goodness and Beauty in Classical Education	17
Chapter Outline	21
1. The Three Estates as a Hermeneutical Lens for Luther's Work	25
Oswald Bayer on the Three Estates	26
Ecclesia	33
Ecclesia in Greek Culture and New Testament Koine Usage	34
Orders of Creation and Orders of Preservation	37
Oeconomia	41
Oeconomia and *Oikonomia*	42
The Roots of *Oeconomia*: Οἰκονομία in the New Testament	44
Oeconomia and Aristotle	49
Oeconomia, Aristotle, and Luther's "Exposition of Psalm 127"	53
Politia	62
Johannes Heckel and *Politia*	65
Eschatology and *Politia*	68
The Three Estates and Luther's Theology	70

2. The Three Estates and Luther's "To the Councilmen of All Cities in Germany that they Establish and Maintain Christian Schools" — 73

    Introduction to "To the Councilmen" and Medieval German Education — 73

        The Educational Problem as Both Spiritual and Temporal — 76

    Education as Present in All Three Estates — 80

        The Role of the Parent in Education — 81

        Politia, Education, and the Two Kingdoms — 83

        The Estates and *On Secular Authority* — 90

    The Languages in Classical Education — 94

        Luther's Translation Work and the Original Biblical Languages — 98

    The Role of Education in Society — 100

        Practicality and Education — 103

        Aristotle and Good versus Bad Books — 104

    The Results of Luther's Reforms — 106

    Relevant Application of Luther's Education Model and the Three Estates — 109

3. Herman Bavinck, Neo-Calvinism, and Reformed Theology — 115

    Lutheran Theology and Neo-Calvinism — 115

    Distinctive Aspects of Dutch Neo-Calvinist Theology — 118

        Common Grace — 119

        The Inspiration of Scripture and the "Organic" — 121

        Creation, Culture, Learning, and the Reformed Tradition — 126

            Stewardship and Creation — 132

            The Doctrine of Sin and Creation — 133

        Sphere Sovereignty — 137

        Providence — 142

    Herman Bavinck within the Scope of Reformed Theology — 144

    Bavinck's Distinctive Theological Positions in Regards to Education — 147

4. Herman Bavinck, Neo-Calvinism, and Education — 149

    Herman Bavinck in Context — 151

        The Historical Setting of the Netherlands in the 19th Century — 154

    Bavinck's Work on Education — 158

Trends in Pedagogy	160
"Classical Education"	161
Bavinck's Views of Classical Education	167
Pedagogical Principles	171
Pedagogy and Neo-Calvinism	174
Classical Education in *Pedagogical Principles*	178
A Model of Education for Bavinck	180
Conclusion: Luther, Bavinck, and Liberal Arts in Practice	183
Classical Education and the Reformed Tradition	184
Contemporary Lutheranism and Classical Education	195
Lutheran Classical Education and the Three Estates	201
Moving Forward: What Can be Learned from this Analysis	205
References	211

Abbreviations

LW — Luther, Martin. *Luther's Works.* American Edition. 55 vols. Edited by Jaroslav Pelikan and Helmut T. Lehman. Philadelphia: Muehlenberg and Fortress, and St. Louis: Concordia, 1955–86.

RD — Bavinck, Herman. *Reformed Dogmatics.* 4 vols. Edited by John Bolt and translated by John Vriend. Grand Rapids: Baker, 2003–2008.

WA — Luther, Martin. *D. Martin Luthers Werke: Kritische Gesammtausgabe.* (The Weimar Edition) Weimar: Hermann Böhlau. Later volumes published by H. Böhlaus Nachfolger 121 vols., 1883-2009.

Acknowledgements

I am thankful for my wife, Joy, who freely chose to follow me to Scotland three years ago and I am glad to enjoy this adventure of life with her. She is truly one of Job's daughters (Job 42:15).

Summary of Salient Points

Introduction: The introduction sets the context for what will be discussed in this thesis. In particular, it introduces the reader to the liberal arts tradition, and in particular the trivium and quadrivium. The introduction also relates the popularity of the liberal arts tradition in the West, and how it has been of interest to many theological minds. The reader is also introduced to the primary two interlocutors of this thesis: Martin Luther and Herman Bavinck.

Chapter 1. The Three Estates as a Hermeneutical Lens for Luther's Work: This chapter serves to provide the reader with a foundational understanding of Martin Luther's use of the three estates of *ecclesia*, *oeconomia*, and *politia*. Particular attention is given to the historical and biblical development of these concepts. This chapter also provides an exegesis of Luther's "Exposition of Psalm 127" and its relation to the estates. The chapter closes by demonstrating how the estates fit into the larger picture of Luther's theology.

Chapter 2. The Three Estates and Luther's "To the Councilmen of All Cities in Germany that they Establish and Maintain Christian Schools": This chapter serves to apply the concepts of Luther's three estates specifically to one of his works. Emphasis in this chapter is placed upon examining what in particular Luther thought would aid in the development of a Christian liberal arts education as well as particularities of what is involved in the development of a Lutheran concept of education when referring to Luther.

Chapter 3. Herman Bavinck, Neo-Calvinism, and Reformed Theology: This chapter introduces the reader to Herman Bavinck's thought within the neo-Calvinist tradition. Contrast also begins to be made between the thought of the neo-Calvinist tradition and the Lutheran tradition. While this chapter serves to provide an overview of Dutch neo-Calvinism, it also focuses on what is distinct in the thought of Bavinck and begins to consider application of his thought to pedagogy.

Chapter 4. Herman Bavinck, Neo-Calvinism, and Education: This chapter begins by introducing the reader to the context in which Bavinck is writing, and then builds upon the foundation set in chapter three by examining Bavinck's "Classical Education" and *Pedagogical Principles*. This chapter endeavors to point towards some of the distinct contributions of neo-Calvinism in regards to pedagogy, and also how this tradition relates to classical education.

Conclusion: The conclusion culminates the thesis by providing interaction with the Lutheran and neo-Calvinist tradition in regards to Christian classical education. Practical application is placed upon the North American context, where Christian classical education is comparatively popular. The conclusion ends by considering the relevance of the material discussed throughout the thesis.

Introduction

The Western tradition has long struggled with the question of how to provide an education for one's young in such a way that they will be prepared to face what challenges may lie ahead in the world. This desire to educate begins in the home with the simple training and teaching of children. For most humans throughout history, the task of survival prevented education going much further beyond this. When further educational opportunities were available, this education was often done to train for a future vocation. For those who have had the leisure, further reflection about how one should be educated has often been a topic of intense discussion. These voices have arisen from the ranks of both secular and religious thinkers.

Historically, the church has had much to say about what role education should play in the life of the follower of Jesus. There has been endless debate concerning how educated one should be, and what resources one should study. Should one follow the example of the former fishermen become disciples of Galilee who proclaimed Jesus' name boldly,[1] or that of Paul, who most likely spent three years in study after his conversion to Christianity prior to his missionary journeys?[2] The question of education certainly underlies some of what is happening in the New Testament canon. In addition, formal education is closely related to the ability to read, and estimates of literacy rates among contemporaries of the New Testament writers varies greatly, but it is usually thought to be in the 10–15% range.[3] Karl Sandnes argues that most likely these rates were even higher among the developing Christian community because

---

[1] Cf. Acts 4:31. All biblical citations will be taken from the English Standard Version unless otherwise noted.
[2] Cf. Gal. 1: 17–18: "nor did I go up to Jerusalem to those who were apostles before me, but I went away into Arabia, and returned again to Damascus. Then after three years I went up to Jerusalem to visit Cephas and remained with him fifteen days." Although the text does not clearly state what Paul was doing during those three years in Arabia (which is also not a particularly definite location), the Christian tradition has long held that this was most likely a time of solitary reflection and study prior to his public ministry. See for example, Richard N. Longenecker, *Galatians,* Word Biblical Commentary, vol. 41 (Dallas: Word Books, 1990), 34, and Herman N. Ridderbos, *The Epistle of Paul to the Churches of Galatia,* The New International Commentary on the New Testament (Grand Rapids: Eerdmans, 1953), 65.
[3] Karl Sandnes, *The Challenge of Homer: School, Pagan Poets, and Early Christianity* (London: T&T Clark, 2009), 5.

they were a people so closely tied together as a textual community.[4] Sandnes further writes, "Although school and education are not directly mentioned in the New Testament, they are clearly assumed as something with which Christians are familiar. Greek education formed a significant part of the world the Christians had to make decisions about. It is therefore not anachronistic to assume the presence of a debate among the first Christians, although the issue is made explicit only later."[5]

The explicit case to which Sandnes refers is most clearly seen in the difference between Clement of Alexandria and Tertullian. The classic case of the church coming to different positions on what role education should play in the Christian's life comes from the positions of Clement of Alexandria (c. 150–c. 215) in favor of the use of philosophy in Christian theology, and Tertullian (c. 160–c. 225) on the other side who argued for a stronger divide between Christian theology and secular philosophy.

Clement, especially in his eight volume work *Stromata*, argues that philosophy was originally given to the Greeks in order to prepare them for the coming of Christ just as he gave the law of Moses to the Jews for the same purpose. In this process Clement is also careful not to award philosophy the same status as divine revelation.[6] Clement argues that because all truth flows from God: "philosophy too is in some manner a work of divine providence,"[7] and "Truth is one."[8] He further writes, "Everything is illuminated when the true light rises. So all who stretched out towards the truth, Greeks and non-Greeks alike, could be shown to possess some portion of the Word of Truth—some a considerable part, others a fraction, as it falls out."[9] Thus it is clear in Clement's opinion that philosophy, or secular knowledge has a valid place in being used in the Christian faith.

On the opposite end of the spectrum, Clement's contemporary Tertullian argued that secular philosophy had very little to do with the Christian faith. His most famous quote is perhaps, "What has Athens to do with Jerusalem?"[10]

---

[4] Ibid., 6.
[5] Ibid., 9.
[6] Alister McGrath, ed. *The Christian Theology Reader*, 3rd ed. (Oxford: Blackwell, 2007), 4.
[7] Clement of Alexandria, *Stromateis: Books One to Three*, trans. John Ferguson (Washington, D.C.: The Catholic University of America Press, 1991), 35.
[8] Ibid., 64.
[9] Clement, *Stromateis: Books One to Three*, 64.
[10] Tertullian, *De Prascriptione Haereticorum Ad Martyras: Ad Scapulam*, ed. T. Herbert Bindley (Oxford: Clarendon Press, 1893), 40–41. The contextual quotation reads in Latin: "*Quid ergo Athenis et Hierosolymis? Quid academiae et ecclesiae? Quid haereticis et Christianis?*" This reads literally, "What has Athens to do with Jerusalem?

Introduction

Tertullian's worry was that philosophy was pagan in its outlook, and therefore would only lead to heresy in the church.[11] It should not be assumed that Tertullian's dismissal of philosophy was a result of his unfamiliarity with the secular Roman and Greek authors. While discussing Tertullian's familiarity with pagan literature Barnes writes:

> Lactantius realized that Tertullian was skilled in every literary genre. And among the genres philosophy occupied no trivial place. Interest or curiosity alone would have led Tertullian to philosophical books, just as it led him to acquire some knowledge of medicine. But he had a strong motive to investigate the subject deeply. The Gnostics attempted a fusion of Greek philosophy and Christian theology. If Tertullian wished to refute them on their own ground, he must show that their comprehension of philosophy was perverse or deficient.[12]

Neither was Tertullian's dismissal of the use of secular philosophy in theology a result of a lack of familiarity with these sources. Despite this knowledge of secular philosophy, Tertullian's opposition to it remained.

Yet despite their differences in the application of secular philosophy, both Clement and Tertullian saw the benefit of learning from secular philosophy and writings. Tertullian certainly would have nothing to do with the later attempts of Origen or those of his contemporary Clement to find reconciliation between pagan philosophy and Christian theology. Tertullian rejected a "Stoic, Platonic or dialectical Christianity."[13] In a wider sense, he was eventually able to reconcile Christianity and classical culture. This was done by taking the benefits of the traditional education structure and using his education to defend and dispense to others the truth of Christianity.[14] For Clement, this benefit was an embracing and application of the truth found in such texts in order to better understand the revelation God has revealed through Scripture. For Tertullian, an education in secular philosophy enables him to better see error when heretics attempt to apply such philosophy incorrectly to the Christian faith.

From this brief review of early Christian thought on the role of education in the Christian faith, one is able to gather that although there have been divergent views concerning the application of knowledge, the lack of knowledge or wisdom has not been considered a Christian virtue. One is also able to surmise from the opinions of Clement and Tertullian that many of the best minds in

---

What the university and the church? What between heretics and Christians?" (author's translation)
[11] McGrath, *The Christian Theology Reader*, 6.
[12] Timothy David Barnes, *Tertullian: A Historical and Literary Study* (Oxford: Clarendon Press, 1971), 205.
[13] Barnes, *Tertullian: A Historical and Literary Study*, 210.
[14] Ibid.

Christian theology have wrestled with questions of education and pedagogy. This thesis will set about the task of interacting with two of those minds, Martin Luther and Herman Bavinck. Prior to directly engaging Luther and Bavinck, I will begin by framing the context in which this discussion will take place. In particular, this thesis will focus upon the classical education tradition. Just as there has been more than one voice in the Christian tradition in regards to the relation of Christianity and culture, so too there have been many voices in regards to how the education of a child should be structured. The context that will be discussed in the next section regards introducing the reader to the classical tradition that will be referred to throughout this thesis.

Setting the Context

A form of education referred to as classical education has a long-standing tradition. As will be discovered moving forward, this tradition has seen a renaissance in contemporary pedagogical circles, and particularly in Christian pedagogy. If this renaissance continues and classical education is an appropriate way to education children, several questions must be asked. Why has there has been an impulse to return to classical education amongst many contemporary Christian pedagogues? Also, what does the Christian tradition have to offer pedagogical practice, and in particular to the practice of classical education? This thesis will not provide a broad history of Western education, but will investigate one particular model that had become dominant by the medieval era commonly referred to as classical education.[15] This model involved education in the Trivium, or the three roads/paths, in which one learned grammar, dialectic, and rhetoric. After the Trivium one progressed to the quadrivium, or the four roads/paths, in which one learned geometry, astronomy, arithimetic and astronomy. One would usually focus on a particular area of interest in the quadrivium most suited to the chosen career choice.

Though the classical education model has a long-standing history, the application of this model faded in the twentieth century in favor of other forms of pedagogy, primarily seen in the form of pragmatism.[16] In the past twenty years there has been a resurgence, particularly in the North American context, of curriculum identifying itself with classical education both at the grade school

---

[15] For a history of European education up to and including the Middle Ages see David L. Wagner, ed. *The Seven Liberal Arts in the Middle Ages* (Bloomington: Indiana University Press, 1983), 1–24; Paul Abelson, *The Seven Liberal Arts, A Study in Medieval Culture* (New York: Russell & Russell, 1965); James Bowen, *A History of Western Education* Vols. 1–3 (London: Methuen & Co., 1972).

[16] John R. Schook and Joseph Margolis, eds. *A Companion to Pragmatism* (Oxford: Blackwell, 2006); George Allen, *Higher Education in the Making: Pragmatism, Whitehead, and the Canon* (Albany: State University of New York, 2004); John P. Murphy, *Pragmatism from Peirce to Davidson* (Boulder: Westview Press, 1990).

and undergraduate university level. The majority of the schools that identify themselves with the classical model also identify themselves with some expression of Christianity. There is no necessary correlation between classical education and Christianity other than its use in Christendom, so it is worth exploring why many contemporary Christians have viewed this form of pedagogy as an appropriate way to educate their young.

Before dealing specifically with Luther and Bavinck, it would be helpful to begin by outlining the main features of the classical education tradition. Because the classical education tradition is a point of commonality and comparison, it will be referred to throughout this thesis. Thus, beginning by explaining classical education and its revival will aid in understanding what it has to offer Christian pedagogy.

For the modern reader, one of the best textbooks on classical education is *The Trivium* by Sister Miriam Joseph originally published in 1937.[17] In this book Joseph sets about to provide a definition of the liberal arts, and how their formulation sets forth a proper education of a child. As far as her background, Sister Joseph was a member of the Sisters of the Holy Cross. She completed her doctoral degree at Columbia University and taught English at Saint Mary's College from 1931–1960. This section will proceed by providing definitions and interaction with the trivium, quadrivium, liberal arts, and classical education.

Sister Joseph's book, *The Trivium*, served as the basis for the core curriculum at Saint Mary's College. In this book she outlines the medieval formulation of the liberal arts as divided into the trivium and the quadrivium. These form the seven branches of the liberal arts. It is referred to as "classical" education because the concept of this type of education harkens back to the ancients. By the time Luther was receiving his foundational education, this formulation would have already been a standard form of pedagogy. Joseph provides a succinct definition of the trivium and quadrivium:

> The trivium include those aspects of the liberal arts that pertain to mind, and the quadrivium, those aspects of the liberal arts that pertain to matter. Logic, grammar, and rhetoric constitute the trivium; and arithmetic, music, geometry, and astronomy constitute the quadrivium. Logic is the art of thinking; grammar, the art of inventing symbols and combining them to express thought; and rhetoric, the art of communicating thought from one mind to another, the adaptation of language to circumstance. Arithmetic, the theory of number, and music, an application of the theory of number (the measurement of discrete quantities in motion), are the arts of

---

[17] Sister Miriam Joseph, *The Trivium: The Liberal Arts of Logic, Grammar and Rhetoric* (Philadelphia: Paul Dry Books, 2002).

discrete quantity or number. Geometry, the theory of space, and astronomy, an application of the theory of space, are the arts of continuous quantity or extension.[18]

A listing of the seven branches of the liberal arts provides a visual representation of this division:

The Trivium:
The three arts of language pertaining to the mind.
    Logic   art of thinking
    Grammar   art of inventing symbols
    Rhetoric   art of communication

The Quadrivium:
The four arts of quantity pertaining to matter.
  (Discrete quantity, or number)
    Arithmetic   theory of number
    Music   application of the theory of number
  (Continuous quantity)
    Geometry   theory of space
    Astronomy   application of the theory of space[19]

As can be observed in this list, the division of the trivium and quadrivium is much more than a random placing subjects for observation and learning. There is a design and beauty to the division of the liberal arts. Each of the skills of the trivium is deliberate in such a way as to build upon its predecessor, and in the same manner the skills learned in the quadrivium takes its lead from what has been learned in the trivium.

Joseph and others argue that one of the primary benefits of a liberal arts education is its unchanging character that prepares individuals for a variety of forms of future vocation and service. Joseph writes:

> Today, as in centuries past, a mastery of the liberal arts is widely recognized as the best preparation for work in professional schools, such as those of medicine, law, engineering, or theology. Those who first perfect their own faculties through liberal education are thereby better prepared to serve others in a professional or other capacity. The seven liberal arts differ essentially from the many utilitarian arts (such as carpentry, masonry, plumbing, salesmanship, printing, editing, banking, law, medicine, or the care of souls) and from the seven fine arts (architecture,

---

[18] Joseph, *The Trivium*, 3.
[19] Ibid., 4.

Introduction

instrumental music, sculpture, painting, literature, the drama, and the dance), for both the utilitarian arts and the fine arts are transitive activities, whereas the essential characteristic of the liberal arts is that they are immanent or intransitive activities.[20]

In Joseph's summation, one of the primary benefits of a liberal arts education is the foundational grounding it provides for a variety of future employment avenues. Modern accounts of a liberal arts education are usually skewed in such a way as to discount the employment value of such an education, but Joseph takes the opposite stance in seeing value in such an education.

The Trivium

As enumerated above, the three arts of the trivium serve as the basis for understanding the application and use of language. Their use in this manner was a gradual development. The development of the verbal arts dates to the early fifth century BCE and represented a fundamental shift in the cultural tradition of the polis. Greek city-states worked to train warriors who could defend their city, and as such physical education was a large portion of one's training. After the defeat of Athens in the Peloponnesian War at the end of fifth century BCE, physical education remained important, but rhetoric became foundational to secondary education and competed with philosophy to become the central focus of secondary education.[21] The trivium formed the foundation of one's education, and is usually seen as preparation for entry into studies in the quadrivium.

As seen in the list on page **Error! Bookmark not defined.**, the trivium is divided into logic, grammar, and rhetoric. While some of the subjects contained in the quadrivium have shifted with time, the subjects of the trivium have remained constant. Each of the subjects of the trivium provides a different lens for how one understands and communicates through language. For Joseph the three arts of language provide disciple for one's mind as well as expression of one's thought in language. The trivium serves for the, "training of the mind for the study of matter and spirit, which together constitute the sum of reality."[22]

The trivium functions to build the mind through critical interaction with the surrounding world. Joseph divides the trivium in terms of how the arts relate to each other metaphysically. In this construction, logic deals a thing as it is

---

[20] Joseph, *The Trivium*, 4.
[21] David Wagner, "The Seven Liberal Arts and Classical Scholarship," *The Seven Liberal Arts in the Middle Ages* ed. David Wagner (Bloomington: Indiana University Press, 1983), 6.
[22] Joseph, *The Trivium*, 8.

known, grammar with how a thing is symbolized, and rhetoric with how a thing is communicated.[23]

In the three liberal arts of the trivium, grammar serves as the foundational art one must learn. In the Middle Ages, grammar was though to discipline both the mind and the soul. The practice of grammar honed spiritual and intellectual practices that could be used for the learning and teaching of the biblical texts by clerics. Jeffrey Huntsman writes, "Grammar was the gateway to the more advanced linguistic topics of rhetoric and logic and this to the study of literature and the Scriptures."[24] Throughout the Middle Ages grammar was seen as the first of the seven liberal arts and at the head of the trivium. It is put in this position because grammar is the grounding element through which one is able to learn the other liberal arts.[25] Coluccio Salutati wrote in 1406 that grammar was, "the gateway to all the liberal arts and to all learning, human and divine."[26] This longstanding tradition of grammar being the foundation through which to gain knowledge in other fields has continued to persist. The practice of grammar has traditionally been done through the learning of a body of knowledge, by which one is able to develop the mind through the act and application of memorization.

In logic (or dialectic) one learns the ability to reason and apply the skills that have been gained through the study of grammar. In grammar one learns facts of language, whereas in logic one learns the practical applicability of these facts. In a definitive statement providing a definition of dialectic, Boethius writes, "The dialectical discipline examines the thesis only; a thesis is a question not involved in circumstances. The rhetorical [discipline], on the other hand, discusses the hypothesis, that is, questions hedged in by a multitude of circumstances. Circumstances are who, what where, why, how, by what means."[27] Logic provides one with the tools to question whether an argument is valid, and also to build a valid argument for oneself. Logic allows one to ask 'Why?' and to understand the relationship between cause and effect.

---

[23] Ibid., 9.
[24] Jeffrey F. Huntsman, "Grammar," *The Seven Liberal Arts in the Middle Ages* ed. David L. Wagner (Bloomington: Indiana University Press, 1983), 59.
[25] Timothy J. Reiss, *Knowledge, Discovery and Imagination in Early Modern Europe*, Cambridge Studies in Renaissance Literature and Culture, 15 (Cambridge: Cambridge UP, 1997), 23.
[26] Ibid., 24.
[27] Quotation taken from Michael Leff, "Rhetoric and Dialectic in the Twenty-First Century," *Argumentation* 14 (2000): 243. For further discussion of the history of logic see Eleonore Stump, "Dialectic," *The Seven Liberal Arts in the Middle Ages*, ed. David Wagner (Bloomington: Indiana University Press, 1983), 125–146.

Rhetoric is usually seen as the summation, or the highest of these three arts. Sister Joseph refers to rhetoric as the "master art of the trivium" because it makes use of both grammar and logic in its application.[28] At its most basic level, rhetoric is the art of discourse and communication. This audible communication could either be for the purpose of persuasion, or simply to convey information. Aristotle focused primarily upon rhetoric being a means of persuasion, whereas Plato found some cause of concern in the art of rhetoric in that it could improperly persuade opinion as a public art. When one is actively involved in the art of rhetoric, he or she must not only deal with the intricacies of an individual paragraph, but also effectively convey what is meant by the presentation as a whole. This bringing together of grammar and logic in the communication of a coherent idea was why rhetoric has been viewed as the third and highest art of the trivium. Whereas grammar and logic teach the student how to use language and how to think critically, it is when the student uses rhetoric that he or she 'joins the conversation' so to speak by conveying his or her ideas.

The timing of the placement of the trivium in the educational curriculum of the child has been a subject of some debate. Some pedagogues argue that the three liberal arts of the trivium should also serve as three stages of learning. As the child advances in age and grade, so the child also advances in the trivium from grammar to logic to rhetoric.[29] Others have argued for a more integrated approach to the trivium and pedagogy throughout the grade school process. Korcok makes the point that emphasis and placement was often related to expedience:

> The ordering of the art was always closely related to ecclesiastical priorities. Thus, the early Evangelicals stressed rhetoric because it taught eloquence and persuasion, which would enable the Evangelical faith to be winsomely presented in the German courts. The Missourians [Lutheran Missouri Synod] had different needs. Their church was growing exponentially through the influx of new immigrants, many of whom had been raised in rationalist or Pietist churches in Germany. The Missourians were concerned that these new arrivals acquire knowledge of sound Lutheran doctrine. Thus, in their schools, it was only natural that grammar should predominate. Since students were not expected to analyze church doctrines, nor were they encouraged to publicly debate them, there was little need for logic or rhetoric. They were, however, required to give a proper assent to these doctrines. This ascent required the mastery of grammar because it enabled them to read and comprehend the sources of doctrine: namely, Holy Scripture, Dietrich's catechism, and the Lutheran Confessions.[30]

---

[28] Joseph, *The Trivium*, 9.
[29] See for example, Steven Hein, "Why Classical Education? A Case for Resurrecting the Old Education," *The Classical Quarterly* 1:1 (March 2007): 3.
[30] Thomas Korcok, *Lutheran Education: From Wittenberg to the Future* (Saint Louis: Concordia Publishing House, 2011), 249–250.

The Quadrivium

The oldest surviving statement in antiquity naming the fourfold curriculum of the quadrivium dates from the fourth century B.C. Its author, Archytas, was a contemporary of Plato, and likely influenced Plato's use of the mathematical arts at the core of his curriculum.[31] Although the exact form of the quadrivium has varied somewhat since its inception, by the Middle Ages the quadrivium included arithmetic, astronomy, music, and geometry. Within this framework the trivium was seen as preparation for the quadrivium and provided a successive sequence in learning. Fant writes:

> The trivium's grammar prepared students to grasp the functionalities of language itself; logic (sometimes called "dialectic") cultivated skills in analysis of thought; rhetoric combined the other two arts by training students to communicate effectively with others. Mastery of those subjects initiated the learner into the quadrivium's advanced subjects, which explored how the universe itself functioned and was ordered, with mathematics providing the primary tool for this exploration. Mastery of the physical world then led to the higher forms of exploration, the world of ideas themselves (philosophy) and of the supernatural or divine (theology). Indeed, the latter field, theology, was once termed "queen of the sciences," the purest form of thought and abstraction.[32]

As Fant notes, mastery of the trivium led to the application of those skills gained in the quadrivium. As indicated in the list on page 6, the quadrivium usually consists of arithmetic, geometry, music, and astronomy. While the trivium served as preparation for studying the quadrivium, often the quadrivium often served as preparation for the study of philosophy and theology. When the quadrivium is applied in contemporary contexts, usually the interdisciplinary nature of the subjects is emphasized. Joseph writes:

> Each of the liberal arts has come to be understood not in the narrow sense of a single subject but rather in the sense of a group of related subjects. The trivium, in itself a tool or a skill, has become associated with its most appropriate subject matter—the languages, oratory, literature, history, philosophy. The quadrivium comprises not only mathematics but many branches of science. The theory of number includes not merely arithmetic but also algebra, calculus, the theory of equations, and other branches of higher mathematics. The applications of the theory of number include not only music (here understood as musical principles, like those of harmony, which constitute the liberal art of music and must be distinguished from applied instrumental music, which is a fine art) but also physics, much of chemistry, and other forms of scientific measurement of discrete quantities. The theory of space

---

[31] Wagner, "The Seven Liberal Arts and Classical Scholarship," 3–4.
[32] Gene C. Fant Jr., *The Liberal Arts: A Student's Guide*, Reclaiming the Christian Intellectual Tradition (Wheaton: Crossway, 2012), 25–26.

Introduction

includes analytic geometry and trigonometry. Applications of the theory of space include principles of architecture, geography, surveying, and engineering.[33]

As such, the subjects of the quadrivium are expanded greater than what may at first be perceived by its four subjects. The classical tradition offers a unified portrait of subjects to be learned and why they should be learned. This tradition is much better equipped than most to answer the 'why' question of why a particular subject should be studied in a school's curriculum. Traditionally, arithmetic was seen as the first of the mathematical disciplines, with music, geometry, and astronomy following to varying degrees.[34] One may not traditionally think of music as being a type of mathematical discipline, but Reiss rightly shows how it was allocated in the quadrivium: Traditionally music has been one element in what Boethius had called the quadrivium, the others being arithmetic, geometry and astronomy. While 'music,' *harmonia*, had once designated for the ancient Greek a broadly conceived *paideia* of physical, intellectual and spiritual harmony, enabling a stable integrated polity of good citizens (as we learn most familiarly from Plato's *Republic*), in the quadrivium it named a mathematics of quantity—multitude—in relations. It made a pair with arithmetic, which analyzed quantity as such, multitude as composed of integral wholes. It was also related to astronomy (exploring magnitudes in motion—geometry treating magnitudes at rest) by virtue of the theory that the harmony of the universe was manifest in musical ways to be analyzed in its terms.[35] Thus far a basic foundation has been laid for understanding what is contained in the classical education tradition. The next section will demonstrate how the liberal arts have intersected with the Western tradition.

Liberal Arts Education and the Western Tradition

The idea of a liberal arts education is a long-standing ideal in the Western tradition. One of the primary strengths of the liberal arts tradition has always been the recognition that it is a system of learning that effectively develops the life of the mind. Education has not always been viewed simply as a means to a particular type of employment, but rather as an expression of human flourishing through the development of the mind. Robert Carlsen states this point well:

> The [liberal arts] tradition stems from the ancient recognition that man does not live by bread alone. To be a man is something more than to carry out the mechanical functions of living. While it is of tremendous importance to us that we learn to perform the functions of staying alive, and a part of our education will be devoted to those things, it is ultimately of greater importance to deal with those things that make us peculiarly and specifically human beings. These include, of course, our ability to

---

[33] Joseph, *The Trivium*, 7–8.
[34] Reiss, *Knowledge, Discovery and Imagination in Early Modern Europe*, 111.
[35] Reiss, *Knowledge, Discovery and Imagination in Early Modern Europe*, 135–136.

communicate, our ability to classify the elements of our environment in mathematical units, our ability to organize ourselves in social units, our ability to preserve a continuity in human affairs through our interest in history, our ability to pass judgments on the facets of our experience, our ability to create satisfying patters of sound, space, color, line, etc. As individuals come to prize and cherish these things, they come closer and closer to the status of true manhood, nearer and nearer ultimate fulfillment.[36]

Carlson argues that the liberal arts provide the necessary function of expanding the mind past mere subsistence. Although he does not incorporate the important theological construct of what it means that man does not live by bread alone, "but by every word that proceeds from the mouth of the Lord,"[37] his purpose is to express that humans have often seen that there is value in asking the question of what it means to be human.

When Luther was advocating classical education, he was in many ways pushing for what he received as a student. German schools in the early 16th century offered a broadly humanistic and religious instruction to its best students. Students were first taught to read, write and sing. Students were then taught the trivium and quadrivium using classical texts as sources. Students who advanced past this stage were trained in biblical and theological topics in training for clerical vocations."[38] Luther appreciated this basic structure, but wanted this education to be available to the wider public while also focusing on training in the Bible rather than leaving this as a study reserved for clergy in training.

Timothy Reiss points to the liberal arts as providing at least a partial answer to the social upheaval taking place in the sixteenth century. He writes:

To note that the European sixteenth century, especially its second half (but then after Reformation, peasant and religious revolts, Spanish, Italian and French wars, and more), was a time of deep and debilitating upheaval in politics, religion, education, economic and social order, and just about every other area of human practice, is scarcely original. As we see, scholarly realms of philosophy and philology, of grammar, rhetoric, logic, and mathematics did not escape this disarray. In many ways they would be crucial to a solution: not because philosophers, philologists or mathematicians intervened practically in concrete events (even though as government officials, lawyers, printers, ecclesiastics and soldiers, many did), but

---

[36] G. Robert Carlson, "English and the Liberal Arts Tradition in the High School," *The English Journal* 44:6 (Sept., 1955): 326. As this article was written in 1955, one should not take the reference to "true manhood" as chauvinistic, but more as a reference to the development of a well-rounded individual.
[37] Deut. 8:3.
[38] John Witte, "The Civic Seminary: Sources of Modern Public Education in the Lutheran Reformation of Germany" *Journal of Law and Religion* 12:1 (1995): 180.

Introduction

because their disciplines eventually gave the analytical tools to describe and explain those events. They made new concepts and practice of meaning, and so of action.[39]

The classical tradition attempts to offer answers to life's greatest questions both in times of peace of upheaval.

The tradition of classical education has seen a revival in recent years in the American context, both in distinctly Christian schools as well as schools without a particular religious tradition. This revival has occurred for a variety of reasons. One of the leading causes has been pedagogues' ambivalence towards the current state of the American education system. A consensus has emerged that throwing more money at the problem of students leaving school without the education needed to excel in society has not worked. The purpose of a liberal education should be to free one to function well in whatever career path that may be followed, and yet many students remained chained by the inadequacy of the education they received. Using tradition as a guide, many have seen the value that classical education has played in Western society and are returning to this way of teaching and learning. Because Western civilization has historically been tied to the practice of Christianity for the last 1,500 years, Christian pedagogues have pointed to the connection between Christianity historically embracing the classical education tradition, despite its secular roots.

A discussion of classical education would not be complete without briefly mentioning the British author Dorothy Sayers (1893–1957). During Sayers' lifetime she was not primarily known for her pedagogical writings. She was best known for mystery novels and short stories set between World War I and World War II. Although one would not expect a person primarily known as a British mystery writer to be a catalyst for the Christian classical education movement in the US decades after her death, her education was actually well suited for the task. In 1912 she won a scholarship to Somerville College, Oxford University where she graduated in 1915 with a first-class honours degree in modern languages and medieval literature. She went on to earn her MA in 1920 during a time when there were not many women entering study at Oxford or Cambridge. In addition to her mystery writing, Sayers was also a translator and Christian humanist. She published a translation of Dante's *Divine Comedy*[40] as well as a variety of books on Christian doctrine.[41] She considered her translation work of Dante to be her greatest achievement. The Anglican

---

[39] Reiss, *Knowledge, Discovery and Imagination in Early Modern Europe*, 79.
[40] Dante, *The Divine Comedy Part II: Purgatory*, trans. Dorothy Sayers (London: Penguin Classics, 1955). Dante, *The Divine Comedy Part III: Paradise*, trans. Dorothy Sayers (London: Penguin Classics, 1955).
[41] Dorothy Sayers, *The Mind of the Maker* (London: Methuen, 1941); *Creed or Chaos?* (Bedford, NH: Sophia Institute Press, 1999); *The Man Born to be King* (San Francisco: Ignatius Press, 1990).

community respected her theological work, and in 1943 Archbishop of Canterbury William Temple intimated that he wished to offer Sayers the Lambeth Doctor of Divinity, which she declined. In 1950 she accepted an honorary Doctor of Letters from the University of Durham.[42]

Although Sayers had an impressive career in many fields, she is perhaps best known today for a lecture she gave in 1947 at Oxford University entitled, "The Lost Tools of Learning." The immediate effect of the lecture was not overwhelming, but it was published in 1977 in *National Review*.[43] As a result of this 1977 publication, the lecture slowly began to gain influence among those who were looking for an alternative to their contemporary state of education. The "lost tools" to which Sayers refers are those of classical education. Sayers argues that one of the primary problems with the state of education in her time was the students' inability to learn, or critically evaluate what it is they are learning. She writes, "Is it not the great defect of our education today that although we often succeed in teaching our pupils 'subjects,' we fail lamentably on the whole in teaching them how to think? They learn everything, except the art of learning."[44] In this manner she goes directly towards the key idea that a liberal education should allow one the epistemological foundation to think through what one is learning. She goes on to explain the trivium and quadrivium, as well as their use in education in medieval society. In her estimation the Trivium should prepare one for the subjects contained in the Quadrivium.[45] She ends the essay by saying:

> What use is it to pile task on task and prolong the days of labour, if at the close the chief object is left unattained? It is not the fault of the teachers—they work only too

---

[42] Peter Webster, "Archbishop Temple's Offer of a Lambeth Degree to Dorothy Sayers," *From the Reformation to the Permissive Society: A Miscellany in Celebration of the 400th Anniversary of Lambeth Palace Library*, eds. Melanie Barber, Stephen Taylor, and Gabriel Sewell (Woodbridge: Boydell and Brewer Press, 2010), 565.

[43] The paper has been published in numerous formats since its original publication. Dorothy Sayers, "The Lost Tools of Learning," in Douglas Wilson, *Recovering the Lost Tools of Learning: An Approach to a Distinctly Christian Education* (Wheaton: Crossway, 1991), 145-164.

[44] Sayers, "The Lost Tools of Learning," 149.

[45] Although most in the American Christian classical education movement have uncritically imbibed the work of Sayers, criticism of her work usually comes on two fronts: 1) At several points in her essay, Sayers delves into psychology, assigning life stages to children that match the trivium. Once the child is fit for university, he or she may then properly explore the quadrivium. 2) Those of a right-leaning disposition that argue for a very specific approach to classical education believe that Sayers' overall corpus of writing is pseudo-Christian and she herself was overly influenced by feminist concerns. See for example, William Michael of the Classical Liberal Arts Academy's article, "Against the Dorothy Sayers Movement," (January 2011): http://www.classical liberalarts.com/library/against_sayers.pdf [accessed December 7, 2012].

Introduction

hard already. The combined folly of a civilization that has forgotten its own roots is forcing them to shore up tottering weight of an educational structure that is build on sand. They are doing for their pupils the work which the pupils themselves ought to do. For the sole end of education is simply this: to teach men how to learn for themselves; and whatever instruction fails to do this is effort spent in vain.[46]

Sayers positions herself in the liberal arts tradition in such a way that the student should be aware that the knowledge being received should be applicable to the well being of one's life.

In his book, *Recovering the Lost Tools of Learning* (which is viewed as a seminal text by many in the American Christian classical education movement) Douglas Wilson argues that amid the current crisis in education, the classical education tradition offers a way forward.[47] It is clear from Wilson's title that he is drawing upon Sayers' work in his presentation of classical education. Wilson builds his case for classical education largely upon the work of Sayers, but then explains how classical education can be incorporated into the Christian faith. Throughout the book Wilson provides more of an overview than a critical interaction with Sayers' work.[48] What is worth noting in Wilson's book is that his is one of the first books on the popular Christian level to blend the classical ideals set forth by Sayers and others with a distinctly Christian education. He is able to form this blend by making three moves: 1) The educational task should fall primarily upon the family. This task involves the family deciding what route is best for their family in such a way as to glorify God (i.e. public school, private school, home school, etc). 2) Classical education offers an educational ideal that has deep rooted history in the Western context. 3) Classical education can be blended with Christian ideals to offer a distinctly Christian education

---

[46] Sayers, "The Lost Tools of Learning," 164.
[47] Douglas Wilson, *Recovering the Lost Tools of Learning: An Approach to a Distinctly Christian Education* (Wheaton: Crossway, 1991). Other popular level books on the American classical education movement include Gene Edward Veith and Andrew Kern, *Classical Education: The Movement Sweeping America*, 2nd ed. (Washington, D.C.: Capital Research Center, 2001); Harvey Bluedorn and Lauri Bluedorn, *Teaching the Trivium: Christian Homeschooling in a Classical Style* (Mucatine, Iowa: Trivium Pursuit, 2001); Randall Hart, *Increasing Academic Achievement with the Trivium of Classical Education: Its Historical Development, Decline in the Last Century, and Resurgence in Recent Decades* (Lincoln: iUniverse, 2006); Douglas Wilson *Repairing the Ruins: The Classical and Christian Challenge to Modern Education* (Moscow, ID: Canon Press, 1996); Douglas Wilson, *The Case for Classical Christian Education* (Wheaton: Crossway, 2002). As these books will attest, in many ways the classical education movement outside of the Lutheran tradition has been a "grassroots" movement of concerned parents and educators looking for an alternative source of education that could be integrated with their Christian ideals.
[48] Wilson, *The Lost Tools of Learning*, 91–97.

that benefits the mind and the soul. This form of pedagogy wants to remain academically rigorous while also benefitting the inner life of the child.

Although this book was not the only catalyst, since its publication the classical education movement has continued to expand in the North American context. Some of the primary areas Wilson points to with which many Christian parents can relate is the feeling that: 1) The child will be overexposed to ways of thinking and activities of other students contrary to the values of the parents, and 2) That the education the child is receiving is inadequate. The idealized American public education of the mid-twentieth century faded into a portrait of the past, and something is needed to fill the gap left behind. The Christian classical education movement is also unique in that:

> Their over-arching concern is not just academic achievement, but educating the whole student: that is, the ethical, moral, and intellectual self. Classical education tends to view the curriculum as a unified whole in which there is an emphasis on relating different areas of knowledge to subject matter. Students are encouraged to delve further into the deeper questions of knowledge, faith and philosophy; and there is a desire to convey joy in learning as opposed to trying to stimulate learning through simple amusement."[49]

These factors have led Christians of various denominations to consider the classical education movement for their children. Wilson is very much encouraging a turn inwards to one's tradition for education. Wilson (coming from a Reformed context) is much more decisive in his advocacy of classical education than were theologians like Luther or Bavinck. This is in part because of the sacred/secular divide that Wilson assumes. The argument proceeds that because handing over the education of children to the state has clearly failed in many if not most instances, perhaps it would be better to return this duty to the church under the watchful eye of the parent. With this paradigm in mind, Wilson sees classical education as a model that can fill the gap of a needed, vibrant Christian education.

Another factor that Wilson could not have anticipated at the time of the publication of his book was the role the internet as well as other technologies would play in decisions regarding pedagogy for children. In urban areas, parents are able to view a plethora of education options available literally at their fingertips. This has led to many hybrid forms of classical education such as networks of parents choosing to practice classical education as a homeschool option. Before interacting directly with the work of Luther and Bavinck, it would be helpful to go a bit further in examining some of the underlying themes in the classical education tradition.

---

[49] Korcok, *Lutheran Education*, 252.

Introduction

Truth, Goodness and Beauty in Classical Education

One theme that appears in the writings of many proponents of classical education is that of truth, goodness, and beauty. For contemporary writers in the field of classical education, a focus upon truth, goodness, and beauty harkens the reader to a purer time of education in a search for real knowledge. Bavinck refers to this triad as being an important part of the impetus in classical education. He writes, "When the humanists thus returned to the sources and became absorbed in the writings of the ancients, their eyes were opened to the beauty that was revealed in the arts."[50] Truth, goodness and beauty as a definite substance found through historical study pervades throughout classical educational writing. Part of the reason for this is that it points to standards by which a thing can be judged. In the writings of classical education proponents Littlejohn and Evans as well as Gene Edward Veith this is an important theme. When commenting on the Lutheran tradition in particular Korcok writes, "This is the heart of all classical education: preparing students for the future by equipping them to study the thinkers of the past and to apply the divine truth and wisdom they uncover to the world they will inherit."[51] In an article entitled, "Why Classical Education? A Case for Resurrecting the Old Education," Lutheran classical education proponent Steven Hein writes, "A classical education nurtures the basic language skills necessary to determine what is true, what is good, and what is beautiful on more profound and comprehensive levels."[52] A search for the objective nature of reality has driven many to see value in this tradition. Another important point in regards to truth, goodness and beauty is that it provides a stability of thought through time in much the same way that the liberal arts tradition itself does. Considering truth, goodness and beauty when approaching classical education by the Reformed and Lutheran traditions can aid a religious educational structure in that it provides knowledge the sense of being unchanging and fixed through time.

Littlejohn and Evans write, "The liberal arts tradition points us back to the truth, goodness, and beauty as foundational values in every person's education."[53] In the previous paragraph Bavinck emphasizes beauty as being something ontologically intrinsic to the arts themselves. Littlejohn and Evans

---

[50] Herman Bavinck, "Classical Education," *Essays on Religion, Science, and Society*, ed. John Bolt, trans. Harry Boonstra and Gerrit Sheeres (Grand Rapids: Baker Academic, 2008), 217.
[51] Thomas Korcok, "Forward to the Past: A Study of the Development of the Liberal Arts in the Context of Confessional Lutheran Education with Special Reference to a Contemporary Application of Liberal Education" (PhD diss., Free University of Amsterdam, 2009), i.
[52] Hein, "Why Classical Education? A Case for Resurrecting the Old Education," 4.
[53] Robert Littlejohn and Charles T. Evans, *Wisdom and Eloquence: A Christian Paradigm for Classical Learning* (Wheaton: Crossway, 2006), 67.

Pedagogy as Theological Praxis

on the other hand emphasize the beauty of the school surroundings as leading to an appreciation of beauty on the part of the students. The authors write:

> Meanwhile [until the school has the money to build something more 'beautiful'], make sure that the buildings and classrooms you currently occupy are decorated with reproduction of classic works of art and photographs of beautiful things and places, not just cartoon characters. If walls need to be painted, paint them. If the church from which the school is renting space will allow a mural to be painted on a wall, paint it. There is no excuse for schools that purport to teach the absolute of truth, goodness and beauty not to make their students' surroundings beautiful.[54]

The authors see this as one practical application for how to teach students to recognize truth, goodness and beauty.

Veith also views this as an important theme to classical education and the liberal arts. He writes, "What follows [in this book] is a story of devoted educators—bold thinkers, visionary administrators, and dedicated teachers—who still believe in the true, the good, and the beautiful, and who cherish their students as human beings of transcendent worth. They are undertaking educational ventures on a small scale, but their significance for the reform of education and the restoration of American culture is far reaching."[55] Whereas the true, good, and beautiful stand for an educational ideal in this model, he also sees it as a travesty when educators leave this model to the wayside. For instance he writes, "[John] Dewey abandoned any claim to be able to know what was good, true and beautiful. He wanted students to learn rational and scientific methods so that they would be equipped to acquire what was useful to them, according to their own interests."[56] This link between truth, goodness and beauty and classical education is made throughout the book. To cite but one more example, Veith writes, "Classical education cultivates wisdom and virtue by nourishing the soul on truth, goodness and beauty."[57] Why does this serve as such an important theme to contemporary writers on Christian classical education?

The concepts of truth, goodness and beauty that these authors are drawing inspiration from are found in the work of Plato. This further links the harkening to the ancients which classical educators view as important. For Plato, truth, goodness and beauty are forms that can be known and are universal. Roy Jackson writes, "For Plato, things that can be qualified do not count as

---

[54] Ibid.
[55] Gene Edward Veith, Jr. and Andrew Kern, *Classical Education: The Movement Sweeping America*, Studies in Philanthropy, vol. 30 (Washington, D.C.: Capital Research Center, 2001), xi.
[56] Veith and Kern, *Classical Education: The Movement Sweeping America*, 2–3.
[57] Ibid., 11.

knowledge. For example, Helen of Troy is beautiful, but not *unqualifiedly* beautiful (she may be ugly when old; therefore 'is and is not' beautiful), or giving back what you owe is not *unqualifiedly* just (for example, giving back a weapon to a madman). What is knowledge is what cannot be qualified. They are not subject to time, place or the perspective of the individual."[58] For Plato, humans are trapped by the world of their senses, but they have the ability to perceive in their souls the true forms. The knowledge to perceive the true, good and the beautiful is innate knowledge contained within the human. Plato writes in *Phaedro*, "The natural property of a wing is to carry something heavy aloft, up on high to the abode of the gods. There is a sense in which, of all the things that are related to the body, wings have more of the divine in them. Anything divine is good, wise, virtuous, and so on, and so these qualities are the best source of nourishment and growth for the soul's wings, but badness and evil and so on cause them to shrink and perish."[59]

In Plato's thought, the guiding principle for the forms was the form of the good:

> Plato believed that there is a hierarchy of Forms. Whereas there are particular Forms for beauty, for justice, for a chair, a bed and so on, there is one Form over and above all there; the Form of the Good. Like the sun, it gives light and life to all other things, including the other Forms. Therefore, when you have awareness of the Form of the Good you have achieved true enlightenment. When the early Church Fathers developed Christian theology, they borrowed heavily from the works of Plato. In Christianity, the Form of the Good becomes God: the source of all things, immutable, eternal, perfect and invisible.[60]

As will be discussed in chapter one, Luther seems comfortable relying in part upon Aristotle in his formulation of the estates. In a similar manner contemporary proponents of classical education seem comfortable relying in part upon Plato in the formulation of their pedagogical paradigm. Karl Morrison states this tension well: "Many scholars insisted that the liberal arts were essential to the work of scriptural interpretation. The same writers were also repelled by the moral standards of pagan antiquity, conveyed through the classic texts of the arts curriculum. They were pulled in two directions, attracted both by erudition, the prideful learning of the world, and by holiness, the humble simplicity of Christ."[61] This tension certainly lives on in Christian thought and pedagogy. As will be seen throughout this thesis, how to approach

---

[58] Roy Jackson, *Plato* (Abingdon: Hodder & Stoughton, 2001), 35.
[59] Plato, *Phaedrus*, trans. Robin Waterfield (Oxford: Oxford UP, 2002), 88.
[60] Jackson, *Plato*, 27.
[61] Karl F. Morrison, "Incentives for Studying the Liberal Arts," in *The Seven Liberal Arts in the Middle Ages*, ed. David Wagner (Bloomington: Indiana University Press, 1983), 33.

the use of worldly wisdom has been dealt with differently by the Lutheran and Reformed traditions, and as such it is important to understand the relationship between truth and its practice. In his commentary on *The Republic*, Nickolas Pappas writes,

> As things stand, everyone wants what is good; in this respect the good differs from justice, since no one needs to be persuaded to seek it (505 d-e). Like the English "good," the Greek word *agathos* can serve both as a narrowly moral concept and as a much broader term of approbation. Even the wicked would rather have good food than bad; they listen to good music without fear of growing saintly. Given this universal desire for what is good, perhaps the ultimate strategy for defending ethics would involve unpacking the meaning of goodness to find a fundamental value on which everyone agrees.[62]

One does not tend to find "the good" as being the highest form among contemporary proponents of Christian classical education. Rather, they have taken the concept of truth, goodness and beauty as being universals (rather than forms). These universals then allow for a place to which one's educational compass may point.

Even if truth, goodness, and beauty is helpful for understanding classical education, one must be careful not to uncritically impose Platonic ways of thinking upon Luther, Bavinck, or others associated with classical education. Robert Benne writes, "The reason that Luther respected was thoroughly ensconced in a Christian worldview. It was a reason that could affirm the Good, the True and the Beautiful in a way that was consistent with Christian presuppositions."[63] This type of reason to which Benne refers assumes that there is correctness in the Christian view of reality. Luther recognized the danger that philosophy could have upon an uncritical reader. McDaniel and Woods write, "While he [Luther] understood classical education (within limits) to be necessary to the proper functioning of German society, Luther feared the metaphysical influence of pagan philosophers on what he believed must be *the* pristine discipline: theology."[64] The point of this excursion into truth, goodness, and beauty is primarily to point to the fact that tradition must be handled with care. As modern proponents of classical education draw upon the past in their formation of education for the present generation, they must also be careful to properly handle the sources with which they are working.

---

[62] Nickolas Pappas, *Plato and the Republic*, Routledge Philosophy Guidebook to Plato (London: Routledge, 1995), 136.
[63] Robert Benne, *Reasonable Ethics: A Christian Approach to Social, Economic, and Political Concerns* (Saint Louis: Concordia Publishing House, 2005), 238.
[64] Charles McDaniel and Vance E. Woods, "John Henry Newman and Martin Luther: balancing heart and mind in higher education," *Journal of Interdisciplinary Studies* 23:1 (2011): 23.

Introduction

Thus far a foundational understanding of classical education has been laid. In addition, some of the tensions that are present when referring to pedagogy and the Christian tradition have been discussed. The next section will provide an outline of how the thesis will proceed. This thesis will set about examining why pedagogy is of keen interest to Christians, and examine how returning to the primary sources of two traditions in particular can further shed light upon practice in that tradition.

Chapter Outline

This thesis will draw upon the work of two theologians in particular: Martin Luther (1483–1546) and Herman Bavinck (1854–1921). The classical tradition that has been examined in the previous section will serve as a backdrop for reading selected pedagogical writings of Luther and Bavinck. In addition, particularities in the thought of Luther and Bavinck will be noted in order to understand their conclusions regarding pedagogy. At first glance one is probably drawn to the differences in the theological method of Luther and Bavinck rather than their similarities. Separated by four hundred years, Luther was the match that lit the Reformation, whereas Bavinck was able to warm himself by the fire of the Reformation through one of its Calvinistic expressions in the Dutch context.

Although the differences between Luther and Bavinck are easy enough to highlight, they also shared much in common. As this thesis will display, both had a keen interest in pedagogy. Luther wrote several letters expressing a desire to reform the state of education in Germany. At the end of his career, Bavinck too wrote several books on the topic of education. Both Luther and Bavinck also expressed interest in the practice of the classical education model of pedagogy. Because Luther and Bavinck are separated by four centuries of history as well as many cultural differences there will not be a complete correlation between what Luther and Bavinck have in mind when they refer to classical education. Despite this, one of the advantages of the classical system of learning is the continuity that its teaching contains. The trivium has remained virtually the same, and the quadrivium has adapted itself to changes in historical circumstance.

The question of what is meant by classical education is an important one. The formulation of one's theology has a direct correlation to how one lives the various aspects of his or her life. These implications will of course be seen in how one thinks about education. In a comparison between Bavinck and Luther, one would conjecture that 1) The differences in their theological positions should have implications for how ethics is practiced by that particular traditions' adherents. In particular this is being applied in this thesis to the practice of pedagogy. 2) Returning to the original sources of Luther and Bavinck should aid the practice of pedagogy in their respective traditions. There can often be a gap between a tradition and what the founders/those who have come before had to say about a particular topic, and a close reading of Luther and Bavinck will assist in better understanding their positions.

Another important feature of this thesis will be in examining how particular aspects of both thinkers' theological positions influence the trajectory of their theology. In chapter one this will be done through exploring Luther's doctrine of the three estates. Examining Luther's estates of *ecclesia, oeconomia,* and *politia* will form a lens through which to view other aspects of Luther's theology, particularly how he viewed education. Particular emphasis will be placed upon how Luther's account of the estates can be helpful in forming a robust theology.

The second chapter will provide application of the three estates to Martin Luther's 1524 letter "To the Councilmen of all Germany that they Establish and Maintain Christian Schools."[65] This letter was written in response to Luther's perception of decline in the education of church-run schools as well as to offset the criticism of some towards Luther that he was anti-educational. This accusation came from Luther's desire to remove hindrances between the Christian and the Word of God. The estates form an appropriate lens through which to read the letter, as much of the letter is devoted to education should be performed in regards to the family unit and the temporal government. In this letter Luther also advocates a form of classical education to which the Lutheran tradition has continued to return. Emphasis will therefore be placed upon how the estates relate to classical education, and how Luther made this application in "To the Councilmen."

In chapter three a shift will be made from focusing upon the work of Martin Luther to that of Herman Bavinck. A similar model of analysis will be carried out in this chapter as in chapter one. There is not a tripartite method such as the estates for Luther that is present for Bavinck, so particular aspects that define broader Dutch neo-Calvinistic theology will be addressed. In addition, facets of neo-Calvinism to which Bavinck made distinct contributions will also be discussed. This chapter will aid not only in defining a distinctly Bavinckian Dutch neo-Calvinist portrait of theology, but will provide some insight into how this position is similar to and different from Lutheran theology.

Chapter four also parallels chapter two in examining some of Bavinck's writings on education, paying particular attention to the subject of classical

---

[65] Most citations from the works of Martin Luther are from *Luther's Works*. American Edition. 55 vols. Edited by Jaroslav Pelikan and Helmut T. Lehman. Philadelphia: Muehlenberg and Fortress, and St. Louis: Concordia, 1955–86. Martin Luther, "To the Councilmen of All Cities in Germany that they Establish and Maintain Christian Schools," LW 45: 341–378.

education. Two of Bavinck's works in particular will be discussed that have direct application to his understanding of pedagogy: one book, *Paedagogische Beginselen* (Pedagogical Principles)[66], and one article entitled "Classical Education."[67] The decision was made in this chapter to deal with two texts rather than one as was done in chapter two for two reasons: 1) Bavinck wrote four books on classical education (*Paedagogische Beginselen* being his earliest), and thus it would provide an incomplete picture not to examine at least one of these works. 2) Because *Paedagogische Beginselen* does not deal specifically with classical education, examining Bavinck's article, "Classical Education" demonstrates that he did in fact have interest in the subject.

At this stage the direction of the thesis has been made clear. Classical education will be an underlying theme, but more importantly, the thesis will be examining how theological positions can have practical implications in the Lutheran and Reformed traditions. It will also emphasize how a return to the work of Luther and Bavinck can have a positive impact upon these two respective traditions. The thesis will conclude by bringing the analysis together. Particular application will be made to contemporary expressions of classical education in the Lutheran and Reformed context in North America. In addition, further application that can be gleaned from examining the original sources of Luther and Bavinck as well as how their particular theological positions can add to contemporary application of classical education. This will end by offering a way forward in further incorporating the tradition of Luther and Bavinck in the practice of classical education.

---

[66] J. Brederveld, *Christian Education: A Summary of Bavinck's Pedagogical Principles* trans. Two Members of the Faculty of Calvin College (Grand Rapids: Smitter Book Company, 1928).
[67] Herman Bavinck, "Classical Education" *Essays on Religion, Science, and Society*, ed. John Bolt, trans. Harry Boonstra and Gerrit Sheeres (Grand Rapids: Baker Academic, 2008), 209–244.

Pedagogy as Theological Praxis

1. The Three Estates as a Hermeneutical Lens for Luther's Work

In this chapter I will provide an explanation of Luther's understanding of the three estates, and how the estates fit into the larger picture of his theology. Particular attention will be given to how his understanding of the estates relates to ethics. Doing so will lead into chapter two, which will examine Luther's "To the Councilmen of all Cities in Germany that they Establish and Maintain Christian Schools"[1] with the three estates in mind. An essential aspect to grasping Luther's theology of education is to understand what is known as the three estates: *ecclesia, oeconomia,* and *politia*. The three estates are not a feature of Luther's theology about which he wrote at length, but they again and again become apparent throughout his work. Luther usually provides passing references to the estates, but more importantly, one is able to discern the effect of the estates in how he views one's relationship to God, humankind, and the rest of the created world. Luther writes, "Firstly, the Bible speaks of and teaches about the works of God without any doubt; these are divided into three hierarchies: economies, politics, and church."[2] "Hierarchy" accurately describes how Luther is attempting to use the estates in his theology. He views *ecclesia* as the highest estate, followed by *oeconomia*, and thirdly *politia*. When reading Luther, his thought is often divided through these categories. Commenting on how there are clearly three orders[3] by which life operates, Luther writes, "This life is profitably divided into three orders: (1) life in the home; (2) life in the state; (3) life in the church. To whatever order you belong—whether you are a husband, an officer of the state, or a teacher of the church—look about you, and see whether you have done full justice to your calling and there is no need of asking to be pardoned for negligence, dissatisfaction, or impatience."[4] In the phrase "to have done full justice" Luther is encouraging the reader towards freely embracing one's place in the estates. When this is done one does not need

---

[1] Martin Luther, "To the Councilmen of All Cities in Germany that they Establish and Maintain Christian Schools," LW 45: 341–378.
[2] Quotation taken from Bernd Wannenwetsch, "Luther's Moral Theology," *The Cambridge Companion to Martin Luther*, ed. Donald K. McKim (Cambridge: Cambridge UP, 2003), 130.
[3] When referencing the three estates, English writers tend to use estates, offices, institutions and orders interchangeably. There are subtle differences in their use, which shed further light on how Luther thinks of the estates. For instance, "office" can often refer to one's vocational function within an estate, "institution" can emphasize God's establishment of the estates, etc.
[4] Martin Luther, "Lectures on Genesis 15–20," LW 3: 217.

Pedagogy as Theological Praxis

to be "pardoned for negligence, dissatisfaction, or impatience" because that person has fulfilled the moral calling of the estates upon one's life.

As will be discussed later, concepts such as common grace and sphere sovereignty played a large part in how Bavinck was interpreting education. In the same manner, Luther's three estates could be used to frame his interpretation. Every theologian has certain themes that can be found throughout their work, and these themes will influence the direction of the work. The purpose of here providing an extensive analysis of the three estates is to better understand Luther's interpretation of education and how his interpretation is orientated by his hermeneutic of the three estates.

One of the first questions that must be asked is where education fits within the three estates. One can see how education could potentially fall under all three categories. If education is simply the gaining of knowledge and wisdom, in *ecclesia* one receives knowledge of God as a worshipper. In *oeconomia* one receives knowledge in the running and maintenance of the home as well as what formal education that may take place in the context of the home. In *politia* one may receive education through a state funded school. The key point here is that education could be interpreted through a variety of functions that take place in daily life.

Oswald Bayer on the Three Estates

Lutheran theologian from the University of Tubingen Oswald Bayer is a modern proponent of placing more emphasis upon how the three estates are relevant to Luther's theology. As Bayer has been one of the main figures to place a renewed interest upon the three estates, he will be the primary dialogue partner of this chapter. Two of Bayer's works available to the Anglophone are of particular interest on the topic of the estates: *Martin Luther's Theology*[5] and *Freedom in Response*.[6] In *Freedom and Response* Bayer focuses more upon the ethical implications and ramifications of the three estates, whereas in *Martin Luther's Theology* the emphasis is more upon providing an understanding of the role of the three estates in the larger picture of Luther's theology. Both works contain rich insight into Luther's construction of the three estates, and as such they will both be dealt with throughout this chapter.

In *Martin Luther's Theology* Bayer sets forth how to understand the three estates as a basis for understanding the world. The three estates involve the interaction of the human with God and with the world around him or her.

---

[5] Oswald Bayer, *Martin Luther's Theology*, trans. Thomas H. Trapp, (Cambridge: Eerdmans, 2008).
[6] Oswald Bayer, *Freedom in Response*, Oxford Studies in Theological Ethics (Oxford: Oxford UP, 2007).

Understanding why this interaction is relevant is helpful in discerning the larger picture of Luther's theology. To further emphasize the importance of the three estates in Luther's understanding of the world, Bayer entitles his chapter on the three estates in this volume "The Order of the World: Church, Household, State."[7] Bayer begins:

> In his overflowing goodness, the Creator creates for his creatures the space that is necessary for life—but he does not retreat afterward so as not to get in the way of his creatures as they act independently. Instead, he uses his communicating Word, by which he provides regulations and guidelines to establish relationships that make communication, exchange, and community possible; he fills everything everywhere and, without begrudging it, exercises the virtue of giving freely.[8]

Bayer reiterates the deeply involved act of the Creator in the life and "space" in which the creature resides. God did not create and then remove himself from the world, but choose to take on an active role in this creation. This communication is performed primarily through the Word by which God reveals himself. God freely provides the creature space for life, and freely allows his creation to respond.

Contemporary theologians who view the three estates as being a central motif to understanding Luther have often cited Luther's work on Genesis 1-5 as being a primary example of how this is the case.[9] Bayer writes, "The freedom that is promised to the human being is to be used to take note of the world around him, to give it order—by assigning names (Gen. 2:19-20)—and to organize it. This activity takes place within a framework of responsibility, which Luther teaches in a principled and yet elementary, catechetical fashion when he teaches about the three estates."[10] As can be seen in the two Bayer quotes provided thus far, Bayer sees a link between the concept of freedom and the activity of God in the world. God gives responsibility and freedom of action to the human being. In the quotation above Bayer provides three adjectives for how he sees Luther teaching the three estates. By "principled" Bayer sees an order in how God creates and decrees to humans. These principles are not only orderly, but also basic to creation. If the three estates are an accurate way to examine the moral world God has created, then the estates should easily be discernable in such a world. Bayer also uses the language of "catechetical" in

---

[7] Bayer, *Martin Luther's Theology*, 120–133.
[8] Ibid., 120.
[9] See Bernd Wannenwetsch "Luther's Moral Theology," 130–131. In this chapter Wannenwetsch provides a brief two-page description of the three estates. Wannenwetsch writes that Luther relates the Genesis 2 mandate to "be fruitful and multiply" to *oeconomia*. See also Brian Brock, "On Generating Categories in Theological Ethics: Barth, Genesis and the *Standelehre*," Tyndale Bulletin 60:1 (2010): 45–67.
[10] Bayer, *Martin Luther's Theology*, 120.

this description. Most references to the estates in Luther's writing appear in a larger context; one will not find a treatise or letter specific to the estates in Luther's writings. Luther refers to the estates when they are of suitable use to make a theological claim. For Luther the stations are based in nature in that they are clearly discernable. They are also based in reason in that "they are necessary and useful for the world—this knowledge is part of the natural law that everyone knows."[11]

The concept of "station" and "estate" derives from the German *Stand*. Bayer notes that that the idea of *station* hardly occurs in contemporary moral dialogue.[12] "Station" carries the connotation of a fixed placed in life. One can also relate station etymologically to "static," meaning unchanging. Today station is most commonly used as (a) a fixed place (such as a train station) or to (b) the place of a soldier. One can see why station is rarely used in moral dialogue. To do so removes one's ability to use rights language. It also removes any anthropological focus. The human is disarmed by no longer being able to speak of social or economic mobility. The focus is positioned upon the God who has placed the human in a given social context. The human is then left to praise the God who has done so. Referring to the estates also as institutions removes some of this static feeling that the estates may carry. These stations are not only fixed, but God also institutes them. An institution is firmly placed in society, and God has made it as such. Brian Brock argues that the use of 'institutions' in describing the estates helps one see the estates "as descriptions of the new patterns of social life that God has promised to found and secure."[13] Emphasizing the estates as institutions helps to see them as the deeply involved act of the creator giving a promise to his creation. This removes some of the static nature of the estates in God's giving of a good gift.

As has been seen, the English word estate can also possess a variety of meanings. In fact, the English 'estate" can have at least three possible meanings. Most often is refers to a piece of property. One could associate estate with social class, such as in the Middle Ages concept of the "estates of the realm." The estates of the realm were a hierarchically divided social class of the clergy, nobility, and commoners. This has also been classified as men who pray, men who fight, and men who work (*oratores, bellatores,* and *laboratories*).[14] Luther would have certainly known the estates of the realm, and

---

[11] Althaus, *The Ethics of Martin Luther*, trans. Robert C. Schultz (Philadelphia: Fortress Press, 1972), 37. Martin Luther, "Psalm 111," LW 13: 369.
[12] Bayer, *Freedom in Response*, 90.
[13] Brian Brock, "Why the Estates? Hans Ulrich's Recovery of an Unpopular Notion," *Studies in Christian Ethics* 20:2 (2007): 180.
[14] Michael Mendle, *Dangerous Positions: Mixed Government, the Estates of the Realm, and the Answer to the xix propositions* (Alabama: University of Alabama Press, 1985), 22–26.

this could have very much influenced his formulation of the three estates. Luther's three estates hold some aspects in common with the three estates of the realm. Luther shares the hierarchical and triune division seen in the estates of the realm. There are other subtle similarities. The king in the estates of the realm was distinct from the three groups and also superior to them.[15] In Luther's estates, it is also God who is over and distinct from the estates. In both Luther and estates of the realm, it is the spiritual order that is the highest; *ecclesia* in the former and the clergy in the latter. Another important aspect that Luther may have held to is the fixed position of the estates. It would have been possible but rare for members of society to "switch" between the estates of the realm. Luther may have appreciated the structure that he saw in the estates of the realm. There are definite religious overtones in practically assigning one's place in life. Mendle notes that the 14th century English preachers John Wycliffe and Sir John Oldcastle took the three estates as commonplace.[16] The order (to borrow Bayer's term) that was seen in the establishment of the estates of the realm is a paradigm to the certain order that is present in God's establishing of the estates. Luther may have also valued the fixity present in the estates, as he saw the first two estates as being present from creation.

A third meaning for estate relates to the condition or position of one's life (most similar to station). Luther's idea of estate seems to be a combination of the second and third meanings. Luther's estates carried the idea of an order in the created world as did the estates of the realm. Both accounts of the estates acted on an individual level, but carried a larger corporate structure. An important distinction between the two is that Luther's estates cut across socio-economic lines. Luther's estates are closer to Hebrews 4:13, "And no creature is hidden from his sight, but all are naked and exposed to the eyes of him to whom we must give account." Luther's estates place the emphasis upon man's accountability to God and his place in creation rather than man's place in society. Theology exerts critical force on existing structures, and the estates are in one sense subversive in that all humans are given an equal place before their creator.

Luther's estates shift the conception from an anthropocentric to a theocentric framing. As mentioned earlier, most people do not want to think in terms of there being a fixed status. Today "estate" is often replaced with status. The human is no longer tied to the hereditary vocation or station of one's fraternal lineage. Though there remain some vocations and positions in which the occupation of the parent plays a major role, the modern Western concept of social status is usually the result of personal achievement rather than the station of one's parents.

---

[15] Ibid., 21–22.
[16] Ibid., 30.

Pedagogy as Theological Praxis

Bayer picks up this point that man does not wish to think in terms of estates, even in theology. He writes, "No moral thinker today would give a central place to 'my station and its duties.'"[17] Understanding the ethical dimension of this line of thinking is crucial to the point Bayer and Luther are tying to put forth. In this construct, the emphasis is removed from achieving more in life, and placed upon worship in one's place in life. As will be further expanded when discussing *oeconomia*, Luther is more concerned with the praise of God than upon worldly manners of achievement. What could be seen by the world as a menial task in work, is actually a God ordained activity. Considering station or vocation as being a divine calling adds divine meaning to what may have previously been menial. Althaus notes Karl Holl's use of vocation and station as being synonymous so that "every Christian, insofar as he belongs to a particular station in life, may also feel that he has been called."[18]

The ethic here draws upon the biblical tradition of self-denial and the giving up of one's preconceived rights that is present in passages such as Matt. 10:39 and parallels, [19] "Whoever finds his life will lose it, and whoever loses his life for my sake will find it." It is not by coincidence that in Matthew 10 these words of Jesus are preceded by the words, "Whoever does not take up his cross and follow me is not worthy of me."[20] The issue at hand here is denial of self in deference to God for the ultimate, but yet invisible reward of acceptance by the Father in heaven (vv. 32–33).[21]

In *Martin Luther's Theology* Bayer forms his interpretation of the three estates from Luther's *Confession concerning Christ's Supper* of 1528.[22] In one particularly clear passage where Luther refers to the estates he writes:

> But the holy orders and true religious institutions established by God are these three: the office of priest, the estate of marriage, the civil government. All who are engaged in the clerical office or ministry of the Word are in a holy, proper, good, and God-

---

[17] Bayer, *Freedom and Response*, 90.
[18] Althaus, *The Ethics of Martin Luther*, 39.
[19] Cf. Matt. 10:39; 16:25; Mk. 8:35; Lk. 9:24; 17:33.
[20] Matt. 10:38.
[21] R.T. France, *The Gospel of Matthew*, New International Commentary on the New Testament (Grand Rapids: Eerdmans, 2007), 411.
[22] Martin Luther, "Confession Concerning Christ's Supper, 1528," LW 37:151–372. This is a rather lengthy treatise that appeared about the same time as Zwingli's Latin work *Friendly Exposition of the Eucharist Affair, to Martin Luther*. At this juncture the Eucharist controversy among the Reformers had erupted. Although Zwingli may have meant for the treatise to be "friendly" as the title suggests, Luther's English editor notes, "He [Zwingli] wrote, however, in a condescending, schoolmasterish tone, and inserted a number of barbed comments (154)." Luther intends this particular work to be his last word on the subject. The particular pages to which Bayer refers in this treatise are 363–365.

pleasing order and estate, such as those who preach, administer sacraments, supervise the common chest, sextons and messengers or servants who serve such persons. These are engaged in works which are altogether holy in God's sight.[23]

Here one sees a reference to the *ecclesia, oeconomia,* and *politia.* This passage comes in Part III and near the end of this work. Part III is by far the shortest of the three in this treatise, at only 12 pages out of 211 in the English translation. In this section Luther's writes that his intention is to confess all the articles of faith that are in opposition to what he considers to be the sacramentarian heresy.[24] This section is set up in a creedal fashion. Luther says that his purpose in doing so is to leave little doubt after his death as to what he believed so that his words would not be misinterpreted. His confession in this section does not deal with the Eucharist and sacrament as much as it does with his Trinitarian understanding of God and rejection of Pelagianism and semi-pelagianism. Luther is at times presented as being anti-clerical in his pronouncements against the Pope and Catholic Church. As this passage demonstrates, it was not that Luther was against the clerical order, but he was against practices of the Church that he believes were performed in a sinful fashion. In this case he encourages those who are ministers of the word. The proper practice of the clerical office is fulfilling the role of *ecclesia.* Luther is able to critique the clerical order in this manner precisely because he has an account of the clerical order in the estates. Those in a clerical role are not special in regards to their status before God, but do have a special role in leading the people of God towards worship. The role of the priest is to teach the Word and administer the sacraments. Luther also encourages those who are servants of the church, but not necessarily in a clerical role. It is "holy in God's sight" when the service of God is done properly through the church. This is the proper working of *ecclesia* in the world: worship of Christ with an upright heart that is acceptable in his sight.

Also, the concept of the estate allows criticism of the actual church, state, or society. The estates are not a theoretical abstract, but serve an extremely practical purpose in theological ethics. Paul Althaus makes the argument that the estates teach humans how they are to live out the Decalogue and the commandment of love in a very practical manner: "This commandment of love, valid everywhere and for all people, becomes specific for us as individuals in the context of the station of life in which God has placed us. Through our station in life we are placed into a definite and particular relationship to one another. And our duty to serve one another thereby takes on very specific form."[25]

---

[23] Martin Luther, "Confession Concerning Christ's Supper, 1528," LW 37: 364.
[24] Ibid., 360.
[25] Althaus, The Ethics of Martin Luther, 36.

Pedagogy as Theological Praxis

It is also worth noting that Luther refers to the estates of marriage and civil government as "religious institutions" in this quote. This chapter will later discuss the implications of such a statement, but for the moment it is simply worth taking stock of what it means that both marriage and civil government fall into religious categories. Though on the surface marriage could be seen as a physical, universal, and secular estate, when it is considered theologically it can take on a much deeper religious meaning. It is impossible to even begin to grasp what a statement such as, "Husbands love your wives, as Christ loved the church and gave himself up for her"[26] apart from realizing the deep religious meaning of the covenant bond of marriage. In regards to the role of civil government, Christian theologians have also wrestled with how the follower of Christ in relation to the state. One catches glimpses of this in passages such as Rom. 13, Eph. 6:21, and in the Revelation of John.

Two paragraphs prior to the above quotation, Luther writes, "I reject and condemn also as sheer deceptions and errors of the devil all monastic orders, rules, cloisters, religious foundations, and all such things devised and instituted by men beyond and apart from Scripture, bound by vows and obligations."[27] Luther's primary problem with these institutions is he believes they lead to salvation through works, rather than to salvation through faith in the mediator, Jesus Christ. Almost in opposition to his previous statement, Luther goes on to write: "It would be a good thing if monasteries and religious foundations were kept for the purpose of teaching young people God's Word, the Scriptures, and Christian morals, so that we might train and prepare fine, capable men to become bishops, pastors, and other servants of the church, as well as competent, learned people for civil government, and fine, respectable learned women capable of keeping house and rearing children in a Christian way."[28] As a former Augustinian monk, Luther was well aware of the workings of a monastery. The problem that he had with all of these religious orders was not their meeting for worship and study, but rather attempting to earn grace through these activities. Luther references all three estates in this quotation, and also alludes to the hierarchical structure of the estates. The proper way to live is to begin with the teaching of the Word. When this is done properly it will have implications in the running of the household ("keeping house and rearing children") and upon the manner in which such Christian teaching will lead to be better structure of civil government. Luther references 1 Tim. 4:1ff as an example of how these institution can be used to seek salvation: "Now the Spirit expressly says that in later times some will depart from the faith by devoting themselves to deceitful spirits and teachings of demons." The implication from this passage is that seeking salvation by one's merit rather than the merit of Christ is the work of the devil, not the work of God. Luther was in favor of such

---

[26] Eph. 5:25.
[27] Luther, "Confession Concerning Christ's Supper, 1528," LW 37: 363.
[28] Ibid., 364.

studying of the Scriptures that led to a better understanding of God's purpose in the world through them, that led to ethical action on the part of the individual, that prepared people for service in the church and the world, and that allowed for a godly and worshipful home life.

Returning to Bayer's interpretation of these pages, he begins by providing quotations of Luther on the three estates from Psalm 113 and Genesis 2:16–17.[29] In Bayer's brief summary of the estates he views the fundamental and base estate as that of the human who is addressed by God. To be human, and to be *imago Dei*, means in some sense to be addressed by God. At a fundamental level God speaking to humans, and the human ability to hear and respond is at the heart of what it means to be religious. Honoring God as creator and redeemer is at the center of being worshipful. Bayer places this ability to respond to God as a human under *ecclesia*. In his paragraph on *ecclesia* Bayer writes, "For the human being to be human means that he is addressed and he can thus hear, and he himself can speak in response, but he also must respond. The divine address and the expectation that the human being will respond set the basic framework for what happens in the religious realm—for honoring God, for the basic way church and religion operate—which is understood here as an order of creation; all human beings and all religions belong to it."[30] The issue here does not seem to be whether the call of God and the human response is penultimate to something else. Placing response under *ecclesia* also heightens the relationship between response and the church. Although response to God is indeed required of all humans, it is through the church that humans are best able to understand how to respond to God. This can be seen in the sacraments, through prayer, the reading of Scripture, corporate worship, etc. It is through the church that one is able to understand the grace received through the sacrifice of Christ. For Luther, there is a difference between man's attempt to know God on his own accord, and God encountering man through his Word. Now that a general overview of the three estates have been provided, explanation of each of the estates individually will be provided.

Ecclesia

In order to provide an analysis of each of the estates, *ecclesia*, *oeconomia*, and *politia* will be discussed in separate sections. Doing so will aid in showing how each of the estates is a unique aspect of Luther's understanding of the relation of God and creation. As earlier discussed, Luther viewed *ecclesia* as the first and highest estate. *Ecclesia* is established at creation when Adam is placed in

---

[29] Luther, "Psalm 111," LW 13:369; "Lectures on Genesis 1–5," LW 1:103–104. As this volume of Bayer's is an English translation it is interesting that Trapp chose to use the word "estate" in the Psalms quotation, whereas the Weimar Edition uses the phrase "divine stations and orders." WA 42:79.3–14.

[30] Bayer, *Martin Luther's Theology*, 122–123.

the garden. At first it seems counterintuitive to think of *ecclesia* as being a creation estate in consideration of there being a church prior to the advent of Christ. In the garden, Luther sees a church "without walls." For Luther the place of Christ in the unfolding of time does not begin at the incarnation. As the eternal Son of God who is "begotten, not made" Christ is present at creation, and plays an active role in creation. As stated in Colossians 1, Christ is the "The image of the invisible God, the firstborn over all creation."[31] In this early Christian hymn, the divine Wisdom and eternal existence of the Father is fully embodied in the Son. Creation is God's realm. Luther is able to observe *ecclesia* in creation because he sees the triune God at work in creation and in the garden. Christ's coming into the world is not like that of an invader entering hostile territory, but rather the eternal God coming to claim what is rightfully his.[32] The idea here is that creation was, and indeed remains Christ's. Through Christ's incarnation God has brought about redemption. In this context, in a prelapsarian state one can understand how there was *ecclesia*. One could experience perfect union with God through *ecclesia* and with fellow man and creation through *oeconomia*. There is a church without walls present in the garden because there are worshippers in the garden.[33]

Bayer himself is somewhat more pessimistic about the remnant of the postlapsarian relationship of the human and *ecclesia*. He writes, "Every human being belongs as a human being—which is what defines one as human—to the church, because it is an order of creation. It no longer actually exists as the church because it has been corrupted by human ingratitude, because of sin."[34] Bayer seems to be distinguishing between two definitions of "church." One is the order of creation in the garden of which all humans partake. The second definition would be that to which he is not referring, those who have been redeemed through Christ as worshippers. The word "church" was appropriate to define *ecclesia* in the Garden because there was no distinction between worshippers and non-worshipers of God. This distinction was only necessary after the fall when man's inclination became rebellion against God.

Ecclesia in Greek Culture and New Testament Koine Usage

Distinguishing between the usual definition of *ekklesia* as a gathered body of Christian believers and what Bayer has in mind here is crucial to understand the idea of creation order to which Luther refers. Bayer views *ecclesia* as being the "foundational estate of the human being." To be in *ecclesia* is fundamentally what it means to be human. It consists in the most foundational human yearning

---

[31] Col. 1:15.
[32] N. T. Wright, *Colossians and Philemon*, Tyndale New Testament Commentaries (Leicester: Inter-Varsity Press, 1986), 67–68.
[33] Luther, "Lectures on Genesis 1–5," LW 1: 103.
[34] Bayer, *Martin Luther's Theology*, 123.

for relationship—relationship with God. Luther's estate of *ecclesia* is not completely equivalent to the biblical notion of *ekklesia*. By Luther's definition, both terms would fall under the notion of church. In the New Testament, *ekklesia*[35] primarily denotes the local worshipping community of the risen Christ. Luther's *ecclesia* has a broader, more universal application of humans as gift receivers of God.

The state of Adam and Eve in the Garden is important for understanding how *ecclesia* should be. This is perhaps why Bayer chooses to use the language of orders of creation to describe the estates. Doing so forms a link between what takes place at creation, and the purpose of the estates in the world. The garden pictures the perfect state of union between God and man. Bayer writes in his chapter on creation in *Martin Luther's Theology*, "The central point of Luther's understanding of creation is that the whole world and all creatures call upon him and that God uses this medium to promise and to give himself completely to us."[36] *Ecclesia* displays the perfect harmony in relationship that exists between God and his creatures.

The word *ecclesia* is probably one of the better known Koine Greek theological words to the non-Greek reader, and is often simply translated as "church." It was used as early as the 5th cent. BC in Greek culture to designate the gathering of the full citizens of the *polis*.[37] Aristotle used the term *ecclesia* on several occasions in *Politics*. In one such instance he writes that all citizens had a right to speak and offer matters of discussion, but a proposition could only be solved if there was a known expert on the matter present.[38] Aristotle will be further discussed in the subsection on *oeconomia*, but at the moment it is sufficient to say Luther had read *Politics*, and at least had some of Aristotle's ideas in mind when formulating his understanding of the three estates. Prior to the New Testament, *ekklesia* carried a political meaning as being a gathering of the citizens to make decisions. Brown notes that *ekklesia* retained its connection not just as any gathering of people, but to the assembly of the *polis*.[39] This is where the New Testament writers took the idea of the *ekklesia* representing their local gathering of worshipers, as it took on special reference to those who gathered to worship the risen Lord.

---

[35] In order to draw a distinction between terms, *ecclesia* will be used to represent Luther's first estate, and the transliteration *ekklesia* will be used when referring to the Koine Greek term ἐκκλησία. A similar construct will be used in the section on *oeconomia*, where *oeconomia* is used as Luther's second estate, and *oikonomia* will be used as a transliteration of the Koine Greek term οἰκονομία.

[36] Bayer, *Martin Luther's Theology*, 111.

[37] Colin Brown, ed. *The New International Dictionary of New Testament Theology*, vol. 1 (Exeter: Paternoster, 1975), 291.

[38] Ibid.

[39] Ibid.

Pedagogy as Theological Praxis

In his volume *Political Worship*, Bernd Wannenwetsch demonstrates the connection between *ekklesia*, *oikos*, and *polis*.[40] One of the most striking aspects noted by Wannenwetsch is the alternate frame of reference taken on by the *ekklesia*, *oikos*, and *polis* in relation to the New Testament church. He writes:

> The secular Hellenistic background of the popular assembly shines through the biblical usage, especially where *ekklesia* is used to describe the specific act of the local community in gathering together. Here the political connection of worship is as clear as the fact that the constitution of the Church's *polis* was based on worship. 'In its meetings for worship, it displays its character.' *Ekklesia* was a wide term which could cover both the individual house-congregation and the church of a town or province, which was made up of house-congregations, and it could reach out as far as 'the church of the nations.' This comprehensive use shows that its political dimension was seen to be distinct from the usual concepts. The *ekklesia* is not tied to any particular external political concept. What turns the different social groupings into the *ekklesia* is rather the inner form of their existence in each case—the same form of life. It is this, and not the way in which the *ekklesia* differs from particular political concepts of sociality, or the need to draw a line between itself and other representatives of the same concept (a particular house as distinct from other houses, a city as distinct from other cities, a people among other peoples), which constitutes its political existence.[41]

The New Testament conception of ἐκκλησία is derived from the root καλεω, which means, "to call." καλεω is a frequently used word in the New Testament. It can carry both a general call such as in Luke 6:45, "Who do you call me, Lord, Lord?" It can also carry more theological weight in God calling to humanity such as in Matt. 2:15, "Out of Egypt I have called my son." When translating "to call" Kittel writes, "We may always translate "to call," though the special nuance suggests the more distinctive sense of "vocation," and this gives rise to the main question from the standpoint of biblical theology."[42] ἐκκλησία was a word used of secular gatherings, but the church added a theological significance to the term, in their being the called out ones. Just as the Hellenistic *ecclesia* referred to the citizens and not the entirety of the population, the biblical *ekklesia* referred to those who are in Christ and members of the local worshipping community.

Kittel goes on to note that ἐκκλησία can have both a secular and a theological purpose in its use in a similar fashion to καλεω. It can mean both

---

[40] Bernd Wannenwetsch, *Political Worship: Ethics for Christian Citizens*, Oxford Studies in Theological Ethics trans. Margaret Kohl, (Oxford: Oxford UP, 2004). In particular, see 137–141; 151–158.
[41] Ibid., 138–139.
[42] Gerhard Kittel, *Theological Dictionary of the New Testament*, vol. 3, ed. Geoffrey W. Bromiley (Grand Rapids: Eerdmans, 1965), 487.

"assembly" and "church."[43] ἐκκλησία occurs primarily in the letters attributed to Paul (62 occurrences out of 114) and in Acts (23 occurrences). The only occurrences in the Gospels take place in Matt. 16:18 and 18:17.[44] The text usually makes it quite clear whether a general assembly is being referred to or what one usually refers to as the church. ἐκκλησία is often associated with the genitive phrase "τοῦ Θεοῦ".[45] This designates the congregation not just as any assembly, but also as the "church of God."[46] Again, *ekklesia* is a specific designation of those who are followers of Christ in the New Testament.

It is primarily in Colossians and Ephesians where further theological significance is given ἐκκλησία. Here one sees in Col. 1:24 where the church is referred to as Christ's body, and in 1:18 Christ is the head of this body. This defines the church as being in a special fellowship with Christ. Paul meant to relate this fellowship to be of such close proximity as to define it as a body. Kittel writes, "To be God's organ is to hearken to God's call."[47] Therefore, *ecclesia* is not only the physical called out community of Christian worshippers, but is also given a spiritual significance in being located in the body of Christ.

Orders of Creation and Orders of Preservation

Transitioning back to Bayer, he views *ecclesia* (as well as *oeconomia*) as being an order of creation in Luther's first and second estates. Luther does not use the terminology of creation order/order of creation in examining the estates. Bayer seems to prefer to speak of the "orders of creation" because they find their basis in creation and will continue until the world's end.[48] It should not be taken for granted that "orders of creation" is the correct phrase to use here, a point made evident by Barth's rejection of the language of "orders" in describing creation

---

[43] Ibid., 503.
[44] Because of this infrequency, some have seen these as a later addition to the text. See for instance Hagner who refers to the use of ἐκκλησία here as "dubious." He views the security of the church, the office of Peter, and the authority of Peter to be anachronistic. Hagner does not completely dismiss these words as being attributed to Jesus, but considers them doubtful as original to the text. Donald A. Hagner, *Matthew 14-28*, Word Biblical Commentary, vol. 33B (Dallas: Word Books, 1995), 465. For an opinion that views ἐκκλησία as likely original to the text, see Craig Blomberg, *Matthew*, New American Commentary, vol. 22 (Nashville: Broadman Press, 1992), 252-253. Blomberg's case rests on (1) the fact that Jesus' instruction to his followers implied that there would be some form of continued community existence after his death, and (2) ἐκκλησία often meant simply "assembly" in the Jewish context (see above).
[45] Cf. 1 Cor. 1:2; 10:32; 11:22; 15:9; 2 Cor. 1:1; Gal. 1:34; plural in 1 Cor. 11:16, 22; 1 Thess 2:14; 2 Thess. 1:4.
[46] Horst Balz and Gehard Schneider, eds. *Exegetical Dictionary of the New Testament*, vol. 1 (Edinburgh: T&T Clark, 1990), 411.
[47] Kittel, *Theological Dictionary of the New Testament*, vol. 3, 512.
[48] Bayer, *Freedom in Response*, 92.

and its post-fall preservation.[49] He preferred Bonhoeffer's theology as being more compatible with his own when compared to the likes of Brunner or Althaus.

In distinction from Bayer, Bonhoeffer preferred to speak of the "orders of preservation" as can be seen in *Creation and Fall* when describing the situation of the world after the fall.[50] Bonhoeffer's preference for using the language of preservation lies in his understanding of the effect of the fall upon creation. Ballor writes, "The radical discontinuity that Bonhoeffer finds in the prelapse state of humankind in the *imago dei* and the postlapse state as *sicut dues* could lead us to conclude that the image of God is absolutely destroyed or no longer existent in human beings after the fall. However, Bonhoeffer's sense of utter loss in the fall is tempered by his doctrine of God's preservation even in the face of creaturely sin."[51] This break from the language of creation is necessary for Bonhoeffer because it emphasizes how the orders of creation are no longer operative in the same manner as prior to the fall. Nonetheless, saying that there are orders of preservation maintains the goodness of God's creation, and God's desire of preservation of that goodness in the world.[52] In distinguishing between orders of creation and orders of preservation, Bonhoeffer writes:

> God looks at God's work and is pleased with it, because it is good. This means that God loves God's work and therefore wills to uphold and preserve it. Creation and preservation are two sides of the same activity of God. It could after all not be otherwise than that God's work is good and that God does not reject or destroy it but loves and upholds it. As God looks at it, that work comes to rest and becomes aware of God's pleasure in it. God's looking keeps the world from falling back into nothingness [Nichts], from complete destruction [Vernichtung].[53]

Bonhoeffer also has a very Christological focus in his orders of preservation. The world is orientated towards Christ, and is being preserved for the sake of Christ.[54]

One of the clearest uses of the estates in relation to creation for Luther is in his commentary on Genesis 2:16–17 which says, "And the LORD God commanded the man, saying, 'You may surely eat of every tree of the garden,

---

[49] Jordan J. Ballor, "Christ in Creation: Bonhoeffer's Orders of Preservation and Natural Theology," *The Journal of Religion* 86:1 (January, 2006): 3.
[50] Ibid., 5.
[51] Ballor, "Christ in Creation: Bonhoeffer's Orders of Preservation and Natural Theology," 5–6.
[52] Ibid., 10.
[53] Dietrich Bonhoeffer, *Creation and Fall: A Theological Exposition of Genesis 1–3*, Dietrich Bonhoeffer Works, vol. 3 (Minneapolis: Fortress Press, 1997), 45.
[54] Ernst Feil, *The Theology of Dietrich Bonhoeffer*, trans. Martin Rumscheidt (Philadelphia: Fortress Press, 1985), 72.

but of the tree of the knowledge of good and evil you shall not eat, for in the day that you eat of it you shall surely die.'" Luther begins his commentary on these verses by writing, "Here we have the establishment of the church before there was any government of the home and of the state; for Eve was not yet created. Moreover, the church is established without walls and without any pomp, in a very spacious and very delightful place. After the church has been established, the household government is also set up, when Eve is added to Adam as a companion. Thus the temple is earlier than the home, and it is also better this way."[55] In this manner the Church has been instituted by the spoken word of God. One should perhaps first ask what is involved in these verses that constitutes Luther referring to the church as being established in the garden. In Bayer's interpretation, he links his conception of creation order in *ecclesia* with the command of God and with the freedom granted by God. A command of both promise and warning is provided in this passage in Gen. 2. There is a freedom given to eat of all but one tree. Bayer's further statement that response no longer belongs to the church seems to be his own estimation of this estate, but not Luther's. Bayer adds the caveat to Luther's exposition that this is "no special church, but a general one."[56] It would seem that Bayer refers to the church here as being general because there are no "called out ones" when there is no fall to speak of. All would have been able to worship and work freely. The question here becomes whether after the fall there remains a general *ecclesia*, or whether this privilege becomes located in the worshipping community of the one true God. To invoke worship and *ecclesia* as being prelapsarian activities, one must also delve into the Christology here being put forth.

Bayer grounds his Christology and understanding of *ecclesia* in the promise of life given in Gen. 2:16, "You may surely eat of every tree of the garden," with God's self-revelation in Ex. 20:2, "I am the Lord your God." The threat of death is given in Gen. 2:17 to guard the life that is promised. Bayer also sees the promise of life given in Gen. 2:16 as being universal. All mankind could have partaken in the life given in the garden. Upon this foundation of life flowing from the worship of God, and death coming from the worship of false gods, Bayer provides a brief sketch of a natural theology in which all men have a partial knowledge of God, but it is through the office of Christ that this knowledge of who God is can be seen in truth. Therefore, there remains a remnant of *ecclesia* for all humans in that all should respond to God, but this knowledge is only brought to fruition through understanding the work of Christ.

There is a fine line here between having an *ecclesia* in the Garden that does not include Christ, and explaining how Christ fits into this paradigm. Bayer aids in resolving this tension in part by pointing to Luther's exposition of the book

---

[55] Martin Luther, "Lectures on Genesis 1–5," LW 1: 103–104.
[56] Bayer, *Martin Luther's Theology*, 126.

of Jonah.[57] Luther interprets Jonah as Christian theology. His key interpretative lens when dealing with this book is Romans 1:18-21:

> For the wrath of God is revealed from heaven against all ungodliness and unrighteousness of men, who by their unrighteousness suppress the truth. For what can be known about God is plain to them, because God has shown it to them. For his invisible attributes, namely, his eternal power and divine nature, have been clearly perceived, ever since the creation of the world, in the things that have been made. So they are without excuse. For although they knew God, they did not honor him as God or give thanks to him, but they became futile in their thinking, and their foolish hearts were darkened.

In particular, Luther uses these verses to interpret the mariners who "each cried out to his god" in Jon. 1:5. Luther writes that reason alone will not be able to identify the true God. Reason, apart from revelation, will lead one as a blind man groping in the dark. Such groping in the dark can only lead to despair and the worship of idols. Luther makes the case that ultimately if one is worshipping apart from the true Christ, they are serving the devil, not God. He writes, "There are innumerable types of idolatry; in fact, there are as many varieties as there are illusions and self-chosen concepts of pleasing God. All but faith in Christ come into this category."[58] Luther's Old Testament exegesis is pervaded with Christ. Therefore, how does one reconcile this Christology with the *ecclesia* seen in the garden?

Sin has made it necessary for Christian theology to point towards a right picture of God. The desire for worship and for *ecclesia* remain after the fall. This is what Luther sees in the mariners' call to their own gods. There remains a desire for worship, and in this case for protection. The incarnation of Christ provided for man this picture of what was lost.

Luther does write in his commentary on Gen. 2:16–17 on the marred relationship that is a result of the fall, but he does not directly state that this task of the church has been removed. Luther writes, "Only this He wants [of Adam]: that he praise God, that he thank Him, that he rejoice in the Lord, and that he obey Him by not eating from the forbidden tree. We have remnants of this worship, since Christ has restored it in some measure amid this weakness of our flesh; for we also praise God and thank Him for every spiritual blessing. But these are truly nothing but remnants."[59] Luther places due emphasis upon the fallenness of postlapsarian society, but he never says that there is not something unique about the proclamation of the Word within the *ecclesia*.

---

[57] Bayer, *Martin Luther's Theology*, 127. Martin Luther, "Lectures on Jonah," LW 19: 3–104.
[58] Luther, "Lectures on Jonah," LW 19: 56.
[59] Luther, "Lectures on Genesis 1–5," LW 1: 106.

Ecclesia is also the place in which the spiritual existence of man is most fully achieved. Luther writes, "Because the church is established by the Word of God, it is certain that man was created for an immortal and spiritual life, to which he would have been carried off or translated without death after living in Eden and on the rest of the earth without inconvenience as long as he wished."[60] The link that is made by Luther in this quotation is between the sustaining power of the Word of God, and the fact that this sustenance bears witness to man being made for "an immortal and spiritual life." *Ecclesia* calls on man to freely respond to the spiritual life he has been given. As will be examined further, the emphasis in *oeconomia* is upon man's earthly life, and in *ecclesia* it is upon his spiritual existence. Luther's estates do not drift into an otherworldly, Platonic state. The estates emphasize understanding Christ at work in the day to day existence involved in being a human, and also in the spiritual aspect of man in his worship of God.

Oeconomia

The next estate Bayer discusses is *oeconomia*. He views this estate as also being a creation order. "Economy" deals with the daily activities that are involved in the relationships of mankind. Bayer writes, "Luther articulates what is meant by this estate as the relationship between parents and children, between a husband and wife, between human being and field, thus as work: the interrelationship of the human being with nature, the acquisition of his means of sustenance, his daily bread."[61] Bayer's view of economy is very earthly. It involves the asking and receiving of daily bread, the working of the land, the personal interchange between intimates. Many of these tasks are routine, even mundane. The plowing of the field or the baking of bread can become second nature. Luther holds in balance the routineness of *oeconomia* with the spiritual significance that accompanies it. Luther's commentary on Genesis 2:16-17 is also helpful in understanding *oeconomia*: "Therefore after the establishment of the church the government of the home is also assigned to Adam in Paradise. But the church was established first because God wants to show by this sign, as it were, that man was created for another purpose than the rest of the living beings."[62] Luther views the relationship of man to the world, even before the creation of woman, as being a creation order. He sees the Edenic state as one in which humans can peacefully exist with the land and the rest of mankind. Thorns and thistles are not a result of hard work, and pain is not the result of childbirth. In the same manner that sin has disabled man's ability to respond to God in the estate of *ecclesia*, sin has thrown disharmony into *oeconomia*. The providing of food for the family and the relationship between family members has become broken,

---

[60] Ibid., 104.
[61] Bayer, *Martin Luther's Theology*, 122.
[62] Luther, "Lectures on Genesis 1–5," LW 1: 104.

and it is through the restoration granted through Christ that these are made right.

Oeconomia and *Oikonomia*

To avoid misunderstanding, examination will be made into what Luther is and is not referring to in the term "o*economia.*" *Oeconomia* is usually translated in English as "economy" and can have multiple meanings. Today it is most generally thought of in terms of the pecuniary activity of a country, or the management of an individual's resources. This is not the definition being approached here. The Greek equivalent to *oeconomia* is "*oikonomia,*" which usually means "management of a household." This has been interpreted theologically in *politia* as understanding God's governance of the world. The relation of *oeconomia* to education could potentially take multiple paths. It is worth examining the fact that to actually understand how God governs the universe, one must have the tools in place to learn and be taught. Parents must actually teach children how to perform the difficult tasks of working and providing food for the sustenance of their future family. Within the household management of God, he has put such parameters in place through which he may be understood.

Understanding the economy of God as God's governance over the world combines two of the New Testament usages of *oikonomia*: one referring to stewardship, and the other referring to the plan of God. Luther was certainly aware of such a usage. In fact, he believed that the concept of *oikonomia* had been grossly misinterpreted by the Church. Kristian Holm, writes that it is *oikonomia* that is at the center of the Reformation. The primary reason for this is in *oikonomia* the human responds to God. This is one of the main ways that the Lutheran concept framework of the three estates differs from the Reformed vision in regards to creation. Reformed theology focuses more upon man being made a steward of creation. This focus is found in the creation mandate of Gen. 2:19 "So out of the ground the Lord God formed every beast of the field and every bird of the heavens and brought them to the man to see what he would call them. And whatever the man called every living creature, that was its name." The Reformed theologian would usually take this verse as a cultural mandate that God has commissioned mankind as a steward over creation.[63] Luther on the other hand would focus more upon the God who is in providing for all creation than upon the man who as a type of steward of creation.

---

[63] See for example, Abraham Kuyper, *Lectures on Calvinism* (Grand Rapids: Eerdmans, 1943). For a more contemporary theologian of this vision, see Craig Barthomelew, *Living at the Crossroads: An Introduction to Christian Worldview* (Grand Rapids: Baker Academic, 2008).

An underlying issue when attempting to understand the concept of the economy of God is to consider whether one is indeed capable of giving something to God. Kristian Holm does excellent work in distinguishing between the Lutheran and Reformed visions in outlining why the transcendent economy of God was so crucial in Luther's theology. Holm writes, "The philosophical answer to the question, 'Can a gift be given?' is equally well known. Gifts cannot be given as long as they are part of an exchange or an economy. Strictly speaking, only non-exchangist gifts remain gifts. . . . One could argue that Reformation theology is about nothing but economy, as has been the case since Augustine and anti-Pelagianism."[64] The point Holm is making considers the context into which Luther was writing. Luther viewed the concepts of merits, indulgences, and prescribed piety as being deeply influenced by an understanding of economy. Salvation and justification were earned by the completion of religious practices. It is therefore through this gift-giving back to God that one is able to receive grace. Holm argues that the Reformation's response was to reorient an understanding of economy and justification. Either one is able to achieve forensic justification through the merit of Christ, or else through some other means. Through his study, Luther rejected any other means for justification than the work of Christ. Luther rebelled strongly against this understanding of economy in his writings as early as his 95 theses were nailed to the Wittenberg church door.

Luther removed the concept of reciprocity from the economic relation of God and man: "Humans are nothing but receivers, and they cannot give to God (*deo suum retribuere*) what is already God's."[65] From this brief analysis one can see that Luther certainly had the concept of the economy of God in mind throughout his writings. This can be seen in *ecclesia* in that God speaks, and man responds. In *oeconomia* it is God who is the giver of daily bread. In *politia* it is God who governs. Luther is referring to the *oeconomia homonis* rather than the *oeconomia Dei*. The classical definition of *oeconomia Dei* is much closer to Luther's estate of *ecclesia* than his *oeconomia*. In *oeconomia*, Luther does not emphasize the economic relation of *God to man*, but rather of *man to God's provision through creation*.

Whereas *ecclesia* for Luther is a primary response to the Word, *oeconomia* is a secondary response. Loving one's spouse or teaching one's children can be a valuable secular activity. It is a good thing to love one's spouse well, but apart from doing so in response to the Word it remains a secular activity. *Oeconomia* is a secondary response to God in that the human is responding through how he or she acts in relation to the familial bonds and to the land. This can potentially open a vast array of directions in discerning the ethical implications of

---

[64] Kristian Holm "Justification and Reciprocity," *Word—Gift—Being*, ed. Bo Kristian Holm and Peter Widmann (Tubingen: Mohr Siebeck, 2009), 90.
[65] Holm, "Justification and Reciprocity," 91.

oeconomia. In the marriage relationship, the bond between man and woman becomes much deeper and more intricate when it is viewed as responding to God. God has placed the call of holiness through faith upon the human, and this holiness is displayed in the sacrificial love of the husband toward the wife, and vice versa. In *oeconomia*, the person lives in response to God in what would normally be considered the menial activities involved in life.

The Roots of *Oeconomia*: Οἰκονομία in the New Testament

To gain a better understanding of the meaning of *oeconomia*, it would be helpful to examine its etymological roots, and specifically how its cognate, οἰκονομία, is used in the New Testament. This section will provide a brief examination of οἰκονομία as used in the New Testament, paying particular attention to how its use is similar or different to *oeconomia*, as well as its use by Luther. In the New Testament οἰκονομία has two usages. The primary definition is closer to what Luther had in mind, so it may be best discuss the secondary use first. The secondary use of this word refers to the "plan of salvation," "administration of salvation," or "order of salvation."[66] There is a definite religious significance tied to οἰκονομία being used in this manner. Such a definition would be appropriate to the theological concept of the economy of God. One such instance of this usage is Eph. 1:10: "making known to us the mystery of his will, according to his purpose, which he set forth in Christ as a plan (οἰκονομίαν) for the fullness of time, to unite all things in him, things in heaven and things on earth." The translation of this word as "plan" seems to be the most common. An older popular translation of οἰκονομία was as "dispensation."[67] Andrew Lincoln is helpful in understanding the meaning of *oikonomia* here: "οἰκονομία can refer to (1) the act of administering, (2) that which is administered, an arrangement or plan, and (3) the office or role of an administrator, a person's stewardship; it is often difficult to decide which nuance is in view with a particular passage. In the Greek world οἰκονομία was

---

[66] Gerhard Friedrich, ed. *Theological Dictionary of the New Testament* trans. and ed. Geoffrey W. Bromiley, vol. 5 (Grand Rapids: Eerdmans, 1967), 152.

[67] Translations that include the translation as "plan" include the Jerusalem Bible and the NRSV. Other less common translations include "administration" (1889 Darby Bible), and "to usher in" International Standard Version. Prior to the twentieth century dispensation was a popular translation. *Dispensatio* is the Latin equivalent on *oikonomia*. The Latin used by the scholastics tended to transliterate this term as *oeconomia*. See Richard A. Muller, *Dictionary of Latin and Greek Theological Terms* (Grand Rapids: Baker, 1985), 93. One could assume that modern biblical translators have chosen to drop the translation as being "dispensation" because this verse has become a chair text for dispensationalism. The most common books against dispensationalism come from covenant theologians. See for example, John H. Gerstner, *Wrongly Dividing the Word of Truth: A Critique of Dispensationalism* (Orlando: Soli Deo Gloria Ministries, 2000).

regularly used for God's ordering and administration of the universe."⁶⁸ Markus Barth further comments that the use of *oikonomia* here forms the "watershed or touchstone."⁶⁹ The commonplace "plan" does not quite express the strength of its meaning here. This plan has been set forth in Christ to unite all things through Christ. Even more, this plan has been made known to the believer in Christ.

A cognate passage to Eph. 1:10 is Eph. 3:9 which states, "To me, though I am the very least of all the saints, this grace was given, to preach to the Gentiles the unsearchable riches of Christ, and to bring to light for everyone what is the plan of the mystery hidden for ages in God who created all things, so that through the church the manifold wisdom of God might now be made known to the rulers and authorities in the heavenly places." In this passage one also sees the connections of οἰκονομία to a mystery (μυστηρίου) and to Christ being over "all things" (τὰ πάντα).⁷⁰ Here, as in Eph. 1:10 *oikonomia* is an active force, whereas the second use refers to Paul's apostolic role and office.⁷¹

A second, and more common, usage in the New Testament of οἰκονομία is that of the household administration. This is similar to the usage that Luther had in mind in his formulation of *oikonomia*. In this usage the word is often translated in the New Testament as "direction" "administration" or "provision." One instance where it is used in this manner is Luke 16:1–2, "He also said to his disciples, "There was a rich man who had a manager (οἰκονόμον), and charges were brought to him that this man was wasting possessions. And he called him and said to him, 'What is this I hear about you? Turn in the account of your management (οἰκονομίας), for you can no longer be manager (οἰκονομεῖν).'" The context of this verse is a parable being told by Jesus in which a rich man has placed a manager over his possessions. Here one sees the household managerial aspect of this word. Paul uses it to refer to the apostolic

---

⁶⁸ Andrew T. Lincoln, *Ephesians* Word Biblical Commentary, vol. 42 (Dallas: Word Books, 1990), 32.
⁶⁹ Markus Barth, *Ephesians 1–3*, The Anchor Bible (Garden City: Doubleday & Company, Inc., 1974), 86. Barth argues that the larger textual evidence makes the meaning of most occurrences of *oikonomia* as stewardship or administration. He argues that nowhere in the LXX does *oikonomia* refer to stewardship or administration, and it is unlikely that Paul would have introduced a new concept (88). This argument is not necessarily as cogent as it may first sound, as Paul was under no obligation not to use the word in such a way as the LXX. It also does not take into account that *oikonomia* could be used in this manner in the wider Greek culture.
⁷⁰ Mystery and stewardship are also linked in Col. 1:25. The cognate οἰκονόμος is linked with mystery in 1 Cor. 4:1.
⁷¹ Lincoln, *Ephesians*, 32.

office and his being entrusted with the gospel.[72] Luther maintains the administration and provisional aspects of *oikonomia*, but one does not find management connotations in *oikonomia* as much in *oeconomia*. This is perhaps because he sees the emphasis in *oeconomia* not as management, but as thankfulness for provision.

To provide one such example of this usage, Paul writes in 1 Cor. 9:17, "For if I do this of my own will, I have a reward, but not of my own will, I am entrusted with a stewardship (οἰκονομίαν)." What does it mean to be "entrusted with a stewardship"? For Paul, he has been entrusted with the gospel as is made clear from the context of this verse. It should be noted that the object with which Paul is entrusted (the gospel) is not a tangible object. Even if the language of "stewardship" is used here in the English translation, Paul is not physically able to give the gospel to another. Paul has been entrusted with the speaking of the gospel, but it is Christ who is ultimately the giver of the gospel, as only he is able to give. Luther provides only a passing reference to 1 Cor. 9:17 in the American Edition of his works. In his commentary on 1 Tim. 1:11 he provides reference to 1 Cor. 9:17 as possessing a similar idea as this verse. He writes, "'Who is believed because he is believed' is exactly the same as *with which I have been entrusted* and 'to me has been entrusted this responsibility.'"[73] Luther here prefers the concept of responsibility to stewardship. Responsibility is certainly closer to the point Luther is trying to get across here in contrast to the sense of possession seen in the Reformed vision of stewardship. As will be demonstrated concerning Bavinck, the Reformed portrait of *oikonomia* emphasizes stewardship, whereas the Lutheran picture with God as gift-giver places greater emphasis upon man's role in receiving and using that gift. Luther would have perhaps preferred the language of "vocation" or "calling" to that of stewardship. When Paul is seen as being entrusted with the vocation of proclaiming the gospel, the weight is upon the God who is proclaimed rather than upon Paul's role as some type of possessor of that which is proclaimed.

Luther's exegesis of being entrusted with the gospel does not place the emphasis upon Paul's role in responsibility. His emphasis is upon the fact that it is the Word that Paul has been entrusted with. The fact that a mere human could

---

[72] Cf. 1 Cor. 9:17; Eph. 3:2; Col 1: 25; 1 Thess. 2:4. For further information see Friedrich, *TDNT*, 151–152. Friedrich also notes that in the prison letters there is a close connection between the two uses of οἰκονομία and it is not always clear to which use Paul is referring. A third use that only occurs once in the New Testament is in 1 Tim. 1:4 where false teachers occupy themselves with myths and genealogies rather than the stewardship (οἰκονομίαν) that is from God by faith. See Friedrich, *Theological Dictionary of the New Testament*, vol. 5, 153.

[73] Luther, "Lectures on 1 Timothy," LW 28: 238.

be given responsibility over such a vital item as the gospel is almost too much for Luther to bear in his exegesis. He writes:

> It strikes us as a chilling phrase: 'Paul, an apostle' (v. 1) and 'the Word has been entrusted to me' (cf. v. 11). I have said that we have no rest or peace unless we know for sure that we have the actual Word of God. It's a great thing to know that one has the very sure and infallible Word is God. This is a gift we cannot explain. Before we were in the Gospel, we were carried about by every wind. . . . The word is a treasure, but not like the treasure of men. He recommends carefully that we must not take up the Word as if it were man's. It is easy to receive the Word, but to receive it as the Word of God, who lives and is blessed forever, that is a truly great thing.[74]

Luther wants the reader to see that it is a sacred responsibility to be entrusted with the gospel, but the emphasis is not upon man's role. In fact, he makes it quite clear that the Word does not belong to man. His focus instead is upon the surety that is found through the Word. This is not a tangible treasure, such as a gold coin, but rather the good news of the giver himself is to be received.

G.G. Findlay writes of the use of *oikonomia* here: "The servant, however highly placed, is a slave whose work is chosen for him and whose one merit is faithful obedience. In Paul's consciousness of stewardship there mingled submission to God, gratitude for the trust bestowed, and independence of human control."[75] This entrusting or stewardship could be that which is given to a slave or to one who rules over much. When *oikonomia* is used as household management in a spiritual sense in the New Testament (such as Paul being entrusted with the gospel), there is a definitive element of the manager submitting himself to the master. This steward is responsible not to man, but to God.[76] These thoughts are very much in line with Luther's idea of one's station in life. Although one has been made a manager or steward over something (whether as a slave or a king), it is important to keep in mind that one has indeed been "made." Humans are creatures, and it is only by the sustenance of God that one is able to fulfill his or her station in life. Stewardship to the Master in Luther's conception of *oikonomia* echoes Paul's conception of himself as, "δοῦλος Χριστοῦ Ἰησοῦ."[77] In one's relationship to man and the world, a person

---

[74] Ibid., 238–239.
[75] G.G. Findlay, *Apostles, Romans, First Corinthians*, The Expositor's Greek Testament, ed. W. Robertson Nicoll (Grand Rapids: Eerdmans, 1983), 852.
[76] Ibid., 796.
[77] Cf. Rom. 1:1. A similar Pauline salutation in which Paul refers to himself as a servant/slave of Jesus occurs in Phil. 1:1 (referencing himself and Timothy as "δοῦλοι Χριστου." Paul is even more direct in his letter to the slave master Onesimus referencing himself as "δέσμιος Χριστοῦ Ἰησου." Whereas δοῦλος can take on the connotation as a servant or a slave, δέσμιος literally means "prisoner." Dunn and others argue that this may not in fact refer to Paul being a slave of Jesus, but rather that he himself is currently in bondage. He is a prisoner of Jesus in the sense that he is quite literally a prisoner for

Pedagogy as Theological Praxis

is in service and worship to God. The literal difference between the usage of *oikonomia* is not always hard and fast in the New Testament. The primary difference seems to lie in whether the word is being used in reference to man or to God.

None of the instances of οἰκονομία in the New Testament refer to the familial relations that are most akin to what Luther had in mind. As has been seen above, the Bible's use of this term takes on more of a managerial and administrative role, whether that is in a clerical or lay sense. This does not necessarily diminish the validity of the estate or the role that it played in Luther's theology. Even if *oeconomia* is not particularly akin to its etymological root in *oikonomia*, the broader structure of the importance of a human's relation to the world is certainly a biblical theme. Despite this difference, there are some similarities between *oeconomia* and *oikonomia*. A few areas of commonality between Luther's *oeconomia* and the biblical use of the word οἰκονομία include: (1) Even if οἰκονομία was not used directly for family relations in the New Testament, there is no reason why it could not have been. This is an argument from silence, but the Hellenistic usage certainly included the family, and there is nothing in the connotations of the word that can be pointed to as a reason why the New Testament writers would have choose not to use οἰκονομία in this manner. Again, this is not a particularly strong point, but the broader Hellenistic usage of οἰκονομία certainly included the family. Luther himself binds *oikos* to the family through his understanding of *Haustafeln*.[78] Wannenwetsch writes that the *Haustafeln*, "are themselves an example of the way the political form of action is brought into the *oikos*. For their tenor is the demand that believers should behave in essentials no differently at home from the way they behave in public worship. The underlying trend of the *Haustafeln* is that a person should respect the other more than him or herself, and that Christians should subject themselves to one another (Eph. 5:21)."[79] (2) οἰκονομία does express the earthly role of relations of humans that Luther wants to include under *oeconomia*. Although the New Testament usage refers more to the role of one who is over others (whether a steward in Jesus' parable or an elder over the church), there remain the close interpersonal ties associated with the word. (3) The spiritual dynamic of οἰκονομία is similar to that of *oeconomia*. As has been examined, οἰκονομία

---

the cause of Jesus. This adds an insightful twist to understanding one's station. In this case Paul is spiritually a slave to his master Jesus in a spiritual sense, and a prisoner for the sake of his master in a literal sense. See James D.G. Dunn, *The Epistles to Colossians and to Philemon* The New International Greek Testament Commentary (Carlisle: Paternoster, 1996), 310; Marvin R. Vincent, *Philippians & Philemon*, The International Critical Commentary (Edinburgh: T&T Clark, 1897), 175.

[78] The *Haustafeln*, or household codes, generally refers to those set forth in Eph. 5:21–33 and Colossians 3:18–25.

[79] Wannenwetsch, *Political Worship*, 155.

primarily serves to express a managerial role, but the word is often also infused with spiritual meaning.[80] Though Luther's *oeconomia* encompasses the familial relationship, which could *prima facie* be seen as a non-spiritual activity, the participation in *oeconomia* is a spiritual activity in response to the Word of God. (4) Friedrich notes that a concept often associated with οἰκονόμος is faithfulness.[81] As examined in Luther's exegesis of 1 Cor. 9:17 it is responsibility, and therefore faithfulness, that is crucial in Paul's being entrusted with the gospel. Paul has been given the responsibility of the Word, and therefore must respond to the giver in the context of the world. With *oeconomia* as a creation estate, this would be quite applicable. It is in faithfulness in the context of *oeconomia* that one is able to have rightly ordered relationships. Luther's concept of *oeconomia* as earthly relationships is more of an overarching theme, rather than deriving its meaning from a single root word.

Oeconomia and Aristotle

Because Luther's understanding of *oeconomia* is not synonymous with the New Testament's usage of οἰκονομία, he certainly had other sources in mind when thinking about the estates. Luther was by no means the first thinker to connect economy[82] with familial relationships. One of those sources was the Greek tradition of familial relations as seen in Aristotle's *Politics*. This section will show the similarity of Aristotle's formulation of domestic relations in *Politics*, and how it can be used as a positive source for understanding the three estates. Today, when one thinks of the word "politics," day to day personal relationships are probably not the first thing that comes to mind. Rather than just viewing the political as the nature of the state or realm of political authority, Aristotle saw it as intrinsically being moral theory.[83] C.C.W. Taylor comments that Aristotle meant *Politics* to be a continuation and completion of the program that was begun in *Nichomachean Ethics*.[84] The reason for this is that the treatises that are present in *Politics* direct one to how to achieve the *eudaemonia*, and this cannot be done apart from the context of a political society. One editor of *Politics* comments on Book 1:13, "The art of household management is a moral art, aiming at the moral goodness of the members of the

---

[80] Such as Paul being entrusted with the gospel, the role of the elder as being entrusted, God's plan in Eph. 1.
[81] Cf. 1 Cor. 4:2; Lk. 12:42; 16:10 f.; Mt. 25:21:21, 23. Friedrich, *Theological Dictionary of the New Testament*, 150–151.
[82] "Economy" is deliberately used here rather than *oeconomia* or *oikonomia*. The purpose being Aristotle would have used *oikonomia* in his writing, but inserting *oikonomia* here would have been confusing as what Luther has in mind for *oeconomia* is not *oikonomia*.
[83] C. C. W. Taylor, "Politics," *The Cambridge Companion to Aristotle*, ed. Jonathan Barnes (Cambridge: Cambridge University Press, 1995), 233.
[84] Ibid.

household; and this is true in regards to slaves as well as to other members."[85] For Aristotle, the relation of husband to wife, husband to child, etc. are not merely perfunctory roles to be filled, but rather have moral meaning attached to them. One is able to build character and virtues to achieve the good life through these relations. For Aristotle, the manner in which the patriarch related to the rest of the family could either serve to make a person more virtuous, or could damage one's morality. Perhaps this idea of the economic household carrying moral weight is what drew Luther to Aristotle's thinking on this subject. Aristotle was correct that there is a proper and an improper manner of running a household, and morality is tied to how one goes about fulfilling these roles.

In Book 1:10–13 of *Politics,* Aristotle addresses the concept of "household management." In 1:10 one finds the type of household manager similar to the manager previously seen in the parable of Jesus in Luke 16. The question Aristotle here addresses is whether the gaining of wealth should be the priority of the household manager.[86] In 1:12–13 Aristotle sets forth an *oeconomia* that is similar to the type of estate for which Luther is arguing. He begins 1:12 by writing, "Of household management we have seen that there are three parts— one is the rule of a master over slaves, which has been discussed already, another of a father, and the third of a husband. A husband and father, we saw rules over wife and children, both free, but the rule differs, the rule over his children being a royal, over his wife a constitutional rule. For although there may be exceptions to the order of nature, the male is by nature fitter for command than the female, just as the elder and full-grown is superior to the younger and more immature."[87] The Greek word used here for household management is οἰκονομής.[88] One can easily see the etymological similarities between what is used here, and the *oikonomia* used in the biblical text of Koine Greek. Aristotle obviously has a patriarchal society in mind when discussing *oikonomia*. Luther would have maintained the father as the head of the family, but this is seen in a Christological light. No longer is the father to act in a domineering fashion, but is to love his wife as Christ has loved the church. The father is not necessarily guiding the family because he possesses the most wisdom, and is therefore able to lead the family best (as in Aristotle). He is leading the family because this is the place in which God has put him. The roles of *oikonomia* revolve around the relationship of the patriarch to other members of the household. These other members are the slave, the child, and the wife.

---

[85] Aristotle, *The Politics of Aristotle*, ed. Ernest Barker (Oxford: Clarendon Press, 1946), 33.
[86] Aristotle, *The Politics*, ed. Stephen Everson (Cambridge: Cambridge UP, 1988), 14.
[87] Ibid., 17.
[88] Aristotle, *APISTOTEDOUS TA PODITIKA: The Politics of Aristotle* 2nd ed., English notes by Richard Congreve (London: Longams, Green, and Co., 1874), 39.

It is interesting that Aristotle chooses to use the phrase "order of nature" to refer to the role of man, woman, and child in the family dynamic. There is a definite symmetry to the manner in which Aristotle sees how the *oikonomia*[89] should be formed. Aristotle also frequently uses the word "natural" to refer to these relationships. For example, in 1:12 the king is the natural superior over his subjects but "remains the same kin or kind with them" in the same manner that the elder is superior to the younger and the father to the son.[90] In 1:13 he argues that all things rule and are ruled, and this is "according to nature."[91] Because the family dynamic is an order of nature, he also argues that the virtues will be displayed differently in men and women.[92] For example, he writes that courage is shown in a man through commanding, but is showing in a woman through obeying.[93] Bayer's "order of creation" is similar to Aristotle's "order of nature" in that both assume there is symmetry present in the order of the world, and therefore a proper manner in which to respond to that symmetry.

Further examining the relation of the biblical and Hellenistic concepts of *oikonomia* to the Latin *oeconomia*, in one Latin translation of *The Politics* the word translated in 12:1 as "household management" is "*yconomicae.*"[94] Beginning a Latin word with "y" is not original to the language, but usually indicates that the word is borrowed from the Greek.[95] The Western transliteration often reads as "*oeconomia.*"[96] This brief etymological study leaves little doubt concerning the roots of this word. As Luther was adept in both Latin and Greek, one wonders why he chose the Latin *oeconomia* (which he linked to Aristotle[97]) over the Greek *oikonomia* in his formulation of this estate. It is a legitimate inquiry to ask why one such as Luther, who clung so tightly to the revealed word and its God, would choose to cite Aristotle rather than Paul for evidence of a creation order. The answer was (most likely) that Luther was not choosing Aristotle over Paul, but perhaps Luther believed Aristotle's concept of economy was closer to expressing what Luther was trying

---

[89] As referenced earlier, Luther quotes Aristotle using *oeconomia* in *Politics*. It has been made clear that *oeconomia* is the Latinizing of the Greek *oikonomia*. As Aristotle was writing in Greek, *oikonomia*, not *oeconomia* will be used in this section to refer to Aristotle's concept. This is also helpful hermeneutically in examining Aristotle by avoiding an anachronism and hence casting meaning upon the word that may or may not have been originally present.
[90] Aristotle, *The Politics*, 18.
[91] Ibid., 19.
[92] Aristotle is in contrast to Socrates on this point.
[93] Aristotle, *The Politics*, 19.
[94] Aristotle, *Politicorvm Libri Octo*, ed. Francis Susemihl (Lipsiae: In Aedibus B.G. Tevbneri, 1872), 51.
[95] Charlton T. Lewis and Charles Short, *A Latin Dictionary*, (Oxford: Clarendon Press, 1879), 2018.
[96] Ibid., 1257.
[97] Martin Luther, "Exposition of Psalm 127," 45: 322–323.

to say with *oeconomia*. There are several advantages to using Aristotle's *oikonomia* rather than the Biblical *oikonomia*.

The first advantage is that when classifying Luther's second prelapsairan estate as "*oeconomia*" one is able to see more clearly how it differs from "*oikonomia*." As discussed previously, the New Testament understanding of *oikonomia* often carries spiritual overtones such as in the case of Eph. 1:10 where a "plan" or "dispensation" is being revealed. This plan in Eph. 1:10 is eschatological; looking forward to a time when Christ will unite all things in himself. Even when Paul uses *oikonomia* to refer to humans as possessing a responsibility it often has spiritual overtones (such as the responsibility of being entrusted with the gospel), and thus does not quite touch the point that Luther wishes to get across with *oeconomia*. It is impossible to say with any degree of accuracy, but perhaps if *oikonomia* carried more connotations of familial relationships in the biblical text Luther may have used it instead. It should also be clarified that it is doubtful Luther wished to remove all spiritual associations of *oikonomia*. The purpose in referring to this estate as *oeconomia* is not to create a sacred/secular divide between *ecclesia* and *oeconomia*. There is certainly a higher degree of sacredness in God revealing his Word to humans, but there is also sacredness in the interaction that occurs between a man and his family and a man and his vocation. Luther made this latter point clear when he spoke of the vocations of the "common man" often being more sacred than that of the clergy. Even though there is spirituality and sacredness in *oeconomia*, Luther literally wanted it to refer to the relationships of humans with other humans, and also with the world around them. The Latin *oeconomia* seldom carried the meaning of plan, but rather referred to "arrangement" or "division."[98] This is also seen in the fact that the Vulgate, the dominant Latin translation of the Bible for a millennium, chose to translate "*oikonomia*" in Eph. 1:10 as *dispensationem* rather than *oeconomia*.[99] The same root word (*dispensatio*) is used for *oikonomia* in the cognate verse Eph. 3:9.

Referring to Aristotle in making a theological point would not have been an odd move for Luther. Luther was not alone among the Reformers in referencing the philosophies of the ancient Greeks and Romans. Luther was well acquainted with Plato, Aristotle, Seneca and other ancient philosophers. In fact, the former lawyer John Calvin weaves the ancient philosophers in a much more prolific manner in *The Institutes* than Luther does in any of his writings.

---

[98] D. P. Simpson, *Cassell's New Latin Dictionary* (London: Cassell, 1959), 409. The vulgate translators prefer to use *dispensatio* even when Paul's stewardship rather than "a plan" as the English equivalent such as in 1 Cor. 9:17; Eph. 3:2; Col 1: 25. To complicate matters further, *oeconomia* and *dispensatio* are not the only Latin words used for *oikonomia*. Two such instances are in Lk. 16:2 and 1 Thess. 2:4.

[99] Roger Gryson, ed. *Biblica Sacra Vulgata* (Stuttgart: Biblgesellschaft, 1969), 1809.

Another advantage of using the nomenclature of *oeconomia* is an historical one. As Latin became the dominant written language of the church, one is able to find more use of *oeconomia* as referring to household management by the church fathers. The fathers primarily used *oikonomia* to refer to the administration of an office, in a similar manner as used by Paul. In fact, Lampe in *A Patristic Greek Lexicon* cites no instances by the fathers where *oikonomia* is used for the familial household management.[100] Related to this point, it became common for the Church to use Latin phrases to express theological concepts. Latin, as expressed through the overwhelming popular use of the Vulgate, had become the tongue of the Church. Remnants of the past glory of this language remain with the Church through the giving of the Mass in Latin. As Luther used Latin for the other two estates (*politia* and *ecclesia*) it would have been odd for Luther to use Greek for this concept, especially when Latin better expressed what he wanted to say about familial relationships.

The crux of Luther's distinction between *ecclesia* and *oeconomia* lies in the need to say that there is something significant about a person's relationship between flesh and the land. *Oeconomia* prevents the Christian life from becoming spiritualized to the point that there is no connection to current world in which God has placed humans. This allows for something real that remains of spiritual significance in one's daily contact where God has placed him or her in creation. An overemphasis upon the doctrine of creation could lead one to a position in which dominance over creation, rather than interaction with creation becomes of most importance.

Oeconomia, Aristotle, and Luther's "Exposition of Psalm 127"

Now that a similarity has been established between familial relations in *Politics* and Luther's use of *oeconomia*, this section will examine Luther's use of Aristotle in his "Exposition of Psalm 127."[101] Doing so will further demonstrate the connection of the influence of *Politics* on Luther's use of *oeconomia*. Throughout Luther's work he writes to awaken the reader to the fact that it is not good works or acts that the Church has condoned as spiritual that saves a person, but rather the work of Christ and faith in the Son of God. The spiritual and the physical are often beautifully intertwined, and both important, in Luther's work. An excellent example of this occurs in his "Exposition of Psalm 127." The focal point of this psalm is upon household management and household relationships. The psalm begins with a theocentric

---

[100] G.W.H. Lampe, *A Patristic Greek Lexicon* (Oxford: Clarendon Press, 1961), 940–943. It is an important to point to the fact that of the wealth of uses Lampe provides for *oikonomia* (ministration, management, charge, office, dispensation, organization, constitution, ordering, prudent handling, etc.), familial household management is never mentioned by the Church Fathers.

[101] Luther, "Exposition of Psalm 127," 45:311–337.

Pedagogy as Theological Praxis

emphasis: "Unless the Lord builds the house, those who build it labor in vain." Luther writes, "I selected this psalm because it so beautifully turns the heart away from covetousness and concern for temporal livelihood and possessions towards faith in God, and in a few words teaches us how Christians are to act with respect to the accumulation and ownership of this world's goods."[102] Luther's emphasis in this statement is upon faith in God being how one understands his or her relationship to the world. It is all too simple for the physical to take emphasis over the spiritual, or vice versa. *Oeconomia* allows one to view the world, and the affairs of the world, in light of *ecclesia*. In a fallen world, it can become all too easy to form a dualism between *ecclesia* and *oeconomia*. Here Luther emphasizes the *ecclesia* being the funnel through which to properly understand the *oeconomia*. Although later verses in this psalm speak more directly of the *oeconomia* in the raising of children and the blessing that they are, he does not leave verse 1 solely in the realm of the spiritual.

Luther's exposition of the first verse of this psalm is one of the clearest in his writings where he shows how he views the *oeconomia*: "First we must understand that "building the house" does not refer simply to the construction of walls and roof, rooms and chambers, out of wood and stone. It refers rather to everything that goes on inside the house, which in German we call managing the household" [haushallten]; just as Aristotle writes, '*Oeconomia*,' that, is pertaining to the household economy which comprises wife and child, servant and maid, livestock and fodder."[103] Luther interprets this verse as not primarily referring to the physical construction of a house, but primarily to the role of God in the construction of a family household.

In his 1539 work *Of the Councils and the Church*, Luther also makes use of Psalm 127:1 to explain the estates. He writes:

> This Psalm 127 [:1] says that there are only two temporal governments on earth, that of the city and that of the home, 'Unless the Lord builds the house; unless the Lord watches over the city.' The first government is that of the home, from which the people come; the second is that of the city, meaning the country, the people, princes and lords, which we call the secular government. These embrace everything—children, property, money, animals, etc. The home must produce, whereas the city must guard, protect and defend. Then follows the third, God's own home and city, that is, the church, which must obtain people from the home and protection and defense from the city.[104]

---

[102] Ibid., 317.
[103] Luther, "Exposition of Psalm 127," 317.
[104] Luther, "On the Councils and the Church, 1539," LW 41:177.

Perhaps Luther's most telling statement of how he views the relation between *ecclesia* and *oeconomia* also occurs in his exposition of this verse. Luther explains that it is not riches that make a newly started family happy and content, as there are those with wealth that squander it, and those without who are content with what they have. Other reasons people marry include desire for each other and desire for children. He writes that the desire for the other may wane, and a household may remain barren, so this cannot be the primary intention of marriage and the building of a household. In a short statement Luther brings together the relation of *ecclesia* and *oeconomia*, "Who is it that so disrupts marriage and household management, and turns them so strangely topsy-turvy? It is he of whom Solomon says: *Unless the Lord keeps this house, household management is a lost cause* (emphasis added). He wishes to buttress this passage [Ps. 127:1a] and confirm its truth. This is why he permits such situations to arise in the world, as an assault on unbelief, to bring to shame the arrogance of reason with all works and cleverness, and to constrain them to believe."[105] The everyday events of *oeconomia* are quickly misguided without one understanding his or her position in relation to God. Luther even says in this psalm, "Solomon's purpose is to describe a Christian marriage; he is instructing everyone how to conduct himself as a Christian husband and head of a household."[106] The Christian stands in a unique position of having received the Word and is able to act upon the moral principles in an attempt to properly establish one's *oeconomia*. Luther believes that the Christian marriage, and therefore the Christian *oeconomia* should be such that it is attractive to others. He argues that young people are hesitant to start a home, or often when they do it falters because they do not understand that it is He who builds the home. Solomon and Luther's wisdom on this subject is as applicable now as it was at the time of their writing. He writes of how extremely difficult it would be for one to attempt to build a house apart from the work of God.

Luther provides an example of this in the marriage relationship. He writes that where there was originally a longing of male for the female and also for children to come of that relationship, there now exists lust, shame in sexuality, and pain in childbirth. As a creation order, there is still a remnant of that past harmony, but in the present state it is little more than a remnant. Without a Christocentric focus in the marriage relationship this remnant is even further diluted. The paradox here is that despite the fact that what is left is a vestige of what was before the fall, the Christian has freedom in this creation order.

Luther also links faith to *oeconomia*: "So we see that the management of a household should and must be done in faith—then there will be enough—so that men come to acknowledge that everything depends not on our doing, but

---

[105] Luther, "Exposition of Psalm 127," 45: 323.
[106] Ibid.

on God's blessing and support."[107] This is a definitive statement of how Luther views the human response in *oeconomia*. In *ecclesia*, it is God who speaks through his Word, and the human who responds directly to God. In *oeconomia*, the human continues to respond to God in faith, but response is played out in the way the person interacts with the world around him or her. For Luther, Psalm 127:1 provides as excellent example of this. The need for shelter is a basic human need, and the building of the house is the labor required to meet that need. The writer of the Psalm provides a dual meaning in that both the physical structure of the home and the building of the family itself must be done in faith, and in response to God. As mentioned earlier, Luther retains that faith is central to one's understanding of *oeconomia*. Without faith, one has no grounding on which to properly build a household. The concept in Ecclesiastes of vanity is appropriate for understanding the building of a house apart from faith. The work of man is vain apart from acknowledgement and faith in the creator.

As Luther cites Aristotle in the exposition of this psalm, it is important to refer back to the way Aristotle was using *oikonomia* and contrast it with Luther's usage. Taylor writes concerning the *oikonomia* as seen Aristotle's *Politics*: "Strictly speaking, then it [household management in *The Politics*] ought to be classed rather as a special sort of *oikonomia* than as a kind of political rule. Household management involves the rule of the developed practical wisdom of the patriarch over slaves, females, and children."[108] These were the three relationships that Aristotle saw as present in the *oikonomia*. Taylor goes on to explain that such a structure is in place because slaves, females and children lack the developed wisdom that is present in the patriarch. Since these other humans lack the developed wisdom of the patriarch, they must make good upon that deficiency by depending on the wisdom of the patriarch.[109]

Luther alters this structure in his interpretation. With both Aristotle and Luther the relation remains essentially the head of the household relating to the rest of the household. In Aristotle, this relationship is how he relates with (a) his wife, (b) his slaves, and (c) his children. Luther's three categories in the "Exposition of Psalm 127" are: (a) wife and child(ren), (b) servant and maid, (c) livestock and fodder.[110] The two thinkers had very different reasons for their classification. Aristotle's groups are as such because they are dependent on the head of the household in three different ways. The society was formed in such a way that the patriarch was the one with the greatest deal power, both physical

---

[107] Luther, "Exposition of Psalm 127," 324.
[108] Barnes, *The Cambridge Companion to Aristotle*, 245.
[109] Barnes, *The Cambridge Companion to Aristotle*, 245.
[110] Luther, "Exposition of Psalm 127, for the Christians at Riga in Livonia, 1524," LW 45: 322.

and financial, in the family. Luther's classes are not based upon levels of dependency. Rather they are three distinct categories of interaction. The nuclear family is that with which the head of household will have the closest relation. Here Luther is relying more upon the *Haustafeln* of Eph. 5:21–33 than upon Aristotle. He acknowledges that there is a uniqueness, distinctness, and spirituality in the bond of husband and wife, as well as the unique role of husband and wife in raising children.

Luther's second category does carry the connotation of those who are at an economic disadvantage to the head of household as stated in the phrase "servant and maid."[111] His purpose in doing so may be because such relationships will be those that relate directly to the family. The servant and maid are involved in the daily running of the house. Despite this involvement these roles will not carry the same weight as the relationship of husband to wife and child. The household is an economic unit, and is the basic locus of production. The servant may have his or her own *oeconomia* with their spouse and child, but there is a sense of transience with the servant that is not present with the wife and child. One may question why relationships with humans in other social relationships (i.e. at the marketplace, sporting event, community gathering, etc.) are not placed under *oeconomia*. The most basic answer to this question is that all economic production happens within the domestic realm. Bayer writes, "*Oeconomia* encompasses for Luther everything that we today, in our economically differentiated situation, place into three different categories: marriage and family, business, and education and academic study."[112]

The role of the servant in Luther's day would have been to aid in raising the family and the provision of food for the family. Though one may balk at referring to someone as a servant in society today, the servant for Luther was one who helps to provide for the physical needs of the family and produces the surplus that drives trade. The servant today may be seen as the factory worker, the farmer, the child minder, etc. The family unit still requires aid of those outside of the familial unit in the provision of the needs of the family.

The contemporary role of the servant in *oeconomia* raises a host of ethical questions. Specifically, one must ask how to relate to those who are in relation to the *oeconomia*, both indirectly in the case of the factory worker the family has never met and the child minder who may in some cases spend more time with the child than the parents. As the family responds to God's word in the *oeconomia*, the role these servants play in the family should be carefully considered. Methods of granting equity to those in this relationship should also be discussed. For instance, in Luther's context he would have most likely seen

---

[111] Ibid.
[112] Bayer, *Martin Luther's Theology*, 142.

it as immoral to underpay a household servant. This is a person in relationship to the household, and deserving of an equitable wage. Similarly, the contemporary family when considering their role in *oeconomia* should consider whether those institutions they support financially through a servant role are also being provided an equitable wage. These ethical issues can become more convoluted the further the family is removed from the farmer, but the underlying current of needing to consider those in servant relationship to the family is crucial.

Another area for moral consideration concerning the role of the servant in *oeconomia* is the socio-economic placement of that person. Bayer comments that as "callings" became more specialized in the Middle Ages, the roles of servants and maids was thought of as "the lowest and most scorned of occupations."[113] Luther transformed this into a holy vocation.

In regards to vocation, this connection to God, man and the land does not necessarily make one vocation more holy than another. Luther writes in his 1530 message "A Sermon on Keeping Children in School,"[114] "I would take the work of a faithful, pious jurist and clerk over the holiness of all the priests, monks, and nuns, even the very best. And if these great and good works do not move you, then you ought at least to be moved by the honor and good pleasure of God, knowing that by this means you thank him so gloriously and render him such great service, as has been said."[115] The place of self-righteousness through religious practices has been removed in favor of Christ the justifier.

This picture of the role of the servant to the family is quite different than that presented by Aristotle. For Aristotle, the patriarch remained in a domineering role over the family and over the servant. The male leader of the family was in a position of power because he supposedly possessed superior wisdom to the other members of the family, and was therefore able to provide protection for the family. For Luther, these family roles take on a completely different dynamic. The family exists in worshipful service to God, and whatever harmony present in the family is present because of Christ. Jesus' prayer in Matt. 6:11, "Give us this day our daily bread," illustrates well how Luther understood *oeconomia*. Though bread is produced by tilling of the soil, the planting of the grain, the harvesting, and the baking, it is God who gives the bread. It is to God one should ask for provision rather than trusting in one's own hand. This is the heart of the message in Luther's "Exposition of Psalm 127." No matter how hard a man works, if it is not in gratitude to God it will be

---

[113] Bayer, *Martin Luther's Theology*, 141.
[114] Martin Luther, "A Sermon on Keeping Children in School," LW 46: 213–258
[115] Ibid., 241.

in vain. Luther does not picture a dictatorial man as the leader of the family, but one who works and lives out relationships in service to God.

Each of the stations a person fills in *oeconomia* is a good, God ordained activity. In one of his most eloquent passages on the beauty of one's station in the estates Luther writes, "A servant, maid, son, daughter, man, woman, lord, subject, or whoever else may belong to a station ordained by God, as long as he fills his station, is as beautiful and glorious in the sight of God as a bride adorned for her marriage or as the image of a saint decorated for a high festival."[116]

Luther's third category of "livestock and fodder" carries much theological significance. This category refers to man's relationship to the organic and inorganic world around him or her. It involves those who work to gather the fruit of the land. Although Luther says *"oeconomia"* is present in Aristotle, this category is not. Aristotle limited the concept to other human members of the household. One must therefore ask why Luther chose to add this category. If *oeconomia* is a biblical concept and creation order as Bayer asserts, what is added by the inclusion of "livestock and fodder"? Luther's purpose here is perhaps to emphasize man's place in and dependence on the created order. Luther's exposition of Gen. 1:26 is helpful: "Thus Adam had a twofold life: a physical one and an immortal one, though this was not yet clearly revealed, but only in hope. Meanwhile he would have eaten, he would have drunk, he would have labored, he would have procreated, etc. In brief words I want to call attention to these facts concerning the difference which God makes though His counsel, by which he sets us apart from the rest of the animals with whom He lets us live. Below we shall deal again with these matters at greater length."[117] Man will always be in need of food, and therefore in need of God to provide that food. The "daily bread" is a necessity just as it was in Jesus' day, and therefore worshipful gratitude to God is also necessary. Again, Jesus statement in Matthew 4 concerning bread also aids in understanding this position: "Man shall not live by bread alone, but by every word that comes from the mouth of God."[118] It is the Word of God that is able to sustain man in daily relationship. It should also be noted that here Jesus does acknowledge necessity of daily sustenance. Food, and thus the land, are good things given by God, however these provisions are not all that is necessary when *oeconomia* is in response to God. Luther referred to this verse often in his writings.[119] In many of these references his purpose in citing this verse is to point the reader to the fact that

---

[116] Martin Luther, "Psalm 111," LW 13:368.
[117] Luther, "Lectures on Genesis 1–5," LW 1:57.
[118] Matt. 4:4.
[119] LW 5:54, 61, 137, 144, 202, 7:128, 9:93, 14:192, 15:173, 25:238, 26:95, 28:143, 29:162, 216, 31:210, 345, 33:155, 35:344, 36:45, 39:200, 43:44, 48:206. References to this verse taken from the *Index to Luther's Works*, LW 55:405.

dependence on God was a necessary quality in the life of those who profess to trust the Word of God. Luther links the relationship between *ecclesia* and *oeconomia* as well as the blessing of God upon his people and the land in his commentary on Gen. 27:28. This verse falls in the blessing of Isaac upon his son Jacob (though Isaac is under the mistaken assumption that he is blessing Jacob's twin Esau): "May God give you the dew of heaven and of the fatness of the earth and plenty of grain and wine." On this passage Luther writes:

> This blessing is far different from and much more sublime than the consecrated water concerning which the papists make many false assertions. They were blessings concerning eternal life over against eternal death. They were priestly and regal blessings that reached into the life to come. Nevertheless, they cannot be administered apart from this life, and it is necessary for us to have physical blessings as well, for we cannot enjoy the eternal blessing without the temporal blessings. God must bless the field, supply bread, meat, and all the other necessities of life. But 'man does not live by bread alone' (Matt. 4:4), and the physical blessings are given because of that eternal blessing. Therefore the spiritual promises always include the temporal promises.[120]

Luther emphasizes the blessings provided in temporal life. In fact, he castigates the papists whom he believes disregard such blessing. He provides a linkage between the earthly reality of the need for provision and the giving of that provision from God.

For Luther, Adam's relationships with the land through labor and with the animals of the land are prelapsarian activities. The concepts of understanding man as *imago dei* and as the keeper of the garden are important for understanding this relationship. Man has been given a special place in tending the garden. Adam was to "work it and keep it" (Gen. 2:15). Prior to the fall, Adam's relationship would have been with God, with Eve, and with the land and animals. Luther's reflections on Gen. 2:12 include the statement that when God punished Adam's sin, he also curses the earth. By "earth" he means not only the physical land, but also "the fish of the sea and the birds of the heaven."[121] The chaos and disorder reaped on the land is a result of man's fall. The destiny of land and animals is in an intricate relationship with that of humans. In Gen. 3:17 God curses the land because of the action of Adam. Just as the relation between husband and wife can go awry in Luther's "Exposition of Psalm 127," man's relationship with the world has been skewed as well.

There is also an eschatological aspect in including animals and the land in *oeconomia*. Creation groans for redemption, as do humans. Luther writes, "Moreover, it appears here [Gen. 3:17] what a great misfortune followed sin,

---

[120] Martin Luther, "Lectures on Genesis Chapters 26–30," LW 5:137.
[121] Luther, "Lectures on Genesis 1–5," LW 1:99.

because the earth, which is innocent and committed no sin, is nevertheless compelled to endure a curse and, as St. Paul says in Rom. 8:20, "has been subjected to vanity." But it will be freed from this on the Last Day, for which it is waiting."[122] *Oeconomia* encompasses the familial relationships, but in these marred relationships on his able to catch glimpse of its pre-fall beauty. This could occur in the marriage relationship when the wife is loved as Christ loved the church. Such a glimpse could occur in the relation with the land in the sense of satisfaction that accompanies the end of a day of work well done. Luther refers to these glimpses as "remnants of the former blessing."[123]

An aspect of Aristotle's *oikonomia* that Bayer picks up in his interpretation of Luther is the concept of freedom in *oikonomia*. Mulgan comments that the rule of this patriarch over slaves is despotic, because the master has his own interests in mind. In contrast, there is freedom in the "rule" of the head of the house over wife and children. Ideally, the husband would act in the interests of his wife and children rather than his own.[124]

In many ways Luther's concept of *oeconomia* is a worthwhile development of which to take note. Luther's personal asceticism and harsh strictness toward the Augustinian order has been well documented.[125] Many of Luther's religious practices of his time as a monk were to find a gracious God and to escape from this earthly life. Such a life could easily lead to a dualism between the flesh and a future heavenly reality. Even with this past, Luther was able to relate man's earthly reality within the context of the cosmos. *Oeconomia* involves the relation of man to man and man to earth.

Of this relation Bayer writes, "There is no question that the life and the theology of the Augustinian monk Martin Luther were characterized by the strictest asceticism up to the time of his reformational turning point. . . . It is most surprising that Luther studies to this point have not pursued the question about how this turn from a radical denial of the world to an impressive affirmation of everything that is of the world and nature took place, which shines forth more brightly in Luther's writings from 1520 on, with ever increasing emphasis."[126] This spiritual connection to the earthly is most clearly seen in the roles of household management and parenthood in the *oeconomia*. Perhaps Luther's development of the earthly aspect of *oeconomia* was a reaction against his earlier has practices as a monk.

---

[122] Luther, "Lectures on Genesis 1–5," LW 1:204.
[123] Ibid.
[124] R. G. Mulgan, *Aristotle's Political Theory* (Oxford: Clarendon Press, 1977), 44.
[125] See, for example, Walther von Loewenich, *Martin Luther: The Man and His Work*, Chapter 7 "The Struggle to Find a Gracious God" (Minneapolis: Augsburg Publishing House, 1982), 72–82.
[126] Bayer, *Martin Luther's Theology*, 140–141.

Pedagogy as Theological Praxis

As discussed throughout this section, understanding *oeconomia* is a vital part of Luther's theology. *Oeconomia* allows man to flourish in the good world that God has created for him. An emphasis upon *oeconomia* can help humans to become comfortable with the context in which one is placed as well as to positively fulfill the station of one's life.

Politia

The next of Luther's estates that will be discussed is that of *politia*. If the estates are seen as a hierarchy, *politia* would be the third of the three estates. For Luther, '*politia*' and 'government' are not synonymous terms. *Politia* is the larger structure under which the government resides. He writes, "However, the stations are not identified with these national systems of law and order because the legal systems change in the course of time but the stations remain basically unchanged in all times—they are stable. God declares that, "these stations must remain if the world is to stand."[127]

Luther does not see the third estate, *politia*, as being a creation estate, but rather as a result of the fall. Bayer understands this estate as, "an order made necessary at the time of the fall into sin."[128] Luther writes:

> Moreover, there was no government of the state before sin, for there was no need of it. Civil government is a remedy required by our corrupted nature. It is necessary that lust be held in check by the bonds of the laws and by penalties. For this reason you may correctly call civil government the rule of sin, just as Paul calls Moses also the minister of death and sin (Rom. 8:2). . . . Therefore if men had not become evil through sin, there would have been no need of civil government; but Adam, together with his descendants, would have lived in utmost serenity and would have achieved more by moving one finger than all the swords, instruments of torture, and axes can achieve now. At that time there would have been no robber, murderer, thief, envier, and liar. What need, therefore, would there have been of laws and of civil government, which is like a cauterizing iron and an awful remedy by which harmful limbs are cut off that the rest may be preserved?[129]

The *politia* therefore spans the working of the world and government that are present in the context of the fall. This estate could also be described as a natural necessity that results from the present state of the world. In the quote above, Luther does not call the civil government itself corrupt, but rather its *necessity* of being present because the world is corrupt. The natural disposition of man is order without the need of civil law, because the law of God governed man. The *politia* also has a close relation to the *oeconomia*. Luther writes in the Large Catechism:

---

[127] Althaus, *The Ethics of Martin Luther*, 37. Luther, "Psalm 111," LW 13: 358.
[128] Bayer, *Martin Luther's Theology*, 123.
[129] Luther, "Lectures on Genesis 1–5," LW 1:104.

The same also is to be said of obedience [as a child to a father] to civil government, which (as we have said) is all embraced in the estate of fatherhood and extends farthest of all relations. For here the father is not one of a single family, but of as many people as he has tenants, citizens, or subjects. For through them, as through our parents, God gives us food, house and home, protection and security. Therefore since they bear such name and title with all honor as their highest dignity, it is our duty to honor them and to esteem them great as the dearest treasure and the most previous jewel on earth.[130]

When considering the role of the civil government in connection to Christian theology, one of the first issues to arise is where the Christian should fall on the spectrum of his or her connection to the state. At one end of the spectrum there is the position that the state is a secular, evil institution full of corruption. The state is necessary because of the depravity of man to prevent men from reaching their full potential of evil. Those who have a more positive view of natural law may hold to a more Aristotelian and Stoic tradition, "that assumes human beings can strive for a consensus that will eventually be cosmopolitan, a consensus of all peoples to be achieved by their powers of reason and that all people can follow in all aspects; rules being broken are the exceptions."[131]

Bayer sees aspects of both of these tendencies in Luther's *politia*. The first is perhaps more obvious in that there being a *politia* is a result of the fall, and is present in the kingdom of the world. The latter tendency is present because ultimately, *politia* derives its meaning in *oeconomia*. Luther's Large Catechism reads, "All other authority flows and spreads out from the authority of the parents," and "The household is the source of all public affairs."[132] The authority of the state takes it authority from the primeval authority granted by God in the familial unit. Because *politia* ultimately finds its meaning in *oeconomia*, "Luther at times relativizes his strict theological assessment that the political estate had to be established because of sin."[133] Because both tendencies can be seen in Luther's work, Bayer argues for a middle path in interpreting Luther that relies on his understanding of "freedom" in Luther. Bayer sees this first path as lacking a sufficient doctrine of creation, and the second as lacking in its doctrine of sin. In his "Sermon on Keeping Children in School" Luther also speaks highly of government:

> Nevertheless, worldly government is a glorious ordinance and splendid gift of God, who has instituted and established it and will have it maintained as something men cannot do without. If there were no worldly government, one man could not stand

---

[130] Martin Luther, "Large Catechism," in *Triglot Concordia: The Symbolical Books the Evangelical Lutheran Church* (St. Louis: Concordia Publishing House, 1921), 590.
[131] Bayer, *Martin Luther's Theology*, 148.
[132] Ibid.
[133] Ibid., 148–149.

before another; each would necessarily devour the other, as irrational beasts devour one another. Therefore as it is the function and honor of the office of preaching to make sinners saints, dead men live, damned men saved, and the devil's children God's children so it is the function and honor of worldly government to make men out of wild beasts and to prevent men from becoming wild beasts. It protects a man's body so that no one may slay it; it protects a man's wife so that no one may seize her; it protects a man's child, his daughter or son, so that no one may carry them away and steal them; it protects a man's house so that no one may break in and wreck things; it protects a man's fields and cattle and all his goods so that no one may attack, steal, plunder, or damage them. . . . It is certain, then, that temporal authority is a creation and ordinance of God, and that for us men in this life it is a necessary office and estate which we can no more dispense with than we can dispense with life itself, since without such an office this life cannot continue.[134]

In this passage government is a good thing given by God to restrain evil men from committing more evil. *Politia* is a necessity in a fallen world, and in this fallen state the world is a better place with government. Because God institutes the estates, there is also "orderliness" in how they should function. When the *politia* causes havoc upon its people, it is because it is not functioning as it should. In his exposition of Psalm 111:3 Luther writes:

The psalmist also says that these undertakings and institutions of God are honorable and glorious, that is, noble and fine, praiseworthy and beautiful, so that whoever knows them must praise them as fine stations. But the ungodly do not understand them, and so despise them. Where such stations operate as they should, there things go well in the world, and there is the very righteousness of God. But where such stations are not maintained, it makes for unrighteousness. Now God declares concerning these stations that they must remain if the world is to stand, ever though many oppose and rage against them.[135]

Although the "deeds" to which the Psalmist refers are not specifically named, Luther writes in such a way that it is clear to him that the estates are glorious and majestic deeds for which one should rejoice. Even if the *politia* is fallen, when it is viewed as glorious, majestic, and redeemable, it is something for which the Christian can take joy. Luther further writes on this verse, "Surely, anyone should laugh in his heart for joy if he finds himself in a station that God instituted and ordained. He ought to shout and dance as he thanks God for such a divine act, because here he hears and is assured that his position is full of honor and adornment before God."[136] Although the *politia* is not specifically named in this exposition, service within the governmental structure would certainly entail the "stations, offices, and duties among men"[137] to which

---

[134] Luther, "A Sermon on Keeping Children in School," LW 46: 237–238.
[135] Luther, "Psalm 111," LW 13: 358.
[136] Luther, "Psalm 111," LW 13: 358.
[137] Ibid.

Luther refers. Luther also chastises those who do not appreciate the station at which God has placed him or her in an estate. He writes:

> But the blind and senseless world will not see this [the value of one's estate]. It despises such stations so shamefully that it makes a pious heart bleed. 'Never!' is says. 'What shall I do with such an unimportant secular station? I will serve God and become a monk or a nun, a priest or a hermit.' And out of this wisdom there has developed such a lively fanaticism that the world is full of monasteries and institutions of so many different orders and factions, and everything fairly crawls and swarms with spiritual people. This was thought to be a good and noble thing, and they applied this verse[138] to themselves and actually said: 'Our work is full of honor and adornment.' This they did not merely rob God's work of its honor and adornment but also polluted, profaned, and blasphemed it. For it deserves to be called a worldly, harmful, and damnable station and life, while their station is sheer goodness and certain salvation. Such people sing this verse as follows: 'The works of God are a shame and a disgrace, filthy and unclean.' But now the Gospel has returned and once more praises God in this His work and ordinance, restoring honor and adornment to these stations. And it exposes the institutions of those people as filth that they are, so that they stand naked and disgraced.[139]

Johannes Heckel and *Politia*

Johannes Heckel's seminal *Lex Charitatis*[140] is helpful in discerning Luther's position on "law" and therefore helps to construct how he understood the *politia*. A brief digression into his work will further clarify what Luther is attempting to do with his understanding of *politia*. Although there is not a section of Heckel's book specifically on the estates, the underlying current of the estates runs throughout the book. For instance he writes, "God provided two legal institutions for the structure of the spiritual communal existence, church and marriage; the former for the promotion of the internal and the external communal life in relationship with the Creation (*cultus dei*), the latter for the God-orientated relationship of people of different sexes with each other."[141] The *politia* is not mentioned in this quotation because of its place as a postlapsarian estate. He writes, "What happened in the kingdom of the world to the institutions of the divine positive law after the Fall? Their history confirms the knowledge which Luther had gained from studying the divine natural law and the secular natural law. Those institutions experienced the same secularization and externalization as did the divine natural law in its infralapsarian misinterpretation."[142]

---

[138] This is still in reference to Ps. 111:3.
[139] Luther, "Psalm 111," LW 13:368–369.
[140] Johannes Heckel, *Lex Charitatis: A Juristic Disquisition on Law in the Theology of Martin Luther* trans. and ed. Gottfried G. Krodel (Grand Rapids: Eerdmans, 2010).
[141] Heckel, *Lex Charitatis*, 52.
[142] Ibid., 70.

Pedagogy as Theological Praxis

Heckel agrees with Bayer that the *politia* must ultimately be a subcategory of *oeconomia* since its space in the world is in the context of human relationship: "The domestic governance of a father is the first legally organized power relationship on earth. Here originates the total order of offices and estates in the *politia*. The civic order in a state, even more, the civic order among mankind, is derived from this source."[143] It is an important link that the nexus Heckel wishes to make between *oeconomia* and *politia* is that of power. The type of power a husband operates over his local family unit is not the same that the state operates over its people. The two types of power are similar in that their goal should be service of another, but again the fall has effected how the *politia* must wield its power. Heckel writes, "Therefore Luther's concept 'marriage' became the nucleus of his concept 'state', with marriage being understood as an infralapsarian institution to be managed according to the secular natural law. For only since the Fall is there power over life and death on earth, only since then is there governmental authority. Because this authority has the competency of punishing, its symbol of office is the sword. As mentioned above, its task is to preserve peace in the kingdom of the world; it is to protect the good and punish the evil."[144]

As will be further discussed in the next chapter, the *politia* serves the purposes of God in the world. As Heckel writes, "God is present also in the secular governance. By his commission, governmental authority is in the first place the executor of the divine punishment in the kingdom of the divine wrath (*vindex Dei in iram*), secondly, it is the tools of God's merciful love; and thirdly, it is the make (*larva*), viceroy, and officer of the divine governance over the world in God's kingdom at the left."[145] There is a balance that must be found between accepting the political order as a fallen institution and seeing God's work in that order. Luther writes in his Genesis commentary, "It is necessary that lust be held in check by the bonds of the laws and by penalties. For this reason you may correctly call civil government the rule of sin, just as Paul calls Moses also the minister of death and of sin (Rom. 8:2)."[146] Luther points to government as a necessary entity because of sin, but Heckel attempts to point to how this can also been seen as a positive necessity.

Another distinctive which Heckel points to is that *politia* can only function properly within the context of the *ecclesia* of Christendom. He writes, "According to Christ's mandate, Christendom is governed in spiritual matters by the clergy so that it forms the universal church (*ecclesia universalis*). On the other hand, in secular matters Christendom is governed by secular rules, and it is called *politia*. *Ecclesia* and *politia* describe the two separate but coordinated

---

[143] Ibid., 77.
[144] Heckel, *Lex Charitatis*, 77.
[145] Ibid., 78.
[146] Luther, "Lectures on Genesis 1–5," LW 1: 104.

structures of the one spiritual-secular kingdom of Christendom, the *respublica christiana*."[147] Heckel also makes a connection between the validity of these estates and how they relate to Luther's doctrine of the two kingdoms.[148]

Luther differs from Aristotle on the relation of the familial *oikonomia* and the *politia* (or *polis* for Aristotle). For Aristotle, through the citizenship of the family, the child is prepared to become a citizen of the state. By the father's rule over his household, he becomes prepared to also rule over the state.[149] In the classical sense, *oikonomia* would have extended its meaning not only to the household, but also to the state.[150] Bayer admits that for Luther, in some sense the *politia* derives itself from the *oeconomia*, and needs to also be interpreted through the implications of household life.[151]

It is important to note that although Luther viewed *politia* as a result of the fall, this estate was not such that God did not work through it.[152] Spitz writes that for Luther, it is through the state that God works for peace and order.[153] Although the world has been corrupted by sin, the state working properly seeks to redeem and negate part of that which was lost. Even in this state of fallenness, this adds an element of freedom to do good, through bringing peace and justice to society.

In addition, Luther saw two purposes in the use of the law. The primary use was the political use, and his secondary use was the spiritual use. In the political use, the purpose of the law was to restrain sinful actions. Here the law takes on a negative role as it serves to prevent mankind from reaching his full potential of depravity. He writes in his commentary on Galatians, "God hath ordained magistrates, parents, teachers, law, bonds, and all civil ordinances, that, if they can do no more, yet at the least they may bind the devil's hands, that he may rage not in his bondslaves after his own lust."[154] Luther writes that the place of those in authority to bind the devil (i.e. institute such laws that would prevent sinful actions) has been ordained by God. One can see how this ordination is not such that it is a creation order for Luther. Prior to the fall there would have

---

[147] Heckel, *Lex Charitatis*, 204.
[148] This relation will be further discussed in chapter 2.
[149] Ernest Barker, *The Political Thought of Plato & Aristotle* (London: G. P. Putnam's Sons, 1906), 400.
[150] T.K. Abbott, *Ephesians & Colossians*, The International Critical Commentary (Edinburgh: T & T Clark, 1897), 17.
[151] Bayer, *Freedom in Response*, 93.
[152] Chapter two will provide further analysis of the relation of *politia* and the fall.
[153] Lewis W. Spitz, "Luther's Ecclesiology and His Concept of the Prince as Notbischof," *Church History* 22:2 (June 1953): 116.
[154] Martin Luther, *A Commentary on St. Paul's Epistle to the Galatians* ed. Philip S. Watson, (London: T & T Clark, 1953), 302.

Pedagogy as Theological Praxis

been no need for restraint of the devil without sin present in the world. The implication still stands that though the world has been tainted, the institution of *politia* remains such that God has instituted it.

Eschatology and *Politia*

Eschatology is an aspect of Luther's theology that is often overlooked, but is important for understanding *politia*. The publication of *Die letzten Dinge* in 1949 by Paul Althaus set a new path in Luther scholarship as this work focused much upon the problem of eschatology in general, and took Luther's own contribution to the subject seriously.[155] Because a theology of the estates relies in part on one's understanding of the fall upon the estates, understanding Luther's views on eschatology is also crucial.

In Althaus's work on Luther he views eschatology as an extremely important part of Luther's theology. This is rooted in his understanding of salvation and his theology of the cross. One may often think of salvation as an event that either took place at a past fixed moment or as some type of future event. Althaus notes salvation as being a present reality for Luther.[156] Christians live in a state of present salvation but also wait for future revelation. Althaus writes, "Theology is and remains theology of the cross; therefore it necessarily becomes eschatology. Faith eagerly waits and hopes for the future when Christ's lordship will be revealed. Luther's theology is thoroughly eschatological in the strict sense of expecting the end of the world. His thoughts about the eschaton are not a conventional appendix but a section of his theology which is rooted in, indispensable to, and a decisive part of the substance of his theology."[157] A theology of the cross in expectation of resurrection does not stand to the accusation that it is not eschatological enough. Althaus also grounds Luther's ethics with the foundational understanding that everything the Christian does presupposes he or she is justified.[158] In this paradigm justification governs the Christian ethos as it governs the Christian's understanding of what the Christian life should be.

Walther von Loewenich writes, "Hence the eschatological character of Luther's concept of faith can be traced to his early years; it is given with his understanding of Hebrews 11:1. But even after the change in Luther's

---

[155] George Wolfgang Forell, "Justification and Eschatology in Luther's Thought," *Church History* 38:2 (1969): 165. Althaus's later work, *Die Theologie Martin Luthers* (Gutersloh: Gutersloher Verlagshaus Gerd Mohn, 1963) is available in English, and as such it will be discussed further.

[156] Paul Althaus, *The Theology of Martin Luther*, trans. Robert Schultz (Philadelphia: Fortress Press, 1966), 404.

[157] Althaus, *The Theology of Martin Luther*, 404–405.

[158] Althaus, *The Ethics of Martin Luther*, 3.

understanding of this passage had taken place, as described above, the eschatological thrust did not disappear."[159] Von Loewenich goes on to explain that throughout Luther's career his theology of the cross was tied to eschatological hope.

Althaus further writes, "Luther's certainty that there will be a new life arising out of death is based on the totality of God's redeeming work in Christ. . . . The heart and center of this whole position is the resurrection of Christ Jesus and the victory over death which he won in it."[160] Even if the *politia* must continue in the present state of affairs, viewing *politia* in light of Christ and the eschaton adds a new dimension. There is a built in assumption that there will be a time when the temporal authority will not be, but there is also an impetus to redeem the *politia* in its current state. If the focus was entirely upon the eschaton, there would be no reason to involve oneself in the political ordering that makes up much of one's life. If this were completely the focus, there would be no need to write a letter such as "To The Councilmen of All Cities in Germany that they Establish and Maintain Christian Schools"[161] as involvement political life would not be necessary.

Forrell notes four essential points of Luther's eschatology:

1. Luther's justification by faith is an eschatological experience.
2. Luther's view of eschatology makes it the seal of his doctrine of justification.
3. Justification by faith without eschatology is a form of subjectivistic and individualistic self-hypnosis.
4. Eschatology without justification by faith is mere utopianism.[162]

One important aspect about the state is that even if the *politia* is a fallen estate, it remains under the control of God. Although there are two kingdoms (one being spiritual and the other secular), "The second is no less a regime of God than the first."[163] Bayer noted that the two kingdoms and the three estates should not be read to the exclusion of one or the other. The dominant theological position at the time of writing "To the Councilmen" would have been that governmental authority derived authority from the Pope. By 1520 Luther was circumscribing the authority of the Pope by saying that secular

---

[159] Walther von Loewenich, *Luther's Theology of the Cross*, trans. Herbert J.A. Bouman (Belfast: Christian Journals Ltd., 1976), 90.
[160] Althaus, *The Theology of Martin Luther*, 410.
[161] Martin Luther, " To the Councilmen of All Cities in Germany that they Establish and Maintain Christian Schools, 1524" LW 45: 341–378.
[162] Forell, "Justification and Eschatology in Luther's Thought," 168.
[163] Edgar M. Carlson, *Luther's Conception of Government*, Church History 15:4 (1946): 259.

rulers derived their power directly from God.[164] In this paradigm, rulers should serve, "as the embodiment of God's temporal government on earth."[165] These rulers are established to punish sin and to sustain law and order among people. To this secular realm the temporal sword has been granted to punish on behalf of God. In this manner temporal secular authorities serve as God's ministers just as much as ministers of the Word, though this is exercised in a different way.[166]

The Three Estates and Luther's Theology

Before discussing the role the three estates plays in Luther's understanding of pedagogy, it would perhaps be helpful to discuss the value of the estates in his theology. This section will conclude this chapter by providing a summary of why the estates are an important part of Luther's theology and also how the estates stand in relation to ethics. American Lutheran theologian Carl Braaten writes, "Karl Barth was right to criticize the Lutheran notion of the "orders of creation" as an autonomous locus of theology completely separate from the revelation of God in Jesus Christ. Our Christian understanding of justice must be related to the gospel of justification. The lack of a Christological center and criterion in the theology of the orders of creation became the legitimate point of departure for the Barthian attack on the Lutheran social ethic."[167] Is there in fact a lack of Christological focus in the estates, or does Barth's emphasis upon Christology lead him to the conclusion that there is not?

Luther's use of the estates point toward the creating God who has provided space in which humans are able to live and thrive. There is a Christological implication in the estates, whether they are seen as orders of creation or as orders of preservation. It is in the garden that one sees a "church without walls"[168] for Luther. This lovely space was made for worship. Barth's critique of the orders of creation finds its location in the statement that the estates are nothing but a form of natural law. Barth's critique is helpful, in that it does not the subjective nature of the estates that can lead to a misinterpretation. The counterpoint from a Lutheran perspective would be that it is abundantly clear that the estates are part of the created order, whether it be called natural law or something else.

---

[164] W. D. J. Cargill Thompson, *The Political Thought of Martin Luther* (Sussex: The Harvester Press, 1984), 63.
[165] Ibid.
[166] Ibid.
[167] Carl E. Braaten, *Principles of Lutheran Theology*, 2nd ed. (Minneapolis: Fortress Press, 2007, 158.
[168] Luther, "Lectures on Genesis Chapters 1–5," 103.

The estates are valuable for understanding Luther's theology because they provided needed boundaries in which humans can grow and flourish. Brock writes:

> The institutions are statements about what Christians believe the Trinitarian God, through scripture, has taught humans to hope for from his speaking, care and governance. . . . The institutions are a hermeneutic for discovering the reality of God's action in the world. They draw on the steady emphases of scripture that express what humans have been told they may hope for from God and in which attentiveness to the neighbour is linked to and draws faith into fresh hearing of God.[169]

The use of the estates in theology acknowledges that God has and is steadily at work in his creation. The estates stand as a promise of the Triune God's care and provision for humanity. Christ's claim upon one's life becomes known through the finding oneself in a position of receiving from God in *ecclesia*.

---

[169] Brock, "Why the Estates?," 182.

Pedagogy as Theological Praxis

2. The Three Estates and Luther's "To the Councilmen of All Cities in Germany that they Establish and Maintain Christian Schools"

In the previous chapter Luther's understanding of the three estates was outlined. Emphasis was placed upon how the practical application of his doctrine of the Three Estates could inform the larger picture of Luther's theology. This chapter will seek to link Luther's account of the three estates to his approach to the topic of education. In Luther's writing the Psalms were informative for understanding the relationship between worship and life. Just as Luther's "Exposition of Psalm 127"[1] served to inform how the three estates related to one's life in the previous chapter, this chapter will serve to show how Luther's understanding of the three estates relates to the topic of education as displayed in his, "To The Councilmen of All Cities in Germany that they Establish and Maintain Christian Schools."[2] The purpose of this reading will be to use Luther's three estates to offer an interpretative grid for specific areas of life, in this case the area of education. This letter, in conjunction with his "Sermon on Keeping Children in School (1530)"[3] are considered to be the most complete for understanding Luther's theology of education.

Introduction to "To the Councilmen" and Medieval German Education

To begin by setting the context for "To the Councilmen," an overview of education in medieval Germany will be provided. Doing so will aid in understanding what Luther was attempting to do in his educational reforms. Walter Brandt notes, "during the Middle Ages the primary means of obtaining an education was through the monastic school."[4] Because of this tradition, formal European education was inherently tied to an ecclesiastical foundation. Witte writes:

> In the centuries before the Lutheran Reformation, the Roman Catholic Church had dominated German education. The church regarded 'teaching' as a special apostolic calling of its clergy, alongside preaching and sacramental administration. Christ's last words to his apostles had been: 'Go ye therefore and *teach all nations*, baptizing them in the name of the Father, and of the Son, and of the Holy Ghost: *teaching*

---

[1] Martin Luther, "Exposition of Psalm 127," LW 45: 313–337.
[2] Ibid., 341–378.
[3] Martin Luther, "A Sermon on Keeping Children in School," LW 46: 207–258
[4] Luther, "To the Councilmen of all Cities in Germany that they Establish and Maintain Christian Schools," LW 45: 341.

them to observe all that I have commanded you: and lo, I am with you always, even to the end of the world.' This calling to teach, the Church believed, had passed, through apostolic succession, to the pope and his prelates. It obligated them both to guard the "faith" set forth in the Bible and to elaborate its meaning for daily life. The Bible would thereby be transmitted faithfully to each new generation, and the meaning of the Bible elaborated through a living Christian tradition.[5]

Formal education was therefore one of the means by which the Church was able to maintain control over who had the authority to teach throughout Christendom. The church established its first schools in Germany in the late seventh century, so by the early 1500's there was an immense network of church schools in this areas governed by canon law and tailored rules by local bishops and synods.[6] This longstanding tradition of the Church being the gatekeeper to education began to be altered by the rise of humanism prior to the Reformation. Humanism sought to revive the liberal education tradition that they saw present in the ancient Greeks. The teachings presented by the humanists at times caused conflict with the established order. The Reformation even further convoluted this order. Because of this connection between the church and education, as men began to question the established tradition and teachings of the church, they also questioned what impact this religious teaching was having upon their children. Brandt writes, "If, as the reformers contended, many of the current doctrines and practices of the church were erroneous and dangerous to salvation, surely parents ought not to send their children to schools where these doctrines were inculcated. Princes, nobles, and municipal authorities, doubtless motivated by greed as much as by their theological principles confiscated the endowments by which schools were supported."[7]

Throughout Luther's writings he is in favor of supporting education that is in line with proper doctrine. Despite this his writings were at times characterized as being anti-educational. One can understand this characterization as in his usual vitriolic language he referred to monastic and cathedral schools as "devil's training centers" and their textbooks as "asses' dung."[8] Because Luther preached the priesthood of all believers, some took this to mean that formal training was not required to take on the role of a priest. The results of an uneducated priesthood had the potential of being catastrophic to the fledging movement of Luther's supporters.[9] Mark Noll writes, "The

---

[5] John Witte, "The Civic Seminary: Sources of Modern Public Education in the Lutheran Reformation of Germany," *Journal of Law and Religion* 12:1 (1995): 179.
[6] Ibid., 180.
[7] Witte, "The Civic Seminary: Sources of Modern Public Education in the Lutheran Reformation of Germany," 180.
[8] Ibid.
[9] This can be seen more directly in the teaching of Karlstadt.

reformers proclaimed that all believers were equal members of a spiritual priesthood. All had the privilege of standing before God without the mediation of any other human beings or human structures. The Holy Spirit was active in all believers. The conclusion, at least to many, was obvious: education as such is *not* necessary for the Christian led by the Holy Spirit. Education can only create a privileged, priest-like class of the learned who impose themselves between God and individuals."[10] One of the most obvious ways that Luther could respond to these errors was through his writings. He wanted an educated public, but for the purpose of the people being able to read Scripture and catechisms rather than to hold positions of authority over others.

While he tried to avoid being characterized as anti-educational, he also had an aversion towards scholastic theology. Early in his academic training, Luther was a member of the *via moderna* rather than the *via antiqua*, but from at least 1515 onwards he was in conflict with this training.[11] Those of the *via antiqua*, such as Thomas Aquinas and Duns Scotus, "held that universal concepts were the expressions of reality itself, since they were the higher reality behind all individuality, nominalists believed that only the individual or the particular was real, and that universals were only names or labels. Because universal concepts were conceived by the mind or based on convention, they possessed no independent reality."[12] Baylor writes, "It was in the period before the 1521 meeting of the Imperial Diet of Worms that Luther's thinking was most heavily influenced by his scholastic training; yet this was also the period in which he came to reject basic features of this training and set about clarifying the growing differences between his own theology and that of the scholastics."[13] Luther's concern with scholasticism was prompted by his growing realization that the chasm separating God and man is one that could not be ultimately overcome by any type of logic or mental effort. This led to the 1517 publication of his "Disputation against Scholastic Theology."[14]

---

[10] Mark Noll, "The earliest Protestants and the reformation of education," *Westminster Theological Journal* 43:1 (Fall 1980): 102.

[11] Michael G. Baylor, *Action and Person: Conscience in Late Scholasticism and the Young Luther*, Studies in Medieval and Reformation Thought, vol. 20 (Leiden: Brill, 1977), 119–121. For a more detailed account of positions of Luther's interaction with the *via moderna* see, Heiko A. Oberman, "Luther and the *Via Moderna*: The Philosophical Backdrop of the Reformation Breakthrough," Journal of Ecclesiastical History 54:4 (Oct. 2003): 641–670.

[12] Leonard S. Smith, *Martin Luther's Two Ways of Viewing Life and the Educational Foundation of a Lutheran Ethos* (Eugene: Pickwick Publications, 2011), 10–11.

[13] Baylor, *Action and Person: Conscience in Late Scholasticism and the Young Luther*, 121.

[14] Marilyn J. Harran, *Martin Luther: Learning for Life* (Saint Louis: Concordia Publishing House, 1997), 140–141. Martin Luther, "Disputation Against Scholastic Theology, 1517," LW 31:3–16.

Pedagogy as Theological Praxis

As has been noted, there are a variety of modes of action that could be considered as education. Karin Maag notes how this plays out at the time of the Reformation:

> Establishing what constituted education in the Reformation is equally complex, not so much because of the absence of data as because of an over-abundance of varieties of formal and informal education being provided at the time. For those living in Protestant Europe in the sixteenth century, education could include training at home by one's parents or by tutors, elementary vernacular schooling, Latin schooling, higher education at university level and catechetical instruction. Obtaining access to these different levels of education was dependent on factors such as social origins, gender and intended occupation as much as (if not more so than) on talent. As stated above, there was little uniformity of educational provision across the board in the Protestant areas of early modern Europe.[15]

Luther certainly has these forms in mind when thinking about pedagogy. When dealing with the councilmen to whom his letter is addressed, Luther's focus was primarily upon education funded by the local councils in an attempt to infuse practices to make for better pedagogy.

The Educational Problem as Both Spiritual and Temporal

Luther begins "To the Councilmen" by attempting to link the decline in universities and monasteries to the spiritual decline taking place in the country. In this manner he addresses the charge laid against him that he was no longer in favor of formal education. It is not that he was not in favor of a university or pedagogical education, but rather he is not in favor of an education that he sees as spiritually dead. He writes that the devil's work was in schools in which the proper service of God was not established: "So he went to work, spread his nets, and set up such monasteries, schools, and estates that it was impossible for any lad to escape him, apart from a special miracle of God. But now that he sees his snares exposed through the word of God, he goes to the other extreme and will permit no learning at all."[16] The analogy that he is drawing here is that though the devil has previously worked in the institution largely sponsored through the church, the Word of God has now exposed those former errors. This should result in a revival of education rather than its neglect.

The problem Luther addresses at the beginning of this letter is ultimately not one of physical and temporal distress, but rather one that is spiritual and eternal. He writes, "If in the cloisters or foundations, or the spiritual estate, they had been seeking not only the belly and the temporal welfare of their children but

---

[15] Karin Maag, "Education and Literacy," *The Reformation World*, ed. Andrew Pettegree (London: Routledge, 2000), 536.

[16] Martin Luther, "To the Councilmen of All Cities in Germany that they Establish and Maintain Christian Schools, 1524," LW 45: 349.

were earnestly concerned for their children's salvation and eternal bliss, they would not thus fold their hands and lapse into indifference, saying, 'If the spiritual estate is no longer to be of any account, we can just as well let education go and not bother out heads about it.'"[17] Here Luther touts the importance of the "spiritual estate", which could be understood as the *ecclesia* as what must be first understood in regards to education. Luther makes a passing reference to Philippians 3:19, "Their end is destruction, their god is their belly, and they glory in their shame, with minds set on earthly things." In this passage Paul makes a comparison between those who are enemies of the cross of Christ (v. 18) and those who are citizens of heaven (v. 20). The problem the people of verse 19 have is that their focus is upon temporal items that pass away rather than that which has an eternal quality. Hawthorne writes, "There exists always the tragic possibility of exchanging the glorious immortal God for some lesser deity. Strangely, this potentiality has the greatest chance of becoming a reality in the realm of the religious, where doctrine and ritual so easily become that to which people wholly devote themselves and to which they commit themselves completely (cf. Rom. 1:21–23)."[18]

The balance in this verse and the balance to which Luther refers is one in which priority must be made between the spiritual and the temporal. The act of educating and learning is inherently a temporal activity, but it is also one that possesses eternal meaning. This is why Jesus warns that it would be better for those who lead children astray that a millstone be hung around their neck and be tossed into the sea. This passage of Jesus' teaching is found in all of the synoptic gospels[19] and serves as a warning against such teaching that could eventually lead to eternal detriment. *Ecclesia* involves God's relationship with man, and man's provision by his or her creator. If the balance of this estate is askew, it will inevitably lead to an imbalance in other areas of life as well. The paradigm Luther forms in his quotation further makes this point. He sets up it as saying that if the spiritual estate no long matters why would it matter what type of education one receives? Luther also provides a response to this question: "Instead, they would say, "If it be true, as the gospel teaches, that this estate is a perilous one for our children, then, dear sirs, show us some way which will be pleasing to God and of benefit to them. For we certainly want to provide not only for our children's bellies, but for their souls as well." At least that is what truly Christian parents would say about it."[20] The spiritual estate is a "perilous one" for children should they be lead astray. Thus Luther sets that stage early in

---

[17] Luther, "To the Councilmen of All Cities in Germany that they Establish and Maintain Christian Schools, 1524," LW 45: 349.

[18] Gerald F. Hawthorne *Philippians*, Word Biblical Commentary vol. 43 (Waco: Word Books, 1983), 167.

[19] Cf. Matt. 18:6; Mk. 9:42; Lk. 17:2.

[20] Luther, "To the Councilmen of All Cities in Germany that they Establish and Maintain Christian Schools, 1524," LW 45: 349.

the letter stating that a parent or teacher who is not spiritually minded is not equipped to teach. As *ecclesia* is the highest of the three estates, it also serves as a foundation by which to understand education in this letter. In this quote Luther also makes the ecclesia as foundational to pedagogy as a logical conclusion. Throughout this letter Luther argues that what is really going on is a spiritual battle in which the devil wages war for the souls of children. To cite but one example, Luther writes, "For it is a grave and important matter, and one which is of vital concern both to Christ and the world at large, that we take steps to help the youth. By doing so we will be taking steps to help also ourselves and everybody else. Bear in mind that such insidious, subtle, and crafty attacks of the devil must be met with great Christian determination."[21] Luther takes it as obvious that it is not one's education or lack thereof that makes one fit service to God. First, one must understand his or her place before God. For Luther, Satan is able to work equally in the educated and the uneducated: "So he [Satan] went to work, spread his nets, and set up such monasteries, schools, and estates that is was impossible for any lad to escape him, apart from a special miracle of God. But now that he sees his snares exposed though the word of God, he goes to the other extreme and will permit no learning at all."[22] For Luther no matter one's educational state, the temptation remains present for one's response to God to be tainted.

Therefore, the setting into which Luther is speaking is one that he sees as academic and spiritual decline. Luther views this former decline as a possible opportunity for the educational system to flourish in his German homeland. He writes that more money should be available for schools since "Formerly he [the citizen] was obliged to waste a great deal of money and property on indulgences, masses, vigils, endowments, bequests, anniversaries, mendicant friars, brotherhoods, pilgrimages, and similar nonsense."[23] Luther argues that as these funds are now readily available they should be used for the glory of God rather than the works of the devil. The primary point conveyed here is that now is a time of opportunity, and it can be used either for the glory of God, or for the works of the devil. It is up to the German people to decide what this outcome will be, hence this letter is addressed to the councilmen of Germany. He goes so far as to refer to that present opportunity which God had provided as a "year of jubilee."[24] The theme that now is the time in which the German people should take advantage of a unique opportunity is one that runs throughout the letter. Later Luther encourages the German people to, "buy while the market is at your door; gather in the harvest while there is sunshine and fair weather; make use of

---

[21] Ibid., 350.
[22] Luther, "To the Councilmen of All Cities in Germany that they Establish and Maintain Christian Schools, 1524," LW 45: 349.
[23] Ibid., 350–351.
[24] Ibid., 351.

God's grace and word while it is there!"[25] Referring to the current time in German history as one which the people must take advantage of was not just a hopeful wish; it was also a historical reality. Volker Riedel writes, "The time between 1485 and 1520 can be described as the high point of humanism in Germany. In addition to the editing and translating of texts, new works were increasingly created, from plays, a number of lyrical genres, letters and treatises to a range of satirical and humorous writings."[26] Luther recognized this wave of knowledge humanism was providing, and sought to take advantage of it as best as he could.

Reidel further notes that after 1520, humanism in Germany was marked throughout by the Reformation. Through the influence of Luther, Zwingli, and Calvin, the *studia humanitatis* (liberal arts) became foundational for how the *studia sacrarum litterarum* (religious studies) were taught. Reidel writes of Luther's contribution to biblical humanism, "Luther showed concern for ensuring that the Greek and Latin languages, and comedy after the model of Terence, were taught, as well as famously translating the Bible into German. He himself translated 13 of Aesop's fables, in such a way as to emphasize their moral, didactic nature."[27]

Little is known of the schools of Wittenberg in 1522 and 1523 just prior to the writing of "To the Councilmen." A later report says that the boys' school was closed during the Wittenberg disturbances. This was due to Karlstadt thinking less of academic education and crediting theological competence to the laity.[28] The schoolmaster George was said to have advocated taking children out of school, and for a time the school building was turned into a bakery shop. The school was reopened in 1523 under a Pastor Bugenhagen.[29] The state of the schools, combined with the decline in university attendance seen at Wittenberg and elsewhere, could have led Luther to see the combination of humanistic and Reformational ideas about education near collapse. In this stricken state one can easily see why Luther felt the necessity to write this letter.

James Kittelson notes that the term "education" can be a very slippery one, and before one approaches the specifics of Luther's words on education at least three questions must be asked: "What is being taught?"; "How is it being

---

[25] Luther, "To the Councilmen of All Cities in Germany that they Establish and Maintain Christian Schools, 1524," LW 45: 352.
[26] Volker Riedel, "Germany and German-Speaking Europe," *A Companion to the Classical Tradition*, Craig W. Kallendorf, ed. (Oxford: Wiley-Blackwell, 2010), 174.
[27] Ibid., 175.
[28] Martin Brecht, *Martin Luther: Shaping and Defining the Reformation 1521–1532*, ed. James L. Schaaf (Minneapolis: Fortress Press, 1990), 138.
[29] Brecht, *Martin Luther: Shaping and Defining the Reformation 1521–1532*, 138.

taught?"; and "What is the desired outcome?"³⁰ Luther was the recipient of the humanist educational critique. This is perhaps why he focused on the liberal arts in "To the Councilmen." As will be explored further in his chapter, Luther was championing a liberal arts education that focused on the classical tradition. Kittelson writes, "The humanists' critique of contemporary learning and education centered on one charge, namely, that propositional knowledge as taught by the schoolmen bore no fruit in daily life and therefore detracted from the proper educational enterprise. Thus, for logic or dialectic, the intellectual cornerstone of scholasticism, they would substitute rhetoric, grammar, and the ancient languages."³¹ Luther took what he saw as the best of the humanist educational structure and formatted so to fit his needs within a larger theological context.

Education as Present in All Three Estates

As the letter continues, Luther transitions from his discussion of now being an ideal opportunity for there to be some type of revolution in the way education is done to an enjoinder for parents to take a primary role in the educating of youth. Luther writes:

> The third consideration is by far the most important of all, namely, the command of God, who through Moses urges and enjoins parents so often to instruct their children that Psalm 78 says: How earnestly he commanded our fathers to teach their children and to instruct their children's children [Ps. 78:5–6]. This is also evident in God's fourth commandment, in which the injunction that children shall obey their parents is so stern that he would even have rebellious children sentenced to death [Deut. 21:18–21]. Indeed, for what purpose do we older folks exist, other than to care for, instruct, and bring up the young? It is utterly impossible for these foolish young people to instruct and protect themselves. This is why God has entrusted them to us who are older and know from experience what is best for them. And God will hold us strictly accountable for them. This is also why Moses commands in Deuteronomy 32 [:7], 'Ask your father and he will tell you; your elders, and they will show you.'³²

The topic of education is not confined to any one of Luther's estates. It was earlier mentioned that one way education relates to *ecclesia* is through the need of the individual to be in right relationship to God for education to bear any meaning as the spiritual takes precedence over the temporal. In the quotation above Luther relates education and *oeconomia*. The dispensing of knowledge is a natural activity to take place in the relationship between a parent and child. In his "The Estate of Marriage" Luther writes, "In short, there is no greater or

---

³⁰ James M. Kittelson, "Luther the Educational Reformer" in *Luther and Learning*, ed. Marilyn J. Harran (London: Associated University Presses, 1985), 96.
³¹ Ibid., 97.
³² Luther, "To the Councilmen of All Cities in Germany that they Establish and Maintain Christian Schools, 1524," LW 45: 353.

nobler authority on earth than that of parents over their children, for this authority is both spiritual and temporal."[33] Luther here also ties the *oeconomia* to the *ecclesia* when earlier in the paragraph he writes, "But the greatest good in married life, that which makes all suffering and labor worthwhile, is that God grants offspring and commands that they be brought up to worship and serve him."[34] In the estate of *oeconomia* there is a bond that connects parent and child. This bond should express *ecclesia* as the child learns in turn to worship. Although the child should receive an education in the things of God in the home, the child should also learn basic skills requisite to *oeconomia*.

The education of one's young is but one example of how the estate of *oeconomia* should be lived when it is seen in the light of *ecclesia*. Luther sees this activity as being natural,[35] and believes it to be a sign of the times that parents should need to be told to educate their young. Luther takes the admonition of educating the young in *oeconomia* very seriously and goes so far as to say that no sin deserves a more severe punishment than neglect in educating one's children.[36] Because of the decline that had been taking place in education, many parents thought it more beneficial for their children to learn a trade than to pursue formal education. Luther saw the desire not to educate one's children for this reason as a panicked misunderstanding that would only wreak further havoc on society.[37]

The Role of the Parent in Education

Once Luther has made the case for parents to educate their children, he proceeds to provide various reasons why parents neglect this sacred duty. The reasons Luther provides here also serve him on a practical level. Luther has already made the case that parents should take the primary duty in educating

---

[33] Martin Luther, "The Estate of Marriage, 1522," LW 45: 46. Quotation taken from Bayer, *Freedom In Response*, 99.

[34] Luther, "The Estate of Marriage, 1522," LW 45: 46.

[35] Luther, "To the Councilmen of All Cities in Germany that they Establish and Maintain Christian Schools, 1524," LW 45: 353.

[36] Ibid. It should also be noted that at this point Luther makes a provocative statement when he follows though with the conviction that there are few sins greater than the neglecting of a child's education. He does so by saying that when he was a boy there was a maxim that stated, "It is just as bad to neglect a pupil as to despoil a virgin (353)" and when he was a child there was no greater sin than that of despoiling a virgin. He goes on to write that the despoiling of a virgin is a much lighter sin than of despoiling a child's mind. His line of argument is that the despoiling of a virgin is a bodily sin that can be atoned for whereas the sin of neglecting a child can have eternal consequences for the child and is seldom atoned for. In this analogy Luther has taken the most heinous sin of the time and attempted to demonstrate why neglecting the education of children is a greater grievance.

[37] Brecht, *Martin Luther: Shaping and Defining the Reformation 1521–1532*, 139.

Pedagogy as Theological Praxis

their children. He does not yet state what this should look like or even what type of education he is referring to. To restate his answer, parents should take a primary role in the education of children because God has entrusted the child to the parent so that the child may be formed into such a person that worships and serves God. If Luther stopped there, the letter would be more aptly entitled "To the Parents of All Cities in Germany that they Establish and Maintain Christian Homes for Children to Learn, Worship, and Serve." Luther realizes that on a practical level there are a variety of reasons why schools are necessary for the training of children. When a child is sent to a school the role of educator passes at least in part from the *oeconomia* to the *politia*. The transition of education from *oeconomia* to *politia* is a crucial step to understand. As discussed in the previous chapter, whereas *oeconomia* is a prelapsarian state, the estate of *politia* came as a result of the fall. The *politia* taking on the role of educator could be viewed as some type of deficiency in the educating provision of the parent because of the fall. Luther therefore maintains a balance between the parent neglecting his duty in the educating of a child and the state taking on that role of educator. Even if education is being done in a fallen state, if it is performed in a Christian context the material taught may be redeemed and profitable for the kingdom of Christ.

The first reason that Luther provides that a parent may neglect the duty of training a child fits well with what Luther has previously said in regards to his contemporary state of parents abdicating this role. He writes, "there are some who lack the goodness and decency to do it, even if they had the ability."[38] In this case the parent acts in a sinful fashion in choosing not do educate a child as he or she should be. When this is the case, Luther argues that a sense of Christian charity and community should lead to the city desiring that such children be educated. Otherwise, "they grow up uneducated, to poison and pollute the other children until at last the whole city is ruined, as happened in Sodom and Gomorrah [Gen. 19:1-25, and Gibeah [Judges 19–20] and a number of other cities."[39] The second reason Luther provides is that parents are unfit for the task. He does not berate this class of people for their lot in life but rather looks to them with pity in that, "they themselves have learned nothing but how to care for their bellies."[40] He provides a third and final reason in that even if parents had the ability and desire to train children themselves, they may not have the opportunity to do so because of the other cares of life. When the majority of one's time is spent working for the providing of daily bread, little time is left for other activities, especially one so time consuming as the education of children.

---

[38] Brecht, *Martin Luther: Shaping and Defining the Reformation 1521–1532*, 139.
[39] Brecht, *Martin Luther: Shaping and Defining the Reformation 1521–1532*, 139.
[40] Ibid.

The Three Estates and Luther's "To the Councilmen of All Cities in Germany"

Politia, Education, and the Two Kingdoms

Because of this state of affairs Luther writes, "*Necessity compels us*, therefore, to engage public schoolteachers for the children—unless each one were willing to engage his own private tutor. But this would be too heavy a burden for the common man, and many a promising boy would again be neglected on account of poverty."[41] Luther has set up an interesting case here. He does not appeal to the state as have been given some type of divine mandate by which it must care for its citizens, and therefore provide them with a proper education. He begins by grounding the education of children as a response to God in *ecclesia* and as something that would ideally take place in *oeconomia*. Because the fall has effected how one can properly respond in *ecclesia* and *oeconomia*, it falls upon the *politia* to primarily fill the role as educator. Brecht writes:

> The reason Luther appealed to the authorities rather than to parents concerning the task of education is that parents were unqualified, and they were in no position to do anything. For him, education was a community responsibility more important than storing supplies or defense, and without it a community would not long endure. Cities needed capable and educated people, and they would not grow by themselves. It was self-evident that it was the Christian state, not the church, that was responsible for establishing Christian schools that would provide a new supply of leaders for church, state, and community. Luther must have presupposed that the finances for them would come from the former property of the church. In a certain sense, the school reform was a preliminary event to the new organization of the reformed churches by the government.[42]

Although the *politia* has its formation in the fall in Luther's conception, he still maintains that the role of the authorities is governed by God. He writes, "It therefore behooves the council and the authorities to devote the greatest care and attention to the young. Since the property, honor, and life of the whole city have been committed to their faithful keeping, they would be remiss in their duty before God and man if they did not seek its welfare and improvement day and night with all the means at their command."[43] He makes the case that the improvement of the educational welfare of the citizens benefits the local government more than anything, because a government is made up of people.

Now that Luther has made his case for the *politia* offering a good education to its citizens, he transitions to some of the specifics that he thinks should be in this education. Luther's starting place for a well-versed education is a classical education in the Roman tradition:

---

[41] Ibid (emphasis added).
[42] Brecht, *Martin Luther: Shaping and Defining the Reformation 1521–1532*, 139.
[43] Luther, "To the Councilmen of All Cities in Germany that they Establish and Maintain Christian Schools, 1524" LW 45: 355.

Pedagogy as Theological Praxis

> So it was done in ancient Rome. There boys were so taught that by the time they reached their fifteenth, eighteenth, or twentieth year they were well versed in Latin, Greek, and all the liberal arts (as they are called), and then immediately entered upon a political or military career. Their system produced intelligent, wise, and competent men, so skilled in every art and rich in experience that if all the bishops, priests, and monks in the whole of Germany today were rolled into one, you would not have the equal of a single Roman soldier. As a result their country prospered; they had capable and trained men for every position.[44]

The Roman system prepared its members for a viable place in society. Anthony Corbeill writes, "Roman education was citizen training."[45] In *Politics*, Aristotle argues that the state should produce three types of classes: artisans, husbandmen, and the military class.[46] In many ways Luther's picture of Roman education may be more of an ideal than a reality. Corbeill further defends that traditionally, at a young age both parents taught their children the basics of mathematics and reading Latin, and later hired private tutors when the parents were no longer able to participate directly in the instruction of the child.[47] Luther's picture is one in which any Roman soldier would have a better education than all the clergy of Germany combined. Corbeill writes:

> In terms of social and economic class these schools [in first century BC Rome] must have been of limited use to any but the most wealthy of the Romans: no systematic teaching of the Greek language existed to prepare students for the study of its literature, so students would need to have been taught at a younger age by personal nurses and pedagogues. As a result, children of members of the non-elite are doubly disadvantaged: at home they lack the atmosphere for assimilating the Greek elements of Roman culture, while in public the attitudes toward acquiring these elements is ambiguous, even openly hostile.[48]

Luther references a time a human flourishing under the establishment of the Roman Empire, and wants to take what he sees as some of the positive aspects of that time and apply it to his contemporary Germany.

---

[44] Luther, "To the Councilmen of All Cities in Germany that they Establish and Maintain Christian Schools, 1524" LW 45: 355. It would also be beneficial to make note of the definition provided by Brandt of liberal arts in his footnote of this passage: "The liberal arts were traditionally seven in number. Grammar, rhetoric, and dialectic comprised the trivium of the medieval elementary schools; music, geometry, and astronomy comprised the quadrivium of the secondary schools. Luther's description has reference to Roman education in the shape it took after the end of the republic, as he has come to know it through his own reading of Cicero, Quintilian, and others (356)."

[45] Anthony Corbeill, "Education in the Roman Republic: Creating Traditions," *Education in Greek and Roman Antiquity*, ed. Yun Lee Too (Leiden: Brill, 2001), 266.

[46] Aristotle, *The Politics of Aristotle*, ed. J. E. C. Welldon (London: MacMillan, 1901), 68–74.

[47] Corbeill, "Education in the Roman Republic: Creating Traditions," 269.

[48] Ibid., 270.

It would be incomplete not to provide some context for how Luther's doctrine of the two kingdoms is relevant to the estates, and well as to his understanding of education as the topic arises several times in "To the Councilmen." This section will therefore demonstrate how the estates and the two kingdoms are complimentary ideas, and how they are relevant to this thesis. As earlier discussed, Luther argued that the *politia* should take on the role of education because in most cases the family would be unable to handle the burden associated with such a task. In this scenario the role of the state seems tenuous at best. When Luther gets to something more specific about what an ideal of education should look like, he refers to a tradition in which he believes the state had an extremely influential role in the education of its citizens. Luther uses this shift to take the burden of education that may have previously been upon the family and place it squarely on the shoulders of the *politia*: "For whose fault is it today our cities have so few capable people? Whose fault, if not that of authorities, who have left the young people to grow up like saplings in the forest, and have given no thought to their instruction and training? This is also why they have grown to maturity so misshapen that they cannot be used for building purposes, but are mere brushwood, fit only for kindling fires."[49] Luther's picture of the state is more generous here than perhaps elsewhere in his writings. In *On Secular* [or temporal] *Authority*, Luther takes a much more negative view of the state in which the state acts primarily as a restrainer of evil actions.[50] In this case Luther expresses his doctrine of the two kingdoms:

> If there were [no law and government], then seeing that all the world is evil and that scarcely one human being in a thousand is a true Christian, people would devour each other and no one would be able to support his wife and children, feed himself and serve God. The world [*Welt*] would become a desert. And so God has ordained the two governments, the spiritual [government] which fashions true Christians and just persons through the Holy Spirit under Christ, and the secular [*weltlich*] government which holds the Unchristian and wicked in check and forces them to keep the peace outwardly and be still, like it or not. It is in this way that St. Paul interprets the secular Sword when he says in Romans 13[3]: 'It [the Sword] is not a terror to good works, but to the wicked.' And Peter says [1 Pet. 2.14]: 'It is given as a punishment on the wicked.'"[51]

Romans 13 and 1 Peter 2 are his chief texts for an assertion that the role of governing authorities is threefold: to keep peace and order in society, to punish evildoers, and to keep order in society.[52] Augustine's concept of the two cities

---

[49] Luther, "To the Councilmen of All Cities in Germany that they Establish and Maintain Christian Schools, 1524," LW 45: 356.
[50] Martin Luther, "On Secular Authority" in *Luther and Calvin on Secular Authority*, Cambridge Texts in the History of Political Thought, ed. and trans. Harro Hopfl (Cambridge: Cambridge UP, 1991), 10.
[51] Martin Luther, "On Secular Authority," 10.
[52] Robert Kolb. *Martin Luther: Confessor of the Faith* (Oxford: Oxford UP, 2009), 188.

shaped Luther's conceptual framework for his understanding of the two kingdoms as being society divided between God's kingdom and the world's system of ruling.

Many Lutheran scholars have emphasized Luther's two kingdom theology much more than his understanding of the three estates. Luther's two kingdoms was a sophisticated version of what one finds in Augustine's *City of God*.[53] Thompson writes that Luther's, "own doctrine of the Two Kingdoms, as it was worked out after 1522 was a much more subtle and complex doctrine than Augustine's, and it went much further than Augustine's in providing a concrete foundation for a genuine Christian political theory."[54] The basic concept of the two kingdoms for Luther was that there was a different kind of love dominating each of the two kingdoms. The kingdom of Christ was compelled by the love of God, and the kingdom of the world was dominated by the love of self.[55] There is a larger divide in the role of human participation in the two cities in comparison to Luther's two kingdoms. This made the contrast between the two kingdoms even more distinct through Luther's understanding of original sin. Heckel writes, "According to Luther, Original Sin completely destroyed the spiritual part of the human nature, that is, that part which is oriented toward God; it left only the corporeal part, that is, that part which is oriented toward God."[56] Because of original sin, man is born into the kingdom of the world. It is through baptism and faith in Christ that the human is taken from the kingdom of the world and taken to the kingdom of Christ, that is the kingdom of grace.[57]

Although Luther begins with the framework of the two cities, he adds his own understanding of the responsibilities in this world to which God has called his people. Kolb writes, "At this point he [Luther] believed that Christians need no control by secular government but willingly submit to one another in love. Nevertheless, they should submit to rulers for the sake of the world, which needs protections against the disorder that the ungodly foment."[58] For Luther, Christian engagement in the *politia* was an act of love. The Christian supports the state out of love for neighbor in that the neighbor may need the benefits bestowed by the state. To act in an anarchist mode is to act contrary to love.[59]

---

[53] Augustine, *City of God*, vol. 2 of The Nicene and Post-Nicene Fathers, ed. Philip Schaff, (Grand Rapids: Eerdmans, 1977).
[54] W.D.J. Cargill Thompson, *The Political Thought of Martin Luther* (Sussex: The Harvester Press, 1984), 3.
[55] Johannes Heckel, *Lex Charitatis: A Juristic Disquisition on Law in the Theology of Martin Luther*, trans. and ed. Gottfried G. Krodel (Grand Rapids: Eerdmans, 2010), 25.
[56] Heckel, *Lex Charitatis*, 25.
[57] Ibid., 31.
[58] Ibid.
[59] Paul Althaus, *The Ethics of Martin Luther*, trans. Robert C. Schultz (Philadelphia: Fortress Press, 1972), 119.

Luther's framework in the two kingdoms effectively rejected the more typically medieval equation of the religious or sacred with godliness and the secular as having lesser worth. Instead, "He affirmed that God effects everything in the realm of faith, the realm which involves the relationship between God and human creatures, while human love acts in the earthly realm, in required obedience to God when sin does not interfere."[60]

The two kingdoms theology has perhaps been held to even more scrutiny than the estates. Possible flaws in the thinking about a dichotomy between public and private life was most evident during the Nazi era in Germany. Many German two-kingdom theorists of the time held that there is no contradiction between giving all of one's allegiance to the German National-Socialistic state on the one hand and to be a Christian on the other.[61] Many of the atrocities of the Second World War were blamed upon the misappropriation of Luther's theology of the two kingdoms and the three estates. Karl Barth was particularly critical and stated that through the Lutheran doctrine of having an independent authority of the state the government, "provided a certain amount of breathing space for German paganism" in that it "separated the created world and law from the gospel."[62] Reinhold Niebuhr was just as critical writing that the two kingdoms made for a dualistic social philosophy which separated the spiritual life of a Christian from his or her social life.[63] The difficulty lies in the degree to which the secular authority is an independent kingdom from the kingdom of God. The answer to the objection to the two kingdoms has repeatedly been that the two kingdoms are by no means independent of each other. The state is under the Lordship of God, and Pannenberg points out that one of the roles of the preaching office is a responsibility towards the ruling power. In the two kingdoms, the preacher should, "inform and instruct all social classes how they should conduct themselves in their offices and ranks, so that they would act justly for God."[64] In the two kingdoms, the religious and the secular are not in antithesis to each other, and are much more closely aligned than in Augustine's two cities. Although they are more closely aligned, they remain distinct with the kingdom of God being higher than the kingdom of the world. The kingdom of

---

[60] Robert Kolb, "Martin Luther and the German Nation," in *A Companion to the Reformation World*, Blackwell Companion to European History, ed. Po-Chia Hsia (Oxford: Blackwell Publishing, 2004), 47. For a definite work on the subject of two kingdoms see Max Weber, *The Protestant Ethic and the Spirit of Capitalism: and other Writings* (London: Penguin Classics, 2002).
[61] Carl Braaten, *Principles of Lutheran Theology* (Philadelphia: Fortress Press, 1985), 152.
[62] Quotation taken from Wolfhart Pannenberg, *Ethics,* trans. Keith Crim (Philadelphia: The Westminster Press, 1981), 112.
[63] Reinhold Niebuhr, *The Nature and Destiny of Man: II Human Destiny* (New York: Charles Scribner's Sons, 1941), 194-195.
[64] Pannenberg, *Ethics*, 113.

the world remains to be the world, "and therefore in comparison with the kingdom of Christ, "a poor, wretched and even a foul and stinking kingdom."[65]

It is also worth noting that Luther combines his distinction between two kingdoms with two ways in which God rules (two "regiments" of God).[66] Pannenberg notes that although the concept of the two kingdoms arose primarily from Augustine, the second in which there are two ways that God rules is traced from medieval theory of there being two forces in Christendom, one secular and one spiritual.[67] The idea of their being two rules of governing arose in medieval Christianity because their was a unified Christian culture in the Middle Ages, and therefore no concrete way to express a *civitas diaboli* that stood in contrast to the Christian church and the *civitas divinitas*.[68] This gave way for the existence of a Christian religious authority, while there also could be a secular authority that is ruled in a Christian manner. Luther interpreted this to mean that while there is a spiritual power and secular power, both are ways God exercises his rule and not as means of power entrusted to humans.[69] This separation establishes the legitimacy of political authority while also limiting power exercised by humans.

Luther's distinction between the two kingdoms and two regiments arose primarily from his antithesis between law and gospel. For Luther, the two kingdoms equate to two ways in which God encounters a sinful world. In his conception the law is dead and it is the gospel that is able to bring life to humans. To the first he encounters, "with the gospel, which gives the Holy Spirit, and the second, with the law, which outwardly checks the consequences for sin."[70] The key for the interpretive grid involving the two kingdoms is determining where the divisions go and how deep they run. For Luther, there is certainly a divide between the Christian and the non-Christian; between one living under the burden of the law and one living under grace. One the other hand, one must question how different one's political life would be from the private life when one's political actions are performed in service to the other.

Pannenberg's as well as Barth's primary critique of the two kingdoms is a political critique. Pannenberg writes:

> Luther did not take into account the question of specifically Christian features in the structure of political life, and therefore reflected only quite inadequately the

---

[65] Gerhard Ebeling, *Luther: An Introduction to His Thought*, trans. R.A. Wilson (London: William Collins & Sons, 1970), 190.
[66] Pannenberg, *Ethics*, 117.
[67] Ibid.
[68] Ibid., 119.
[69] Ibid., 125.
[70] Ebeling, *Luther: An Introduction to His Thought*, 185.

historical basis on which his own theological treatment of the theory of secular power rested. His abstract concept of secular authority, divorced as it was from the historical circumstances of Christendom, explains how Luther's political theory remained so remarkably unaffected by the tendencies of his time to give independent authority to the German states and to develop political absolutism, and how any church that followed Luther's teaching proved to be defenseless against these tendencies. In historical terms, Barth's judgment on the significance of Luther's doctrine of the two kingdoms does not deal adequately with the circumstances of Luther's era, but it still remains true that the gaps which remained in Luther's synthesis provided the occasion for historical tendencies to take hold in the portion of the Christian tradition influenced by Luther. These were consequences which Luther neither was aware of nor anticipated, and which thus had the historical consequences that Barth and other critics have rightly described as disastrous.[71]

David Steinmetz, writing more recently, appropriately balances Pannenberg's criticism with five goals that Luther hoped to achieve through his political theory. Steinmetz also notes that it is important to remember that these are goals Luther hoped to achieve in his context, not in some type of modern democratic state:

1. Christian ethics, though not all human morality is grounded in justification by faith alone.
2. All Christians have a civic and social responsibility to discharge and that some Christians may discharge that duty by assuming public office in the state.
3. The Sermon on the Mount is not merely a monastic ethic or an ethic for the future Kingdom of God but applies to the life of every Christian, even if its moral demands are not applicable to every decision which Christians must make as public persons.
4. The state has been established by God to achieve divinely willed ends that the Church cannot and should not attempt to achieve.
5. God, who rules the Church through the gospel, rules this disordered world through the instruments available to the state—namely human reason, wisdom, natural law, and the application of violent coercion.[72]

One of the primary questions that the two kingdoms doctrine must answer is just how limited its use may be by its historical circumstances. Pannenberg writes, "On closer examination, Luther's doctrine of the two kingdoms and of God's two 'regiments' is seen as an expression of political thought deeply colored by the thought of its own time in the context of the transmission of Christian theology. This raises the question of what its permanent significance

---

[71] Pannenberg, *Ethics*, 127.
[72] David C. Steinmetz, *Luther in Context*, 2nd ed. (Grand Rapids: Baker, 2002), 121–123.

Pedagogy as Theological Praxis

maybe."[73] If Pannenberg is correct that much of the use of the two kingdoms is time bound, could one conjecture that the use of the estates are also time bound? In the previous chapter the idea that Luther could have drawn upon the medieval concept of the estates of the realm was discussed, so Luther was drawing upon his historical situation in the formulation of the estates as much as he was in the formulation of the two kingdoms. There are at least a few points that differentiate the theological use of the estates as compared to the two kingdoms. First, Luther grounds the estates in creation.[74] As stated by Wannenwetch, for Luther the estates were "con-creatures" of humankind.[75] Luther assumed the estates to be a part of God's created world, and as such spent little time attempting to justify their use. Even if Luther was aided by Aristotle and the estates of the realm as his primary sources, he saw them as a concept that was natural to the world, and therefore one would expect others (religious or otherwise) to grasp the basic concept of the estates. Another difference between the use of the two kingdoms and the estates is the universal applicability of the estates. Although the estates are best understood and practiced within a Christian context, all humans are involved in some type of relation to God, other humans and the created world.

Bayer also sees the faults of an overemphasis on the two kingdoms in comparison to the three estates. He writes, "If greater weight were given to Luther's teaching about the three estates when his writings are appropriated for today, many futile discussions could be avoided. There is danger when it comes to Luther's teaching about the two realms that one can single out sexuality, marriage, family, rearing, education, and business and assign such topics to the political sphere as "temporal" rule, playing these off against "spiritual" rule. One might even go so far as to summarize the contrast of the two realms by reducing it to a simplistic contrast between state and church."[76] As previously highlighted by Braaten, there is a danger in making too firm of a dichotomy between these realms in the practical workings of life.

The Estates and *On Secular Authority*

Another important work of Luther's that should be referenced here is his *On Secular Authority*.[77] This section will provide an excursus into Luther's *On Secular Authority*, which will be particularly helpful in further coming to terms

---

[73] Pannenberg, *Ethics*, 127.
[74] Luther, "Lectures on Genesis 1–5," LW 1: 95.
[75] Bernd Wannenwetsch, "Luther's Moral Theology," *The Cambridge Companion to Martin Luther*, ed. Donald K. McKim (Cambridge: Cambridge UP, 2003), 130.
[76] Bayer, *Martin Luther's Theology*, 125.
[77] Martin Luther, "On Secular Authority" in *Luther and Calvin on Secular Authority*, Cambridge Texts in the History of Political Thought, ed. and trans. Harro Hopfl (Cambridge: Cambridge UP, 1991), 1–43.

with Luther's understanding of *politia*. Luther does use the term "estate" (*Stand*) in *On Secular Authority*, but usually not referring directly to the three estates. His use in this case is to refer to a person being either in the estate of a Christian or the estate of a non-Christian. For instance, he writes, "And for the rest God has established another government, outside the Christian estate and the kingdom of God, and has cast them into subjection to the Sword."[78] *On Secular Authority* serves more as a call for religious tolerance than it does for openness to the state teaching the Christian religion as seen in "To the Councilmen." This tract presents Luther at his most antagonistic towards secular authority. "True religion is presented here as being more divorced from the life of the civil community than in any earlier or later account, as more private and more personal; a more restricted jurisdiction is assigned to rulers; and the true Church is portrayed as more independent of their authority."[79] The writing of *On Secular Authority* was brought about for at least two reasons. A well-known jurist of the time, Count John Henry von Schwarzenberg published *Lex Bambergensis* in 1507, and this work served as a model for imperial law.[80] Prior to the writing of *On Secular Authority* Schwarzenberg sent Luther some of his writings on points of faith. In reply, Luther said he agreed with all points save one: "I disagree with Your Grace entirely when you make the point that the use of the sword by temporal authorities can be made to agree with the gospel. So I intend to publish a little book on this subject especially."[81] A second reason for the writing of *On Secular Authority* was occasioned in part by the resistance he encountered in the publication of his translation of the New Testament. His translation was banned in Ducal Saxony and other territories. Any copies that were found were to be confiscated by the authorities.[82]

One important phrase that Luther uses in "To the Councilmen" that relates well to his earlier work *On Secular Authority* is, "After all, temporal government has to continue."[83] He locates *politia* as something that is permanent in the present state of things. Throughout Luther's writings he makes the argument that the estates will continue until the end of the world. At first glance it would seem an oxymoron to say that something that is temporal must continue. This reinforces Luther's concept of *politia* as a fallen estate. He is

---

[78] Luther, "On Secular Authority," 10.
[79] Luther, "On Secular Authority," x. Perhaps the timing of the two pieces of writing could account for some of the differences in attitudes towards secular authority. *On Secular Authority* was published in March 1523 (ix). "To the Councilmen" was published just a year later in 1524.
[80] Heinrich Bornkamm, *Luther in Mid-Career 1521–1530*, ed. Karin Bornkamm, trans. E. Theodore Bachmann (London: Darton, Longman & Todd, 1983), 112.
[81] Ibid.
[82] Ibid., 113.
[83] Luther, "To the Councilmen of All Cities in Germany that they Establish and Maintain Christian Schools, 1524" LW 45: 357.

taking an eschatological view in which at the second coming of Christ one way mankind will be delivered is from *politia*. To say that temporal government must continue is not to say that temporal government must continue in an eschatological form.

When the two kingdoms are taken to an extreme, there forms a clear divide between one's public life and private life. In such cases, "There is a certain dualistic interpretation of the two kingdoms which completely paralyzes the nerve of the church on issues of human rights. What do human rights have to do with a gospel that relates only to the inner life of faith and afterlife of hope?"[84] Bornkamm makes the point clear that it is asinine to think that a person can somehow live in one of the kingdoms but not the other. He writes, "They [Christians] live in them only when, by means of the one or the other "regime," they do the will of God, who holds them together. This requires of the Christian an ever new and conscientious making of decisions for which there is but one norm. What is here the appropriate form of love, to endure injustice or to exact justice?"[85]

The role of temporal authority in *politia* is raised throughout "To the Councilmen." Luther's case thus far for government intervention into the education of the people has been primarily a religious one. He has dealt with the need for the people to learn biblical languages so that they can be apt interpreters of Scripture, and for the state to step in because for one reason or another most parents are not equipped to educate their children. As the letter progresses, he attempts to make more of a secular case for the need for the state to educate children. He writes, "To this point we have been speaking about the necessity and value of languages and Christian schools for the spiritual realm and the salvation of souls. Now let us consider also the body. Let us suppose that there were no soul, no heaven or hell, and that we were to consider solely the temporal government from the standpoint of its worldly functions."[86] The case that he makes is that there is both a spiritual and physical benefit to having an educated class of people. He writes that on a practical level good schools are much more beneficial to the physical realm than to the spiritual. He weighs his argument against "the sophists" who show no concern for temporal government.[87] Luther's argument offers an extremely healthy balance between the spiritual and the physical, between the *ecclesia* and the *oeconomia*. In the *ecclesia* humans respond to the gift of God. Earlier in this letter Luther stressed how terribly important it is to understand the consequences of leading children astray. Just as important is the role of education in *oeconomia*. Because

---

[84] Carl E. Braaten, *Principles of Lutheran Theology*, 123.
[85] Bornkamm, *Luther in Mid-Career 1521–1530*, 115.
[86] Luther, "To the Councilmen of All Cities in Germany that they Establish and Maintain Christian Schools, 1524," LW 45: 366–367.
[87] Ibid., 367.

oeconomia involves the physical interaction of humans, the better educated one is, the better equipped one may be to serve one's role well in *oeconomia*. The body and soul both benefiting from education is an important part of this letter. Here we have the physical and spiritual joined for a common purpose. Richard Marius writes, "Luther at the heart of his religious being believed in incarnation, the goodness of creation, the capacity of physical and spiritual to be joined together. . . . Sin might infect creation, but Christ would finally restore God's work to its original purity."[88]

In this context Luther makes another one of his interesting asides about the role of temporal government: "It is not necessary to repeat here that the temporal government is a divinely ordained estate (I have elsewhere treated this subject so fully that I trust no one has any doubt about it)."[89] The most likely work he is referring to as having earlier been written on the subject is *On Secular Authority* written the previous year in 1523. Referring to government as a "divinely ordained estate" is a very telling phrase. This expression provides temporal government with a place of legitimacy in the sight of God and man. The sword and the government function as a form of "divine service."[90] A large portion of Part I of *Secular Authority* involves Luther's case that the sword has been used throughout Judeo-Christian history as a means of government. Its actual function begins post-fall: "The law of this temporal sword has existed from the beginning of the world. For when Cain slew his brother Abel, he was in such great terror of being killed in turn that God even placed a special prohibition on it and suspended the sword for his sake, so that no one was to slay him [Gen. 4:14-15]. He would not have had this fear if he had not seen and heard from Adam that murderers are to be slain."[91] Even if the sword is "from the beginning of the world" Luther does not trace its actual function until after the fall. The first account of the sword one sees in the Bible occurs in Gen. 3:24, "He drove out the man, and at the east of the garden of Eden he placed the cherubim and a flaming sword that turned every way to guard the way to the tree of life." God is the one who has placed the sword at the entrance to the garden. Luther says that service (and hence service in temporal authority) should be a Christian activity. He goes so far as to say, "For the sword and authority, as a particular service of God, belong more appropriately to Christians than to any other men on earth. Therefore, you should esteem the sword or governmental authority as highly as the estate of marriage, or

---

[88] Richard Marius, *Martin Luther: The Christian between God and Death*, (Cambridge, Mass: The Belknap Press of Harvard University Press, 1999), 385.
[89] Luther, "To the Councilmen of All Cities in Germany that they Establish and Maintain Christian Schools, 1524," LW 45: 367.
[90] Martin Luther, "Temporal Authority: To What Extent It Should Be Obeyed, 1523," LW 45: 103.
[91] Ibid., 86.

husbandry, or any other calling which God has instituted."[92] The section has demonstrated at least two important points. First, the two kingdoms and the three estates need not be bifurcated when studying Luther. Both are weaved throughout Luther's work, and can be integrated when studying Luther. Second, although at times Luther takes a positive, neutral, and negative stance towards government, in each case he maintains its validity in the current state of the world. This is important for understanding Luther's positions on education, as the state possesses a divinely ordained place in the order of the world, and therefore one would assume it plays some type of role in the important task of educating citizens.

The Languages in Classical Education

Returning to "To the Councilmen," the first specific admonition Luther provides in his formulation of education is a push for the teaching of the languages. The learning of biblical and classical languages plays an important role in both the humanist and the classical traditions. This section will provide some context for Luther's use of the languages in his formulation of classical education. When he begins to discuss the use of the languages, Luther asks the question, "What is the use of teaching Latin, Greek, and Hebrew and the other liberal arts?"[93] He replies that there are two reasons why these should be taught. The first is a better understanding of the Scriptures. "Languages and the arts, which can do us no harm, but are actually a greater ornament, profit, glory, and benefit, both for the understanding of Holy Scripture and the conduct of temporal government—these we despise."[94] By "we" Luther means that the German people in their current state despise that which would do them much good—"languages and the arts." The second reason he provides coincides with his earlier thoughts, namely, that the education of the population will lead to a people who are better fit to serve in government and elsewhere.

The so-called "biblical humanists" emphasized textual study of the original languages rather than focusing on Latin citations by earlier scholars in biblical study. This move to ancient sources with a focus upon the biblical text and the church fathers was sparked by the publication of Lorenzo Valla's *Adnotationes in Novem Testamentum* (1444).[95] Many biblical humanists appreciated Luther's

---

[92] Ibid., 100.
[93] Luther, "To the Councilmen of All Cities in Germany that they Establish and Maintain Christian Schools, 1524," LW 45: 357.
[94] Ibid., 358.
[95] Robert Kolb, *Martin Luther: Confessor of the Faith* (Oxford: Oxford UP, 2009), 37. Valla is perhaps best remembered today for his undermining papal claim of authority over Christendom by proving the Donation of Constantine to be a forgery for its many anachronisms. For more information see Richard Marius, *Martin Luther: The Christian*

work and his study in the ancient texts. Robert Kolb writes, "Not only did Luther embrace many of the humanists' concerns and methods; many of those engaged in humanistic pursuits embraced his cause as his calls for reform began to spread. Not without ambiguity and imprecise understanding if what he was really proposing, many of his age or younger greeted Luther enthusiastically and supported him, lavishing praise upon him, at least until the crisis of his condemnation by pope and emperor."[96] Luther's desire for this return to the ancient languages was cemented in his belief that knowledge of the Scriptures in their original language would lead to an increase in the godliness of the people as they attained a better understanding of the Scriptures. He viewed the languages as a "fine and noble gift of God."[97]

For Luther it was providential that the textual and philological techniques that were needed for reform were put at his disposal through the humanist movement.[98] The ancient languages served purposes in both of Luther's two kingdoms: they provided a better understanding of the Bible and aided in governing in the secular realm.[99] It is fairly clear why the languages are helpful in the religious realm, but perhaps not so for the secular realm. The ancient languages are helpful in the secular realm in that they provide one with ready access to the classics of Greek and Roman culture. Luther bases many of his ideas in this chapter on what he believes to be the Greek and Roman system of education. Luther at times self-castigates in this letter because of his lack of knowledge of ancient literature and poetry because he believes this will aid in his mental development and capacity.[100]

The subjects of "language" and "the languages" play an important role in this letter. Luther believed that it was a providential event that the gospel had been recovered at the same time that the biblical languages were being once again studied.[101] In Bornkamm's words, "The gospel and the languages belong together inseparably. Only when one ponders God's revelation though Word and Scripture does one grasp the purpose of the languages."[102] Bornkamm is here echoing Luther's pronouncement, "In proportion then as we value the

---

between God and Death (Cambridge, Mass.: The Belknap Press of Harvard University Press, 1999), 14.

[96] Kolb, *Martin Luther: Confessor of the Faith*, 38.

[97] Luther, "To the Councilmen of All Cities in Germany that they Establish and Maintain Christian Schools, 1524," LW 45: 358.

[98] Alister McGrath, *The Intellectual Origins of the European Reformation* (Oxford: Basil Blackwell, 1987), 59.

[99] Brecht, *Martin Luther: Shaping and Defining the Reformation 1521–1532*, 140.

[100] Luther, "To the Councilmen of All Cities in Germany that they Establish and Maintain Christian Schools, 1524," LW 45: 360.

[101] Walther von Loewenich, *Luther's Theology of the Cross*, trans. Herbert J. A. Bouman (Belfast: Christian Journals, LTD., 1976), 243.

[102] Bornkamm, *Luther in Mid-Career 1521–1530*, 139.

Pedagogy as Theological Praxis

gospel, let us zealously hold to the languages. For it was not without purpose that God caused his Scriptures to be set down in these two languages alone—Old Testament in Hebrew, the New in Greek."[103] Noll expresses similar sentiment in his explanation of why the reformers focused much attention on language, whether it be one's native tongue, or Latin, or the biblical languages: "In so doing [emphasizing language] the reformers remind us as Christians that our knowledge of God and of ourselves, our proper knowledge of the world and of society, is bound up with Holy Scripture."[104] Over the next few pages Luther goes to great lengths to stress the importance of the languages and the crucial role they play in a right understanding of the gospel. In one of his most eloquent passages in the letter Luther writes, "And let us be sure of this: we will not long preserve the gospel without the languages. The languages are the sheath in which this sword of the Spirit [Eph. 6:17] is contained; they are the casket in which this jewel is enshrined; they are the vessel in which this wine is held; they are the larder in which this food is stored; and, as the gospel itself points out [Matt. 14:20], they are the baskets in which are kept these loaves and fishes and fragments."[105] Without knowledge of the original languages and philological exegesis it is doubtful that Luther would have taken up his position of struggle against the pope and scholasticism that he did.[106]

One must question whether Luther's focus upon the languages and their importance to the gospel is justified. Luther provides the reader with a practical example of the importance of the languages. He believes that because the languages were being revived in his time, knowledge was available to the Christian who studied the Scriptures as had never before been available. On a practical level he writes that Augustine often erred in his interpretation of the Psalms because he lacked sufficient training in Hebrew. For one example of where the Vulgate is insufficient he cites Psalm 110: "Let me give you an example: It is rightly said that Christ is the Son of God; but how ridiculous it must have sounded to the ears of their adversaries when they attempted to prove this by citing Psalm 110: '*Tecum principium in die virtutis tuae*,' though in the Hebrew there is not a word about the Deity in this passage! When men attempt to defend the faith with such uncertain arguments and mistaken proof texts, are not Christians put to shame and made a laughingstock in the eyes of adversaries who know the language?"[107] He argues throughout this letter that interpretation handed down can be of little use if he cannot search the Scriptures for himself

---

[103] Luther, "To the Councilmen of All Cities in Germany that they Establish and Maintain Christian Schools, 1524," LW 45: 359.
[104] Noll, "The earliest Protestants and the reformation of education," 115.
[105] Luther, "To the Councilmen of All Cities in Germany that they Establish and Maintain Christian Schools, 1524," LW 45: 360.
[106] Brecht, *Martin Luther: Shaping and Defining the Reformation 1521–1532*, 140.
[107] Luther, "To the Councilmen of All Cities in Germany that they Establish and Maintain Christian Schools, 1524," LW 45: 361–362.

to see whether the interpretation is in fact valid. For Luther, being able to read the original language of Scripture allows the Christian to grasp the word of God in a manner that a secondary language cannot. It is a point of both faith and apologetic to be able to truly understand what the words of Scriptures mean. It is through language and 'the languages' that the human is able to return adoration and worship to God.

Luther's casting of some of the church fathers as having an imperfect knowledge of the Scriptures because of their lack of knowledge of the original languages serves as an important argumentative tool for Luther. Surely the councilmen to whom Luther writes would have thought their interpretation of the Scriptures to be inferior to that of the church fathers.[108] Nonetheless, he argues that this knowledge is available that the fathers did not possess. Such knowledge will excuse what errors one may find in the fathers: "As sunshine is to shadow, so is the language itself compared to all the glosses of the fathers."[109] He does not blame the fathers for what they lacked, but argues that they would have more than gladly known the knowledge available to Luther and his contemporaries: "O how happy the dear fathers would have been if they had had our opportunity to study the languages and come thus prepared to the Holy Scriptures! What great toil and effort it cost them to gather up a few crumbs, while we with half the labor—yes, almost without any labor at all—can acquire the whole loaf!"[110]

The points of faith, apologetics, and languages are also important for the Reformation. Many people were in bondage to the translation and interpretation of Scripture that had been handed down to them. Even those who could read the Vulgate were still in captivity to a translation.

Luther's own work sets up a scenario in which he has to weigh his belief that knowledge of original languages is crucial for the biblical expositor with a healthy dose of reality that not all Germans would actually have access to Greek and Hebrew. Thus, one of Luther's most important contributions to the German language was his translation of the New Testament into German in 1522. Luther finished his translation of the entire Bible in 1534.[111] At this time German was still not a unified language, and his translation was one that he believed the

---

[108] In addition to calling attention to Augustine's imperfect knowledge of Hebrew, Luther also points to some of the interpretations of Hillary of Potiers and Bernard of Clairvaux as being suspect because of their lack of the original languages.
[109] Luther, "To the Councilmen of All Cities in Germany that they Establish and Maintain Christian Schools, 1524," LW 45: 364.
[110] Luther, "To the Councilmen of All Cities in Germany that they Establish and Maintain Christian Schools, 1524," LW 45: 364..
[111] Revised editions of his translation continued to appear throughout his lifetime, and the last before his death was published in 1545.

common people could understand.[112] His translation soon became a point of unification for the German language. Just as one of the reasons he believed many parents would be unable to properly educate their children was simply the demands of life, so too many would not possess a sufficient knowledge of Greek and Hebrew because of other pressing concerns.

Luther's Translation Work and the Original Biblical Languages

Although Luther at times deprecates deprecate his ability in biblical and classical languages, his biblical expositions from Greek and Hebrew as well as his translation of the New Testament into German are some of his most lasting contributions to Protestantism. This section will indicate the relation between Luther's translation work and his use of the biblical languages.

There is a seeming inconsistency between Luther's mode of translation and his argument for the original languages. At times Luther took a freer view of translation, and did not always translate literally if he did not think the German people would understand what was being said. The most famous example of this is in his translation of the Magnificat.[113] It is often translated in the English, "Hail Mary, full of grace." In the Vulgate it reads *ave Maria gratia plena.* Luther would not offer a literal translation because:

> He thought the Germans would not use the word 'full' in connection with grace because it was usually linked with being "full" with beer or money. Instead he translated, 'Thou gracious one' (Ger. *Du holdselige*). The common people would have the angel say, 'Hello there, Mary,' meaning 'God greet you, you dear Mary' (from the popular German greeting on arrival, *Gott grusse dich, liebe Maria*, comparable to the English 'God be with you'). Using such common language, Luther mused, would have made his hypocritical pious opponents hang themselves because he would have destroyed the salutation for them. But he did settle on the translation 'dear (*liebe*) Mary' because the German word 'love' (*Liebe*) expresses a sentiment that rings through the heart as it is reflected in the Greek *kecharitomene* (Luke 1:28), which means something or someone very lovely and attractive. Luther insisted on being right since no one had tried harder than he did to communicate with Germans in daily life.[114]

Luther's focus here was to communicate the truth of Scripture to the German people in their own tongue. It would seem that this type of translation would lead to the same type of error that Luther is warning his listeners to avoid in "To the Councilmen." Perhaps a counterbalance between these two positions is that it is doubtful Luther saw his translation as timeless. His main reason for

---

[112] Loewenich, *Luther's Theology of the Cross*, 210.
[113] Lk. 1:28.
[114] Eric W. Gritsch "Luther as Bible Translator," *The Cambridge Companion to Martin Luther*, ed. Donald K. McKim (Cambridge: Cambridge UP, 2003), 67.

arguing against the Vulgate as being the final definitive source for interpretation of Scripture is that it is secondary to the original languages, and was not readable by the majority of Germans. In the same manner, his translation is secondary and as such he would have surely encouraged the reader the check the original texts if something in his translation seemed to be in doubt. His assumption would have been that this translation is for the people, but is not final. This is why revisions of the "Luther Bible" continued to appear throughout his lifetime. In addition, translating the Bible so that the people reading it can understand the meaning is quite different from making theological propositions based on an inaccurate reading of the original languages. His translation of the Bible into German could also be a reflection of his understanding of *ecclesia* and *oeconomia*. The home is the place in which the interactions of daily life occur. This interaction is not a secular activity. This was seen in the previous chapter in his "Exposition of Psalm 110:1," which reads, "Unless the Lord build this house, those who build it build in vain." A German translation of the Bible for the "common people" would have served to bring the Bible into the home of the German people in a manner unheard of before. Reading the Bible in one's native tongue serves to make for a worshipful community. Gritsch writes, "When Luther's Bible appeared it was greeted like a new-born baby. Theologians, pastors and ordinary people expressed their delight that finally the Bible had come to be a part of their lives."[115] It also served to unite the German people's language. Whereas local dialect differed greatly in 16th century Germany, the translation itself influenced the German people's understanding of the language.

Luther did provide some insight into his mode of translating in two publications. The first was published in 1530 and entitled *On Translating: An Open Letter*. In this piece Luther responds to a friend who wants to know why Luther included the word "alone" in his translation of Romans 3:28: "We hold that a person is justified without the works of the law, by faith alone."[116] His second piece on translation was written a year later and subsequently published in 1532 under the title *Defense of the Translation of the Psalms*. This work served as an introduction to Luther's German translation of the Psalms and dealt primarily with his use of Hebrew.[117]

In addition to the languages, Luther also encouraged the study of the classics in "To the Councilmen." Lewis W. Spitz writes, "Luther's 1524 letter *To the Councilmen of All Cities in Germany* is the best source for his views on the classical languages."[118] Luther often took a self-deprecating stance towards

---

[115] Gritsch "Luther as Bible Translator," 71.
[116] Gritsch "Luther as Bible Translator," 66.
[117] Ibid., 66; 68.
[118] Lewis W. Spitz "Luther and Humanism" in *Luther and Learning*, ed. Marilyn J. Harran (London: Associated University Presses, 1983), 81.

Pedagogy as Theological Praxis

his knowledge of the classics as well as the original languages, but it is clear that he does in fact have a solid knowledge of the Greek and Roman classics in addition to biblical languages.

Luther's next transition in "To the Councilmen" is to pneumatology. This transition is made through a warning he gives concerning the "Waldensian Brethren" who he characterizes as not believing the languages necessary.[119] The justification given is that they "boast of the spirit,"[120] and in doing so downplay the importance of Scripture. Luther argues that they have misunderstood the Spirit, but even more so they have misunderstood Scripture. He writes, "So I can by no means commend the Waldensian Brethren for their neglect of the languages. For even though they may teach the truth, they inevitably often miss the true meaning of the text, and thus are neither equipped nor fit for defending the faith against error.... For there is great danger in speaking of things of God in a different manner and in different terms than God himself employs."[121] His primary issue here is that without knowledge of the original languages, there can be no certainty in one's interpretation of the Bible.

The Role of Education in Society

Now that Luther has made a strong case for temporal government as being something in which Christians should be involved throughout "To the Councilmen," one must ask how to get "good and capable men"[122] involved in this institution. This section will explain why this is important to him and how understanding this relationship is important in the context of the chapter. After making this statement concerning "good and capable men," Luther's next writing is quite telling for his understanding of *oeconomia*:

> Now if (as we have assumed) there were no souls, and there were no need at all of schools and languages for the sake of the Scriptures and of God, this one consideration alone would be sufficient to justify the establishment everywhere of the very best schools for both boys and girls, namely, that in order to maintain its temporal estate outwardly the world must have good and capable men and women, men able to rule well over land and people, women able to manage the household and train children and servants aright. Now such men must come from our boys, and such women from our girls. Therefore, it is a matter of properly educating and training our boys and girls to that end.... Therefore, dear councilmen, it rests on

---

[119] Luther, "To the Councilmen of All Cities in Germany that they Establish and Maintain Christian Schools, 1524," LW 45: 365.
[120] Ibid.
[121] Luther, "To the Councilmen of All Cities in Germany that they Establish and Maintain Christian Schools, 1524," LW 45: 366.
[122] Ibid., 367.

you alone; you have better authority and occasion to do it [the educating of children] than princes and lords.[123]

In his analogy of educating people without souls, his purpose is to show that even apart from the *ecclesia*, education still maintains a valuable function for *oeconomia* and *politia*. In many ways Luther is novel in this passage in that he is arguing for the education of both men and women. In sixteenth century Europe only the daughters of kings and other important rulers would have received any type of formal education.[124] Luther argues that all humans should have an opportunity to be able to read and have at least the basics of an education. He sees both sexes as having a valuable function in society. He draws a distinction in roles between men and women, but not between the value of those roles. The phraseology of *oeconomia* used in this passage is similar to what one finds elsewhere in Luther. One has man's relationship to the land, his wife, his children, and servants. The state of welfare of the *oeconomia* has a direct correlation to how well the *politia* will function. For the temporal government to function well, the individual homes and relationships of the people must also be functioning as they were meant to be. Luther ends the passage by again laying the burden of education upon the councilmen.

Luther next addresses some of the specifics as to why public education is good for society. He writes that though discipline can be taught at home, education through a public structure allows the individual to interact and converse with others, and to assist and seek the counsel of others.[125] Luther writes, "But if children were instructed and trained in schools, or wherever learned and well-trained schoolmasters and schoolmistresses were available to teach the languages, the other arts, and history, they would then hear of the doings and sayings of the entire world, and how things went with various cities, kingdoms, princes, men, and women."[126] Whereas the languages and the arts had previously been discussed in this letter, Luther now adds to the mix the study of history. He explains that the purpose of the study of history is twofold: First, it serves to give the student knowledge of particular places and what has happened there. Second, the study of history allows one to learn wisdom from the lives of others: "they [students] could gain from history the knowledge and understanding of what to seek and what to avoid in this outward life, and be able to advise and direct others accordingly."[127]

---

[123] Ibid., 368.
[124] Noll, "The earliest Protestants and the reformation of education," 122.
[125] Luther, "To the Councilmen of All Cities in Germany that they Establish and Maintain Christian Schools, 1524," LW 45: 368.
[126] Ibid.
[127] Luther, "To the Councilmen of All Cities in Germany that they Establish and Maintain Christian Schools, 1524," LW 45: 369.

Pedagogy as Theological Praxis

Luther continues to add to the subjects that he believes appropriate to a well-rounded education. He makes a facetious statement that since children have so much energy, they may as well apply that energy to study. He writes, "If we take so much time and trouble to teach children card-playing, singing, and dancing, why do we not take as much time to teach them reading and other disciplines while they are young and have the time, and are apt and eager to learn? For my part, if I had children and could manage it, I would have them study not only languages and history, but also singing and music together with the whole of mathematics. For what is all this but mere child's play? The ancient Greeks trained their children to these disciplines; yet they grew up to be people of wondrous ability, subsequently fit for everything."[128] Luther adds more playful skills as well as mathematics to his list of what he believes should be taught. Again, Luther also believes that he is harkening back to a better time of education in his prescription, and basing his system upon the ancient Greeks and Romans. Music was part of the ancient Greek system of education, but it also held a special place for Luther. Heinrich Boehmer writes, "For music was to him [Luther] of all gifts of God the highest and most precious, saving only God's Word—the soul's comforter, which unfailingly "revived him and delivered him from sore distress," so that "his heart overflowed" if he but thought of it."[129]

It is clear that the type of education Luther has in mind here is the trivium and quadrivium based upon the ancients and solidified in the middle ages. As discussed in the introduction, the trivium consists of grammar, logic, and rhetoric. Trivium simply means the 'three roads' or 'three ways.' In most cases, the trivium served as preparation for the quadrivium: of arithmetic, geometry, music, and astronomy. These seven areas of learning are what has been traditionally known as the "liberal arts." David Wagner writes, "In a strict sense, the term designates those arts as they were codified by the Latin encyclopedists of the fifth and sixth centuries A.D., whose works provided the basic content and form of intellectual life for several centuries."[130] Marilyn Harran notes that Luther would have been trained according to the trivium. She writes that prior to entering the University of Erfurt his education would have centered upon grammar. At Erfurt, there was a definite emphasis upon logic, especially that of Aristotle, and grammar and rhetoric would have received much less attention.[131] While his studies would have focused upon the trivium

---

[128] Ibid., 369–370.

[129] Heinrich Boehmer, *Luther and the Reformation*, trans. E. S. G. Potter (London: G. Bell and Sons, Ltd., 1930), 170.

[130] David L. Wagner, "The Seven Liberal Arts and Classical Scholarship," *The Seven Liberal Arts in the Middle Ages*, ed. David L. Wagner (Bloomington: Indiana University Press, 1983), 1.

[131] Marilyn J. Harran, *Martin Luther: Learning for Life* (Saint Louis: Concordia Publishing House, 1997), 63–64.

for his Bachelor of Arts, they would have expanded to the quadrivium in his Master of Arts. Harran writes, "Having completed his B.A., Luther turned to climbing the next rung on the academic ladder, gaining his Master of Arts degree. While his first studies had focused on the *trivium*, those that concerned him now were the *quadrivium*, including geometry, arithmetic and music, and astronomy."[132] The liberal arts were well established by the time Luther is encouraging that children be educated in them in "To the Councilmen." What is unique about Luther's proposal of the liberal arts is his desire for them to be infused with Christian truth. Luther is not simply rehashing to the councilmen the education he received as a child, but argues for pedagogy that is more focused upon the Bible and ethical matters which will then be integrated into a liberal arts program.

Practicality and Education

Luther tries to balance his system with some practicality. In this section I will explain how Luther attempts to make his system of education attainable to a wider cross-section of society. Luther is unique in that he is attempting to make some level of education available for virtually all youth in Germany. Although it may at first seem daunting to engage in the type of education he is calling for, he writes that it is best to have a balance between work and study. In fact, he says that his idea is to have the boys in a school for just one or two hours a day, and the rest of their time be spent "working at home, learning a trade, or doing whatever is expected of them."[133] In the same manner, he believes that an hour or two per day could easily be found by which girls can go to school and still take care of what duties may be at home. He believes that the only thing that is lacking at the moment is the desire to engage boys and girls in such study.

Again, practicality tempered with innovation is his mode of thinking about education. Luther realizes that different classes of people will require different levels of education. Exceptional students who could go on to hold future positions as teachers, preachers or other clerical positions should be allowed to continue their education further Luther writes. "We must certainly have men to administer God's word and sacraments and to be shepherds of souls. But where shall we get them if we let our schools go by the board and fail to replace them with others that are Christian?"[134]

Luther also appeals to the estates in his formulation of education. He writes, "It is highly necessary, therefore, that we take some positive action in this matter [education of children] before it is too late; not only on account of the

---

[132] Ibid. 81.
[133] Luther, "To the Councilmen of All Cities in Germany that they Establish and Maintain Christian Schools, 1524," LW 45: 370.
[134] Ibid., 371.

Pedagogy as Theological Praxis

young people, but also in order to preserve both our spiritual and temporal estates."[135] The comment raises the question of what Luther here means that through education society is able to preserve the spiritual and temporal estates. No matter how aberrant the expression of the estates may become, they could not be completely destroyed because of God's word. The most likely direction he is going with this statement is that through education, citizens are better equipped to serve in the *politia*. As discussed in the previous chapter, Bonhoeffer and Barth preferred to speak of the "orders of preservation." In a fallen world, the estates exist and will continue to exist, but will only function properly when understood by society. Therefore, the "positive action" that can be taken in the preservation of the estates is the education of society's youth.

Luther's next transition is to say that in addition to having good schools and the languages established in Germany, believes that every effort possible should be made to establish libraries. He writes, "For if the gospel and all arts are to be preserved, they must be set down and held fast in books and writings (as was done by the prophets themselves, as I have said above). This is essential, not only that those who are to be our spiritual and temporal leaders may have books to read and study, but also that the good books may be preserved and not lost, together with the arts and languages which we now have by the grace of God."[136] Libraries serve an essential function for Luther because it is primarily through written language that humanity possesses knowledge of the various fields of study he is encouraging to be undertaken. Luther also writes that there is a historical precedent in which the collection of knowledge in written form makes for a flourishing society. He writes that the best example of this is the people of Israel. Moses began the practice of a written history, which was kept in the ark of God.[137] He writes that this "library" was added to by Joshua, Samuel, David, Solomon, Isaiah, etc. He follows this through to the monasteries, which kept some semblance of culture through their keeping of libraries.

Aristotle and Good versus Bad Books

Luther writes that a period of darkness in human history has come about because the languages, arts, and libraries have been allowed to deteriorate. Through this God rightly punished humans for their ingratitude by restraining the flow of knowledge. He writes, "Isn't it a crying shame that heretofore a boy was obliged to study for twenty years or even longer merely to learn enough bad Latin to become a priest and mumble through the mass...That is the reward of our ingratitude, that men failed to found libraries but let the good books

---

[135] Luther, "To the Councilmen of All Cities in Germany that they Establish and Maintain Christian Schools, 1524," LW 45: 373.
[136] Ibid.
[137] Deut. 31:25–26.

perish and kept poor ones."[138] The effects of a lack of proper education are physical in that people are not properly equipped to serve in society, but they are also spiritual in that priests are not equipped to administer their function as servants of God. Throughout this section there is also the pervading idea that more learning or more books will not solve the problem. He states that the monasteries have declined because they were reading the wrong kind of books, and further that a wrong sort of emphasis has occurred in theology because of a focus on Aristotle rather than the Bible. This is combined, "with countless harmful books which drew us farther from the Bible."[139] Such an argument that not just any kind of education is needed to bring the German people from their present state cuts a particular path for Luther to follow. He is able to counter any accusation that the universities and schools are flourishing if they are not learning in such a way that is profitable for their place in the estates. Luther writes that it would be more profitable to be selective in what one chooses to read and study: "My advice is not to heap together all manner of books indiscriminately and think only of the number and size of the collection. I would make a judicious selection, for it is not necessary to have all the commentaries of the jurists, all the sentences of the theologians, all the *quaestiones* of the philosophers, and all the sermons of the monks. Indeed, I would discard all such dung, and furnish my library with the right sort of books, consulting with scholars as to my choice."[140] Luther seems to leave the question open to the reader as to what books should be included in such a selection, but he follow this with what he thinks should be included in such a library.

He begins with the Bible in Latin, Greek, Hebrew, German and any other language in which it may be available. This is followed by biblical commentaries (the older the better) in Greek, Hebrew, and Latin. Next on his list is books that would help one learn the languages, "such as the poets and orators, regardless of whether they were pagan or Christian, Greek or Latin, for it is from such books that one must learn grammar."[141] This is followed by, "books on the liberal arts, and all the other arts. Finally, there would be books of law and medicine; here too there should be careful choice among commentaries."[142] He also encourages the Germans to write down their histories. He says that historically those cultures that do not have a written history little is known, and therefore it would be wise for the German people to come out of their laziness and keep a written history.

---

[138] Luther, "To the Councilmen of All Cities in Germany that they Establish and Maintain Christian Schools, 1524," LW 45: 375.
[139] Ibid.
[140] Luther, "To the Councilmen of All Cities in Germany that they Establish and Maintain Christian Schools, 1524," LW 45: 376.
[141] Ibid.
[142] Ibid.

Pedagogy as Theological Praxis

At this point in the letter Luther returns to his refrain that now is a time of opportunity for the German people: "Now that God has today so graciously bestowed upon us an abundance of arts, scholars, and books, it is time to reap and gather in the best as well as we can, and lay up treasure in order to preserve for the future something from these years of jubilee, and not lose this plentiful harvest."[143] This is followed by a warning that this time of opportunity will surely not last as the devil will again persuade people to read and study materials that are worthless.

Luther concludes the letter by encouraging the councilmen to take heed to what he has thus far said. He writes that his work has not been for his own advantage, but for the people of Germany. He ends the letter with a blessing and a call to action on behalf of the youth: "May he soften and kindle your hearts that they may be deeply concerned for the poor, miserable, and neglected youth, and with the help of God aid and assist them, to the end that there may be a blessed and Christian government in the German lands with respect to both body and soul, with all plenty and abundance, to the glory and honor of God the Father, through our Savior Jesus Christ. Amen."[144]

The Results of Luther's Reforms

At this point it is fair to take a look at history and ask whether any of Luther's proposed reforms were actually put into place. This section will examine the immediate context of Luther's and his follower's reforms. Martin Brecht traces some of the immediate results that came as a consequence of "To the Councilmen." On 25 April, 1524 Luther requested Jacob Strauss to establish a school in Eisenach. He wrote to Strauss that the gospel would be seriously threatened here if a school were not established. He also wrote a letter in 1524 to the city of Riga in which he complained about how his message concerning education had largely been received with apathy.[145] Later during the Peasants' War Luther blamed the ignorance of God's law as being the reason for the decline of schools.

In some circles Luther's appeal for educational reform were taken to heart. In 1524 reforms were being undertaken in the schools of Madeburg, Nordhausen, Halberstadt and Gotha.[146] On 16 April 1525 Luther traveled with Melanchthon and Agricola to Eisleben at the request of Count Albrecht of Mansfield for the purpose of establishing a Christian Latin school. After this encounter Luther held up Count Albrecht as an example to the government of

---

[143] Luther, "To the Councilmen of All Cities in Germany that they Establish and Maintain Christian Schools, 1524," LW 45: 378.
[144] Ibid.
[145] Brecht, *Martin Luther: Shaping and Defining the Reformation 1521–1532*, 141.
[146] Ibid.

Electoral Saxony in addition to the cities of Magdeburg, Danzig, and Nuremberg.[147] A year later Luther sent a German schoolmaster to aid in the education work being done in Eisleben. In May 1525 the council of Zerbst asked him what should be done with monastic property. Just as in "To the Councilmen," he advocated that it be turned into a boys' and girls' school, "for the greatest power lies in the education of the young."[148] In 1527 Luther asked a former nun from Nimbeschen, Else von Kanitz, to take charge of the girls' school in Wittenberg in order to set an example for others of how such a school should be run.[149] The historical record bears witness that after this letter Luther and Melanchthon were increasingly looked to for the establishing of schools and the provision of schoolmasters. Today Melanchthon is remember much more than Luther for his educational reforms, as was given the amiable title of "Teacher of Germany," but Melanchthon's work most likely could have not been performed without the foundation laid by Luther. Brecht writes, "In general, the effort to establish schools proved not to be without results—as Luther had initially feared—but it still was a long-term task. The development of an educational system in the evangelical territories was usually initiated in connection with the reorganization of the church, and it thus provided an educated new generation. Not least did this also contribute to a consolidation against enthusiasm. In the long run, the evangelical schools proved to be important sustainers of a Protestant culture."[150] It should also be noted that the time of the writing of "To the Councilmen" in 1524 was one of transition in Luther's thinking about education. Karin Maag writes:

> Up until the early 1520's, Luther believed the most effective form of education was on combining religious training in the home, led by the head of the household, and academic study in schools, which were supported and funded by parents and the magistrates. However, after the shock of the German Peasants' War and the increasing realization that appealing to the voluntary support of the parents and civil authorities was not producing any concrete results, Luther's views changed. By the late 1520's and early 1530s, he argued vigorously for compulsory schooling, to be organized and overseen by secular authorities. Yet even this form of education did not touch the entire population: children whose education ended when they completed the curriculum of their local vernacular school, youngsters (particularly in rural areas) with no access to schooling on a regular basis, and of course older people, were left out of this educational scheme. Hence Luther and other German reformers, such as Johannes Bugenhagen, also strongly urged the importance of catechetical instruction to provide basic doctrinal education for a broader range of people. Works such as Luther's Small Catechism of 1529 were designed to help the general population in rural as well as urban areas to learn the basics about their faith through a question-and-answer format to be memorized and learned by rote. Indeed,

---

[147] Ibid.
[148] Ibid.
[149] Ibid.
[150] Brecht, *Martin Luther: Shaping and Defining the Reformation 1521–1532*, 141–142.

there are signs that the reformers favoured catechetical instruction over unlimited access of the population to the Bible, because the catechism did not raise the spectre of multiple interpretations. In others words, the advocacy of catechetical study by the reformers was motivated in part by their perception of the catechism as a safe learning tool in the hands of otherwise ignorant populations.[151]

Luther's system of education also affirms that the Christian has something unique to offer in the public realm. Luther writes, "I have pointed out that the common man is doing nothing about it [the education of children]; he is incapable of it, unwilling, and ignorant of what to do."[152] In Luther's opinion it is a Christian task to provide children with a proper education. Only the Christian properly understands his or her station in the estates,[153] and therefore only the Christian would be able to achieve the high goals in education Luther demands.

Does this exclude non-Christians from Luther's brand of liberal arts education? It is important to remember that Luther is appealing to secular authority when asking for aid in education. The overlaying of Christendom upon the two kingdoms results in the meshing of Christians in the secular kingdom, and ergo Christian involvement in secular activities. It is also worth noting that the type of school Luther is advocating seems to be a Christian school. It would be of little use for one who does not desire to read or intensely study the Bible to engage in the study of biblical languages, which is at the heart of Luther's educational reforms. If nothing else, such study would hopefully lead to further desire for the things of God through such study.

At the university level, Luther had early on attempted to incorporate the study of languages as a key part of the curriculum. In 1518 Wittenberg became the first German university to have chairs in Hebrew, Greek, and Latin. Melanthchon took up the chair in Greek, and aided in setting the course for German education.[154]

As enumerated earlier, the Christian is best equipped to serve in the *politia* because he or she enters a governmental station out of love. Luther makes a teleological argument to the councilmen that in their decision to sponsor public education they will be improving the citizenry and thus provide for the future stability of the state. Although there are a variety of spiritual and physical reasons why a liberal arts education is beneficial to the pupil, it is also

---

[151] Maag, "Education and Literacy," 536.

[152] Luther, "To the Councilmen of All Cities in Germany that they Establish and Maintain Christian Schools, 1524," LW 45: 368.

[153] Althaus, *The Ethics of Martin Luther*, 37–38.

[154] Robert Rosin, "The Reformation, Humanism, and Education: the Wittenberg Model for Reform," *Concordia Journal* 16:4 (October, 1990): 310.

beneficial to the teacher because he or she is properly exercising the God given station of providing a good education to the other out of neighbor love. Luther says that the stations should "serve God and the world,"[155] and the exercise of this in education is but one example of how this could be done. Luther particularly emphasizes the working of the estates as vocation when referring to secular vocations,[156] of which pedagogy would be one.

This should be qualified by the fact that one would assume there would be more of a noticeable outward effect in some stations more than others. For instance, in a station such as farming, where both a Christian and a non-Christian are both good at what they do and enjoy their job, a cursory glance would probably offer little in the difference between how these two farmers fulfill their duty. On the other hand, in a spoken station such teaching, especially teaching the liberal arts infused with biblical languages and theology as advocated by Luther, there could be a noticeable difference in what is said and done on the part of the Christian teacher desiring to fulfill his or her duty when compared to the non-Christian teacher. This is due in part to the biblical concept that, "out of the overflow of the heart the mouth speaks,"[157] and a public station will lend itself to a more obvious differentiation in the fulfilling of the station.

It should also be acknowledged that Luther's educational reforms were not restricted to just his immediate context. A recent PhD thesis by Thomas Korcok has traced the educational reforms of Luther, Phillip Melanchthon, and Johannes Bugenhagen from the Reformation to contemporary education.[158] In the long-term two main effects arose out of Luther's educational reforms in Germany: the provision of schools becoming the role of the civil authority and obligatory weekly catechism sessions for the young.[159]

Relevant Application of Luther's Education Model and the Three Estates

After providing a detailed analysis of "To the Councilmen" a few points have become clear. The content of the letter can be divided into theological reflection and practical reform. Theologically, much of the letter is spent proposing a paradigm shift in how one studies the Bible, and the purpose for which the

---

[155] Luther, "A Sermon on Keeping Children in School," LW 46: 252. Quotation taken from Althaus, *The Ethics of Martin Luther*, 38.
[156] Althaus, *The Ethics of Martin Luther*, 39.
[157] Cf. Matt. 12:34; Lk. 6:45.
[158] Thomas Korcok, "Forward to the Past: A Study of the Development of the Liberal Arts in the Context of Confessional Lutheran Education with Special Reference to a Contemporary Application of Liberal Education" (PhD diss., Free University of Amsterdam, 2009).
[159] Maag, "Education and Literacy," 537.

government educates and trains its citizens. The importance of learning the biblical languages is a thread that runs throughout this letter. This is Luther's belief that foundationally no human can stand between a person and God as revealed in the Scriptures. In his volume of Luther's view of the authority of Scripture Mark Thompson writes:

> Luther could and did speak of the Scriptures proceeding from the mouth of God and carrying the authority of God. . . . The inheritance into which Luther entered entailed a commitment to the divine inspiration of the Bible and its consequently unique authority, despite the fact that in some quarters the theological tradition had emerged as a second source of authority which tended to circumscribe that of Scripture itself. Further, and particularly in the period prior to the indulgence controversy, Luther appeared to have no consciousness of departing from the accepted teaching of the church on this subject.[160]

Because the Scriptures lead to a true knowledge of God, avoiding the errors of false interpreters will lead one to truth in Luther's conception. Luther's educational idea of incorporating the languages into curriculum would hand the truth of the Scriptures to a younger generation.

There is also a very important political motif running through this letter. Because the kingdom of the world is still God's kingdom, Christians should be actively involved in governmental life. Luther's primary appeal on secular and religious grounds for the education of youth is that this will make for good citizens who are fit to serve in various forms of civic life. Luther is somewhat ambiguous as to the application of *politia*. Because it is a postlapsarian estate, in some instances it is seen as a sort of necessary evil through which the Christian must endure. In other instances, such as in the secular kingdom of the two kingdoms theory it is a divinely commanded institute through which the Christian works. Bernd Wannenwetch also notices that inconsistency: "As for the institution of *politia*, he [Luther] seems to be somewhat inconsistent. On the one hand, he sees it as a postlapsarian function of God's providence against the anarchic power of sin (*usus politicus*); but on the other, he entertains the existence of politics in a prelapsarian sense: namely as an ordered way of loving together harmoniously under God's rule without the coercive feature that marks political authority after the fall."[161] In "To the Councilmen," Luther takes both a positive and negative view of the governmental order. If there would have been a sharp divide between the sacred and the secular in Luther's thought, it is doubtful he would have petitioned governmental officials to establish what were essentially Christian schools. He views the governmental function to be at

---

[160] Mark Thompson, *A Sure Ground on Which to Stand: The Relation of Authority and Interpretive Method in Luther's Approach to Scripture* (Carlisle: Paternoster Press, 2004), 119.
[161] Bernd Wannenwetsch, "Luther's Moral Theology," 130.

least in part to establish a common Christian morality among the people of Germany, which he believes is done through the education of its citizens. The grounds by which he establishes governmental intervention in education are also both positive and negative. Negatively, it is the government's responsibility to education because parents are not up to the task. The implication here is that if parents were fit to educate, the task for doing so would fall primarily upon them. On a positive note, latter in the letter Luther writes, "Therefore, dear sirs, take this task to heart which God so earnestly requires of you, which your office imposes upon you, which is so necessary for our youth, and with which neither church not world can dispense."[162] A few pages prior to this quote he argues that education is in fact more proper to a public, rather than private home setting, because it is through a public setting that one is able to be instructed by someone who is well trained to teach and also because one is able to engage with a wider variety of ideas and individuals. This could simply be a rhetorical tool by which Luther has convinced the councilmen that it is their task to educate children because it is a divinely ordained function of the *politia*. He seems to prevaricate, however, and his position moves from one of necessity because of the unfitness of the *oeconomia* to educate to one of education intrinsically being a part of *oeconomia*.

Part of the answer to this dilemma is that the estates are basically static entities in the sense of being a superstructure into which all of humanity and the events of creation must conform. Wannenwetch notes Luther's use of the term "con-creatures" to describe the role of the estates.[163] This term brings out the concept of the estates being created alongside of humans, "in order to provide the social spheres that are necessary for a flourishing and obedient life."[164] Although something such as the relation between a husband and wife is clearly seen in its fullest expression in *oeconomia*, the topic of learning and receiving knowledge is not so clearly placed in just one of the estates. Pedagogy and education is not confined to any one of the estates, though it is grounded in *ecclesia*. In *ecclesia* one is educated in a variety of functions such as worship, obedience, gratitude, etc. Through *ecclesia* one receives knowledge of God. At the death of David he instructs his son and heir to his kingdom, "And you, Solomon my son, know the God of your father and serve him with a whole heart and with a willing mind, for the Lord searches all hearts and understands every plan and thought. If you seek him, he will be found by you, but if you forsake him, he will cast you off forever."[165] The type of knowledge advocated here is relational. Solomon is commanded to have an intimate knowledge of God that will lead to service and obedience on the part of the participant. In

---

[162] Luther, "To the Councilmen of All Cities in Germany that they Establish and Maintain Christian Schools, 1524," LW 45:372.
[163] Wannenwetsch, "Luther's Moral Theology," 130.
[164] Ibid., 131.
[165] 1 Chronicles 28:9.

numerous biblical passages, particularly the Psalms one is told either to know a particular attribute of God, or God himself is commanding to be recognized as God.[166] In Jesus' words on John 17:3 he prays, "And this is eternal life, that they know you are the only true God, and Jesus Christ whom you have sent." Paul echoes this concept in Galatians 4:9, "But now that you have come to know God, or rather to be known by God, how can you turn back again to the weak and worthless elementary principles of the world, whose slaves you want to be once more?" This type of learning who God is, and learning what it means to be known by God is certainly best expressed in *ecclesia*. One is benefitted by education in *eccelesia* in Luther's classical education model in that through the study of the languages and the study of the space in which one is placed, that person is better equipped to understand and worship the creator. In the same manner one is privy to be benefitted in *oeconomia* through classical education. The study of history or the Bible can equip one to better understand and serve in his or her station in *oeconomia*.

In *oeconomia* a child should naturally learn the affection of family, one may learn a trade from a parent and sundry other skills necessary in life. Luther says that training in proper discipline could be best learned in the home.[167] Even within the liberal arts, it is not as if one cannot be taught in the home. The problem Luther raises with receiving a liberal arts education in the home is that most parents have not been trained to be a schoolmaster or schoolmistress.

The point Luther seems to be making is that the type of education he is advocating is best performed by the *politia* because the *politia* is best equipped to provide a Christian and liberal arts education. This equipping is primarily due to the resources and structure that the state can provide. It is the responsibility of the state to promote peace among its citizens, and one manner in which this can be performed is through the education of its citizens.

Luther's use of the estates in "To the Councilmen" is also important because of his advocacy for the education of women. It is true that the type of education for which he is arguing is not completely egalitarian, but he is novel in saying that both young boys and girls would benefit from receiving a publicly funded education. Luther argues that it would be beneficial to educate boys and girls because both have a valuable place in society. Although the place of the female was primarily in the home in Luther's contemporary world, he certainly advocated learning something more than "homemaking" skills. These types of valuable skills (cooking, cleaning, raising a household, etc) would be best suited to training in the *oeconomia* rather than a public education, unless the

---

[166] Cf. Ps. 46:10; Ps. 59:13; Ps. 100: 3.
[167] Luther, "To the Councilmen of All Cities in Germany that they Establish and Maintain Christian Schools, 1524," LW 45: 368.

necessary skills were lacking in the adults in the family. If it were just homemaking skills Luther was referring to for girls, then he would not have said, "a girl can surely find time enough to attend school for an hour a day, and still take care of her duties at home."[168] It would be oxymoronic to take a girl away for taking care of the home in order to teach her to take care of the home. Even if the station of a woman were to "manage the household and train children and servants aright,"[169] they would also benefit from Luther's liberal arts educational system.

The concept of the estates being best understood by Christians is also important for their relation to education. Although all humans partake in the estates (as noted by Bayer in the previous chapter when he refers to *ecclesia* as being universal) only through the triune God of Christianity can one properly understand the place of the estates in the world. Althaus writes, "only the Christian knows that these stations have been established by God. They are instituted, presupposed, recognized and honored by the Scripture and are therefore "contained and involved in God's word and commandment. Christians alone know and teach that these are divine ordinances and institutions. Therefore, they alone can truly give thanks and pray for them in their churches."[170] One who is not a follower of Christ can have glimpses of God's intention in the estates, but cannot truly grasp how God is using the estates for the benefit of mankind. This is surely one reason why Luther uses the estates to make an argument for a Christian form of education. The follower of Jesus through the estates can learn how to fulfill his or her role in the good world that God has provided.

Maag notes that when trying to understand the impact of the Reformation upon education it is difficult to untangle what is a result of the Reformation and what is the result of other factors. She writes:

> The main difficulty in assessing the impact of the Reformation on educational provision in Protestant areas during the sixteenth century lies in establishing whether the developments which occurred were due solely or in part to the Reformation itself, or to other factors. Indeed, one line of argument suggests that it was the increased availability and participation in education that led to more general acceptance of the Reformation, especially in cities, and not the other way around. In this perspective, the development of education is tied much more to humanism and growing urban self-confidence than to religious change. And yet one cannot ignore the major increase in the number of Latin schools, academies and universities across Europe in the Reformation period. Leading reformers and their successors saw the creation of schools at all levels as part of their more general plan to transform

---

[168] Brecht, *Martin Luther: Shaping and Defining the Reformation 1521–1532*, 370.
[169] Ibid., 368.
[170] Althaus, *The Ethics of Martin Luther*, 38. Martin Luther, "Confession Concerning Christ's Supper, 1528," LW 37: 365; "Psalm 111," LW 13:370.

society. The schools were instruments to train the young, and through them, it was hoped, older generations too would come to a fuller knowledge of Lutheran or Reformed doctrine. Increasingly as the decades wore on, however, both the ecclesiastical and civic authorities concentrated their attention and their resources on the education of the lite, both in an attempt to train up worth successors to themselves and in response to the seemingly muted impact of the Reformation and its teachings on the population at large. For instance, visitation records from the second half of the sixteenth century in the German lands suggest that few people were able to give a satisfactory account of the faith in their own words to the visitors. Even those who had memorized and could recite the catechism could not necessarily explain the meaning of what they had learned.[171]

Ultimately, "To the Councilmen" supports the essential elements of humanism that Luther favored, but it is also combined with his Reformation ideals. He is able to argue in favor of a liberal arts education and strike a middle ground between his disfavor of scholasticism and his charge of being anti-educational. Thus, Luther achieved his purpose in "To the Councilmen" of presenting a proposal of education that would provide reform to the lackadaisical state it was in. Though Melanchthon would later take the helm in leading educational reform in Germany, it was these early insights in "To the Councilmen" through which Luther paved the way. Thus far this thesis has provided background in the classical tradition, examined Luther's three estates, and provided application of the estates to Luther's 1524 letter "To the Councilmen of all Cities in Germany that they Establish and Maintain Christian Schools." The thesis will now transition to an examination of Dutch Reformed theology, and the contributions of Herman Bavinck in particular.

---

[171] Maag, "Education and Literacy," 541.

3. Herman Bavinck, Neo-Calvinism, and Reformed Theology

At first glance, the strands that hold together a thesis providing a comparison between Martin Luther and Herman Bavinck may not seem particularly obvious. As was mentioned in the introduction, one of the primary unifying themes is that both figures had an interest in classical education, as well as pedagogy in general. Lutheran and Reformed streams of thought hold much in common, but there are also critical differences that will affect how the two camps understand education. Just as chapter one showed how the three estates serve as a lens through which to view Luther's theology as well as his understanding of education, this chapter will provide an overview of Dutch Reformed theology and the particular conceptual moves that Herman Bavinck offered to this theological tradition.

To understand Herman Bavinck's position regarding the role of education in the life of the believer it is helpful to begin by examining the underlying presuppositions of Bavinck's theology. This will be executed by looking at some of the distinctive aspects of Bavinck's expression of Reformed theology as well and how these fit into a larger picture of Reformed theology. This chapter is not an exhaustive account of the intricacies of Bavinck's theology, but will focus upon the areas that could have ramifications on his views of education as well as some areas in which he is similar to or differs from Luther. This will lead into chapter four, which will examine two of Bavinck's writings on education: an article entitled "Classical Education" and a book entitled *Pedagogical Principles*. These two chapters together will form a robust picture of the relation of pedagogy and theology in Bavinck's work.

Lutheran Theology and Neo-Calvinism

As this thesis involves an analysis of the distinctions between Bavinck's and Luther's theological positions and how this led to different paths through which they understood education, it is helpful to examine what Bavinck had to say concerning Lutheran theology. Here is Bavinck's account of the fundamental theological difference between Lutheran and Reformed theology is in the area of emphasis:

> The primary question asked by Lutherans was anthropological: 'How can I be saved?' Works-righteousness was seen as the great departure from gospel truth. The Reformed, by contrast, sought to explore the foundations of salvation in the electing counsel of God and asked the theological question: 'How is the glory of God advanced?' Avoiding idolatry is the major concern for the Reformed. Doctrines such

as election, justification, regeneration, and sacraments were richer and more multifaceted among the various Reformed churches than in the Lutheran.[1]

This quotation comes at the beginning of Bavinck's chapter on Reformed dogmatics, which immediately follows his chapter on Lutheran dogmatics. One must first ask whether Bavinck is indeed correct in the distinction he draws between Lutheran and Reformed dogmatics, and second what difference such a distinction could in fact make.

Bavinck is correct that the emphasis of Lutheran dogmatics is a move away from any form of work-based righteousness, but to leave that as the representation of Lutheran theology is trite at best. Even if the question "How can I be saved?" is an anthropological question, it is also a theological question. As was examined in chapter 1, Luther's estate of *ecclesia* represented the divine role of the Godhead in creation and provision for mankind. Asking how one is saved places the emphasis upon the God who justifies and redeems apart from the goodness of man. Bavinck is quick to emphasize that Lutheran and Reformed theology hold much in common, and as such it is important to determine where the distinction between the two lies. Bavinck's contemporary in neo-Calvinism Abraham Kuyper takes the same position as Bavinck in the divide between the anthropological and the theological. He writes, "Luther as well as Calvin contended for a direct fellowship with God, but Luther took it up from its subjective, anthropological side, and not from its objective, cosmological side as Calvin did. Luther's starting-point was the special-soteriological principle of a justifying faith; while Calvin's extending far wider, lay in the general cosmological principle of the sovereignty of God."[2]

Bavinck appreciates many of the insights of Luther, and throughout *Reformed Dogmatics* Luther remains a dialogue partner concerning a number of theological topics.[3] He argues that though the Lutheran stream remains an important piece of the Christian tradition, Reformed theology is able to become "richer" because of the emphasis upon how the glory of God is advanced. This emphasis upon the glory of God is closely related to the cultural mandate[4] because the glory of God is meant to be advanced in all areas of life.

---

[1] Herman Bavinck, *Reformed Dogmatics, Vol. 1: Prolegomena*, ed. John Bolt, trans. John Vriend (Grand Rapids: Baker, 2003) 175.
[2] Abraham Kuyper, *Calvinism* (Edinburgh: T&T Clark, 1899), 20.
[3] Bavinck, *Reformed Dogmatics: Vol. 4: Holy Spirit, Church, and New Creation*, ed. John Bolt, trans. John Vriend (Grand Rapids: Baker, 2008), 921. This reference is to the subject index of the four volumes of *Reformed Dogmatics*. Dialogue with Luther occurs on twenty-eight subjects. The most extensive of these is concerning justification and the sacraments.
[4] Cf. Gen. 1:28. The concept of a Reformed "cultural mandate" will be further discussed in regards to Reformed theology in this chapter.

Another similarity that has recently been pointed out by David VanDrunen is the role of natural law and the two kingdoms in Bavinck's work. VanDrunen is fairly novel in his approach, noting that neo-Calvinism usually tends to emphasize the kingdom of Christ penetrating all of human life rather than there be any type of dualistic two kingdom theology.[5] VanDrunen outlines what he considers to be the traditional Reformed doctrine of the two kingdoms:

> The two kingdoms teach that God rules all things in his Son, yet does so in two fundamentally different ways. As the Creator and Sustainer, through his Son as the eternal Logos, he rules over all human beings in the *civil* kingdom. This civil kingdom consists of a range of nonecclesiastical cultural endeavors and institutions, among which the state particular prominence. As the Redeemer, through his Son as the incarnate God-Man, God rules the other kingdom, sometimes referred to at the *spiritual* kingdom. This spiritual kingdom is essentially heavenly and eschatological but has broken into history and is now expressed institutionally in the church. Both kingdoms are good, God-ordained, and regulated by divine law, and believers participate in both kingdoms during the present age. From this distinction between a twofold kingship of the Son of God and the consequent distinction between two kingdoms by which he rules the world, Reformed orthodox theology derived a series of distinctions between political and ecclesiastical authority. According to one particularly helpful summary of these distinctions, political and ecclesiastical authority differ in regard to origin, subjects, form, end, object, effects, and mode. The civil kingdom is provisional, temporary, and of this world. The spiritual kingdom is everlasting, eschatological and not of this world.[6]

VanDrunen's basic case for Bavinck's use of the two kingdoms is that it is not explicit, but rather he utilizes the categories made available to him by the two kingdoms in his doctrine of creation. For Bavinck, Christ is lord over creation and re-creation.[7] To make this distinction Bavinck often assigned the title of *Logos* to the eternal Son as the creator of the cosmos, and the title *Christ* as the incarnate Son who has brought about redemption.[8] This distinction is not to completely bifurcate the roles of the Son, but to represent two *modus opperandi* of the Son. This separation leads to the Reformed take on the two kingdoms in which Christ holds kingship over all creation, but also has a redemptive kingship particular to followers of Christ.[9]

---

[5] David VanDrunen "'The Kingship of Christ is Twofold': Natural Law and the Two Kingdoms in the Thought of Herman Bavinck," *Calvin Theological Journal* 45:1 (2010): 147. For further information on this relation see VanDrunen's volume, *Natural Law and the Two Kingdoms: A Study in the Development of Reformed Social Thought* (Grand Rapids: Eerdmans, 2010).

[6] VanDrunen, "'The Kingship of Christ is Twofold': Natural Law and the Two Kingdoms in the Thought of Herman Bavinck," 148–149.

[7] Bavinck, *RD*, 2.276.

[8] Bavinck, *RD*, 2.75; 3.225, 470, 4.33.

[9] VanDrunen, "'The Kingship of Christ is Twofold': Natural Law and the Two Kingdoms in the Thought of Herman Bavinck," 151. Concerning this point Bavinck also

In both the Lutheran and the Reformed account of the two kingdoms there is acknowledgement of God as being over both kingdoms. VanDrunen believes that the distinction between these two positions is, "The Lutherans tended to constrict the "kingdom of the right hand" to the church's spiritual ministry of the Word and sacraments and the "kingdom of the left hand" to the external church government. Thus, they often handed over church government to the civil government. The Reformed, conversely, insisted that Christ's kingship over his church includes an interest in its government, therefore, they defended the church's right to exercise discipline and to administer its own affairs."[10] Bavinck follows the Reformed tradition here and makes a firm separation between ecclesiastical government and civil office.[11] This is an important difference because it makes two separate spheres of power.

Distinctive Aspects of Dutch Neo-Calvinist Theology

In this section I will examine aspects of Bavinck's theology that are particular to him as well as to the Dutch Reformed tradition. Doing so will aid in demonstrating the distinct contributions Bavinck made to theology as well as pedagogy. As has been stated, Herman Bavinck's theological heritage is that of Dutch Neo-Calvinism. Neo-Calvinism is most closely associated with Abraham Kuyper, and it is difficult to speak about the movement without speaking of Kuyper. Being seventeen years younger than Kuyper, Bavinck had the opportunity to distill many of the theological concepts that Kuyper put forth. Neo-Calvinism as a movement came about as a result of Kuyper's desire to reform both the state and the Dutch Reformed Church as it existed in mid-19th century Netherlands. Following two years at a pastorate in Utrecht, Kuyper came to the conclusion that the existing church order in the Netherlands was in need of reform. The ties between the church and state were drawn closely together in the Constitution of 1814, but they were notably relaxed during a new Constitution set forth in 1848. Despite this the state continued to exercise a great deal of control over the church, and Kuyper therefore saw reform in both the church and state as necessary.[12] In many ways Bavinck was seen as the theological and political heir of the Dutch neo-Calvinism movement during Kuyper's later years. Thus Bavinck inherited many of the particulars of neo-Calvinism while also adding some of his own. The rest of this chapter will

---

relates common grace to his understanding of the two kingdoms *RD*, 4.436. He also associates the Noahic covenant of nature with the work of the Son as *Logos* in distinction from the work of the Son as Christ as the mediator of the covenant of grace *RD*, 4.33, 436.

[10] VanDrunen, "'The Kingship of Christ is Twofold': Natural Law and the Two Kingdoms in the Thought of Herman Bavinck," 151.

[11] Bavinck, *RD*, 4.340, 359, 368–370, 379, 409–410, and 413–414.

[12] Justus M. van der Kroef, *Abraham Kuyper and the Rise of Neo-Calvinism in the Netherlands*, Church History 17:4 (Dec. 1943): 317.

examine some of the distinctive aspects of Dutch neo-Calvinism as well as some of the characteristic features of Bavinck's theology. Kuyper and Bavinck were public theologians in two very different ways. George Harinck writes, "Bavinck was a better analyst than general [with Kuyper being the general]. He, too, fought his battles but never relished them. In his heart, Bavinck was not attracted by conflict; he engaged the problem. He did not want to confront others as opponents but engage them as partners."[13] This is an important distinction, as throughout Bavinck's career he was keen to engage his opponents, but not in such a way as to make them enemies. He attempted to learn what truth could be found in the positions of others, while also maintaining his Reformed worldview.

Common Grace

One of the distinctive doctrines neo-Calvinism is known for is the place of common grace in its theology. Common grace is called "common" not in the sense that it is cheap grace, but rather it is grace that all humans hold in common.[14] This is a separate category from redemptive grace by which humans are able to receive salvation. Michael Allen writes, "Second [after redemptive grace], there is grace that does not result in salvation *per se*, even as it leads to good works in the here and now. God's restraining and invigorating grace allows for good things to flow from unredeemed people: see the gifting of Cain, so that he could build a city (Gen. 4:12, 15) or the covenantal promise given to Noah (Gen. 8:21–22; 9:9–11)."[15] Allen also stresses that such giving of grace to culture should be seen as a blessing in that all of God's creatures are given the opportunity to take part in the grace given by God. This is an important link for how the neo-Calvinist vision of common grace transfers to their understanding of culture.

James McGoldrick writes that the role of common grace was one of the most distinctive elements of Abraham Kuyper's theology:

> One of the most prominent themes in the theology of Abraham Kuyper is the distinction he made between common grace and special grace. He held that divine grace combats the effects of human sinfulness in two principle ways. Common grace restrains the human tendency towards destructive evil and encourages people to perform actions that are beneficial to the human race as a whole. Special grace transforms the sinful nature of God's elect so that they renounce unbelief and sinful

---

[13] George Harinck, "Herman Bavinck and Gerhard Vos," *Calvin Theological Journal* 45:1 (April, 2010): 19.
[14] Dietrich Bonhoeffer, *Discipleship* (Minneapolis: Fortress Press, 2003), 43.
[15] R. Michael Allen, *Reformed Theology*, (London: T&T Clark, 2010), 162.

behaviour to serve the God who has redeemed them. Both kinds of grace are unmerited gifts from God.[16]

Kuyper argues that his position regarding common grace is firmly grounded in the Reformed tradition. Although common grace was an important and distinctive aspect of Kuyper's theology as well, it's meaning and outworking was distilled much more by Bavinck. John Bolt notes that there was contradiction in Kuyper's use of common grace. He writes:

> At times he [Kuyper] speaks of common grace as independent of special grace, at other times as preparation for special grace and a necessary condition for redemption. The precise relation between special and common grace as the fruit of the redemptive work of Jesus Christ is not clear either, though he does finally achieve a *formal* systematic unity of thought by grounding both special and common grace in the eternal decree of God. Kuyper was less concerned with a systematically worked-out and consistent definition of common grace that with its polemical value in combating the cultural alienation of many orthodox Dutch Reformed people.[17]

Compared to Kuyper, common grace was an even more relevant part of Bavinck's theology.[18] VanDrunen writes, "For Bavinck, common grace is common in the sense that God bestows it on all people—the good and the evil together. Grounded in the covenant with Noah, which Bavinck termed the covenant of nature in distinction from the covenant of grace, common grace restrains sin and evil in a fallen world (special grace, in contrast, renews and redeems the world and conquers sin). Although he affirmed the Calvinist doctrine of sin, Bavinck recognized remarkable accomplishments of fallen humanity."[19] Bavinck's primary theological expression of his understanding of common grace appeared in *The Princeton Theological Review* under the title "Calvin and Common Grace."[20]

With this understanding of common grace, Bavinck and other neo-Calvinists were able to affirm what truth they saw in science and the arts. McGoldrick argues that the importance of stating there is such a thing as common grace in Reformed theology is linked to the need to make God's sovereign working in the world explicit. He writes, "Reformed believers have showed serious interest

---

[16] James E. McGoldrick, *God's Renaissance Man: The Life and Work of Abraham Kuyper* (Darlington: Evangelical Press, 2000), 141.
[17] John Bolt, *A Free Church, A Holy Nation* (Grand Rapids: Eerdmans, 2001), 221–222.
[18] One dissenting voice stating that common grace is a minor part of Bavinck's theology is E. P. Heideman, *The Relation of Revelation and Reason in E. Brunner and H. Bavinck* (Assen: Van Gorcum, 1959), 178.
[19] VanDrunen, "'The Kingship of Christ is Twofold': Natural Law and the Two Kingdoms in the Thought of Herman Bavinck," 156. Bavinck, *RD*, 3.120–121.
[20] Herman Bavinck, "Calvin and Common Grace," *The Princeton Theological Review*, 1909.

in common grace . . . [because they] have appreciated sufficiently the implications of God's sovereignty. Their understanding of this matter means that Calvinists do not become concerned with personal salvation to the point where they have little interest in mundane affairs that lie outside the realm of saving grace."[21] Although neo-Calvinists emphasized common grace more than most Christian theologians, they argued that this was not a new invention in doctrine, but found its initial expression in John Calvin.[22] One particular place to which the neo-Calvinists could look is III.XIX of John Calvin's *Institutes* entitled, "Christian Freedom."[23] Near the end of this chapter Calvin argues that there are two kinds of government by which man is ruled: a spiritual government and a political government. Calvin writes:

> Therefore, in order that none of us may stumble on that stone, let us first consider that there is a twofold government in man: one aspect is spiritual, whereby the conscience is instructed in piety and in reverencing God; the second is political, whereby man is educated for the duties of humanity and citizenship that must be maintained among men. These are usually called the 'spiritual' and the 'temporal' jurisdiction (not improper terms) by which is meant that the former sort of government pertains to the life of the soul, while the latter has to do with the concerns of the present life—not only with food and clothing but with laying down laws whereby a man may live his life among other men holily, honorably, and temperately.[24]

The importance of common grace to the Dutch neo-Calvinist tradition is seen in that for one to teach at the Free University of Amsterdam (which Bavinck did from 1902 until the end of his career), all professors had to subscribe to 'Reformed principles', which primarily referred to the doctrines of creation and grace.[25] The role of creation is Dutch Reformed theology will be explored later in the chapter.

The Inspiration of Scripture and the "Organic"

Another important aspect of Dutch neo-Calvinist theology (or any group's theology for that matter) is its understanding of Scripture. Developing an understanding of the neo-Calvinist position regarding Scripture, and Bavinck's in particular, is important because it directs how Scripture bears upon practical issues such as education. One of the unique concepts of neo-Calvinist theology is its use of the term "organic." Both Bavinck and Kuyper use the term

---

[21] McGoldrick, *God's Renaissance Man*, 150.
[22] Ibid., 153.
[23] Jean Calvin, *Institutes of the Christian Religion*. The Library of Christian Classics, ed. John T. McNeill trans. Ford Lewis Battles (Philadelphia: Westminster Press, 1960), 833–849.
[24] Ibid., 847.
[25] McGoldrick, *God's Renaissance Man*, 155.

"organic" in relation to their understanding of the inspiration of Scripture.[26] Kuyper, in the tradition of Princeton theologian B.B. Warfield took a more mechanical view of inspiration while using the word organic. When using the word organic, Kuyper emphasized the particular of the organism forming a whole rather than its organic development. He writes in his *magnum opus*, the *Encyclopedia of Sacred Theology*, "By the organism of theology we mean what is commonly called 'the division of the theological departments.'"[27] He further writes that theology is an "organic whole" which in itself is, "an organic member of the all-embracing organism of science."[28]

For Bavinck, organic, "refers to the fact that all revelation occurs through means. The revelation of God in the inspiration of Scripture has come to us via historical and psychological mediation. In a strict sense there is no immediate revelation either in nature or in grace because God always uses means. 'Even when he reveals himself internally in the human consciousness through the Spirit, this revelation always occurs organically and therefore mediately.'"[29] Bavinck allowed for a degree of subjectivity in the Scriptures being "living and active."[30] Warfield's view of the inspiration of Scripture as mechanical is typified by his comparison of authors of the Bible as being musical instruments that are made, tuned, and played by God as the musician.[31] Warfield acknowledges the work of the Spirit being present in the process of inspiration, but it remains a mechanical sort of inspiration. For Bavinck, the incarnation serves as an illustration for his understanding of revelation. The eternal Word became organic flesh and the spoken Word of Scriptures of which both modes of revelation are intimately connected.[32] Gaffin writes of Bavinck's use of the organic in inspiration:

> For Bavinck organic inspiration in not a matter of a divine, redemptive subject matter that is then left to the biblical writers in their freedom to be given its specific human, verbal form. . . . Organic inspiration means that, without violating the personalities of the writers, in the act of writing the Spirit produces the particular mode of expression suitable to *his* thought. The thoughts of the human writers, their style and word choice—in short, the human *form*, no less than and inseparable from

---

[26] For further information on the role of the "organic" in the larger scope of Bavinck's theology, see James Eglinton, *Trinity and Organism: Towards a New Reading of Herman Bavinck's Organic Motif* (London: T&T Clark, 2012).
[27] Abraham Kuyper, *Encyclopedia of Sacred Theology*, (London: Hodder and Stoughton, 1899), 600.
[28] Ibid.
[29] Henk Van Den Belt, *Authority of Scripture in Reformed Theology: Truth and Trust*, vol. 17 of Studies in Reformed Theology (Leiden: Brill, 2008), 256. Bavinck, *RD* I, 309.
[30] Cf. Heb. 4:12.
[31] Van Den Belt, "Herman Bavinck and Benjamin B. Warfield on Apologetics and the *Autopistia* of Scripture," *Calvin Theological Journal* 45:1 (2010): 37.
[32] Bavinck, *RD*, I.434.

the divine message, is primarily and directly attributable to the Spirit's inspiring activity.[33]

Bavinck understands revelation as a past historical event that continues to retain validity.[34] Warfield critiqued this view of inspiration as allowing for less than infallible views of the Bible to creep in under the guise of being organic. Bavinck was more concerned with inspiration being an ongoing activity of the Holy Spirit than with what one meant by the Scriptures being infallible.[35] Andrew McGowan writes, "It is precisely Bavinck's rejection of [Charles] Hodge's 'empirical' view and his own adoption of an 'organic' view that enables him to offer a real Reformed alternative to the 'inerrantist' views that came out of Old Princeton, particularly in the writings of B. B. Warfield and of Charles Hodge's son, A. A. Hodge."[36]

There are several places in *Reformed Dogmatics* where this concept of the "organic" arises. In one such example Bavinck writes, "In Christ, in the middle of history, God created an organic centre; from this centre, in an ever widening sphere, God drew the circles within which the light of revelation shines. . . . Presently the grace of God appears to all human beings. The Holy Spirit takes everything from Christ, adding nothing new to revelation. . . . In Christ God both fully revealed and fully gave himself. Consequently also Scripture is complete; it is the perfected Word of God."[37]

The first thorough exposition of the use of the organic in Bavinck was by Jan Veenhof in his 1968 dissertation *Revelatie en Inspiratie*.[38] Veenhof's thesis in this book is that the concept of organic as used by Kuyper and Bavinck has its roots in the German idealism of Hegel and Schelling.[39] German Idealism emerged in 1781 with the publication of Kant's *Critique of Pure Reason* and continued for fifty years until the death of Hegel in 1831.[40] Dudley writes:

> The modern insistence that belief and action be rationally justified is, in principle if not always in practice, radically egalitarian and radically liberating. If wisdom and

---

[33] Richard B. Gaffin Jr., *God's Word in Servant-Form: Abraham Kuyper and Herman Bavinck on the Doctrine of Scripture* (Jackson, MS: Reformed Academic Press, 2008), 85.
[34] Ibid., 54.
[35] Eglinton, *Trinity and Organism*, 181.
[36] A. T. B. McGowan, *The Divine Authenticity of Scripture: Retrieving an Evangelical Heritage* (Downer's Grove: InterVarsity Press, 2007), 146. McGowan provides an excellent extended overview of Bavinck's understanding of Scripture in this volume, 139–161.
[37] Bavinck, *RD*, 1.383.
[38] Jan Veenhof, *Revelatie en Inspiratie* (Amsterdam: Buijten & Schipperheign, 1968).
[39] Ibid., 267.
[40] Will Dudley, *Understanding German Idealism* (Stocksfield: Acumen, 2008), 1.

power are vested in a special authority, such as a monarch or priest, ordinary people must defer to that authority for instructions regarding what to think and what to do. But if good reasons are the only legitimate authority, then everyone can lay equal claim to being able to participate in the process of offering and evaluating the arguments that justify our theoretical and practical commitments. And those who do participate in the process achieve emancipation in the extent that their thoughts and actions are no longer determined by external authorities, but rather by themselves. Such modern agents are, in virtue of the exercise of their own rationality, self-determining or free.[41]

German Idealism is characterized by mind-dependence of reality, thought over sensation, universalized ethics, and natural teleology.

Brian Mattson picks up on this theme: "The difficulty [of the neo-Calvinist use of organic] presents itself in that it has all the markings of a favorite emphasis in the Idealism of Hegel and Schelling, the German 'history of religions' school, and the Dutch Ethical Theologians, not to mention the explosive rise of such language in the natural sciences following in the wake of Darwin's evolutionary hypothesis. It cannot be denied that the simultaneity of neo-Calvinism's 'organic' emphasis with these wider cultural and intellectual movements is indeed striking."[42] A cursory glance would seem to lead one to the conclusion that the neo-Calvinist position borrowed the term and position from the German Idealists. The primary incongruence with this position is that throughout Kuyper and Bavinck's work they drew a strong antithesis between theistic and atheistic worldviews. It would seem doubtful that a public theologian as insightful as Bavinck would miss so important a point as to be co-opted by a system of thought to which he would be opposed. Throughout *Reformed Dogmatics* Bavinck criticizes the position of German Idealists.[43]

In the last few years Brian Mattson and James Eglinton have challenged this thesis by Veenhoof.[44] The basic critique of the Veenhoof thesis is in making a historical trajectory from German Idealism to neo-Calvinism without allowing Bavinck's Reformation tradition to speak into the issue. Mattson writes:

> Veenhoof assumes, relying as he does on his late-19th century sources, that any interest in organic 'unfolding' or 'development' must have its source in something other than the tradition of Reformed orthodoxy; if that were the case, then indeed, there is no better candidate than post-Kantian philosophy, particularly Hegel and

---

[41] Ibid., 2–3.
[42] Brian Mattson, *Restored to Our Destiny: Eschatology & the Image of God in Herman Bavinck's Reformed Dogmatics*, Studies in Reformed Theology (Boston: Brill, 2012), 47.
[43] Bavinck, *RD*, 1. 254–258; 290–295; 2. 114–115; 155–156; 230–233; 410; 3. 52–53; 177–178; 260–261; 275; 351–352; 547–550; 4. 591–593.
[44] Mattson, *Restored to Our Destiny*, 46–54. Eglinton, *Trinity and Organism*, 51–78.

Schelling. However, *contra* the late-reigning view of Reformed orthodoxy as a rationalistic, a-historical dogmatic system, it in fact manifested a strong interest in historical development and the gradual unfolding of God's salvific purposes for creation.[45]

At this point Mattson is drawing upon Richard Muller in describing Reformed theology as a historical-theological tradition out of which Bavinck drew the concept of the organic, even if German Idealists used the term. This is the most logical conclusion for how to reconcile German Idealists and Bavinck's use of organic.[46]

Contra the Veenhoof thesis, James Eglinton proposes that Bavinck's use of the organic motif is primarily to draw a distinction between theistic and atheistic worldviews. Eglinton writes:

> He [Bavinck] asserts that, at the most basic level, only two worldviews exist: the theistic, and the atheistic. Bavinck associates a mechanical worldview with the latter, and thus demonstrates his dissatisfaction with the theistic mechanism of his Leiden professors, Scholten and Rauwenhoff. The notion of a closed-system universe operating solely by uninterrupted cause and effect—in essence, a mechanical cosmos—is, for Bavinck, irreconcilable with Christian theism. A worldview founded on a Trinitarian doctrine of God must move toward a nonmechanical interpretation of the universe.[47]

At the core of Bavinck's use of the organic is "seeing the universe as the general revelation of God's trinity."[48] Eglinton further writes, "By *organic*, Bavinck understands the cosmos as a unity in diversity, in which unity precedes diversity and the several parts cooperate toward a shared ideal culminating in a nonreductionist *eschaton*."[49]

Reformed dogmatician Richard Muller makes the case that it is an error to equate the doctrines of the inspiration and the authority of Scriptures into one.

---

[45] Mattson, *Restored to Our Destiny*, 49.
[46] A counterargument should be noted. The concept of containing a "grain of truth," is closely aligned with Bavinck's understanding of common grace. In this paradigm all systems of thought are likely to contain at least some truth because grace is given to all humans by which they may obtain some means of truth. The objection to this is that were the grain of truth of German Idealism being the organic, it is doubtful Bavinck would have taken one of his most important theological concepts from it without acknowledgment, especially with the amount of critique he levels at the German Idealists.
[47] James Eglinton, "Bavinck's Organic Motif: Questions Seeking Answers," *Calvin Theological Journal*, 45:1 (2010): 62.
[48] Ibid., 63.
[49] Ibid., 66.

He makes the case that in the Reformation, it was never the issue of inspiration that was up for debate, but rather that of authority. He writes:

> The doctrine of the inspiration of Scripture, quite contrary to the impression given by much twentieth-century discussion, was not an issue elaborated at great length either by the Reformers of by the Protestant orthodox of the late sixteenth and early seventeenth centuries. . . . This is not to say that the doctrine of inspiration was unimportant to the Protestant thinkers of the sixteenth and seventeenth centuries: it is to say, however, that a right understanding of the old Protestant doctrine of inspiration arises out of a sense of its place and role in the larger doctrine of Scripture rather than out of a mistaken equation of the doctrine of inspiration with the doctrine of Scripture. The fundamental issue addressed by the Reformers and orthodox alike was the issue of authority and certainty.[50]

The importance of the argument for this thesis lies in that the organic theme as well as the use of Scripture for ethical application are important for Bavinck's understanding of pedagogy. The organic will also come into play in Bavinck's pedagogy as he works towards developing an integrating type of education that will affect both the heart and the mind of the student.

Creation, Culture, Learning, and the Reformed Tradition

In this section I will explain the relation of creation and culture to Bavinck's account of the Reformed tradition. Doing so will provide a strong counterpoint with Luther, for whom creation also stood as an important theological theme. One aspect of the Reformed tradition that has been emphasized more since the mid-twentieth century is the role of Reformed theology and culture. John Leith writes:

> Neither rejecting culture nor identifying with culture, it has sought to transform culture. This relationship to culture is based upon the conviction that culture, as part of the creation to God, is good and therefore is convertible. It is also based upon the conviction that culture is fallen or disordered and therefore needs transformation. History provides abundant evidence that the Reformed community has been energetic in the pursuit of the transformation of culture, particularly in the ethical and political areas. The vigorous way in which the Reformed tradition has stimulated political and social change has not, however, been matched by any equal vigor and fruitfulness in the arts and in those concerns of culture that have to do with the physical, the emotional, and the aesthetic.[51]

---

[50] Richard A. Muller, *Post-Reformation Reformed Dogmatics*, 2nd ed., vol. 2 (Grand Rapids: Baker Academic, 2003), 230–231.

[51] John Leith, *An Introduction to the Reformed Tradition* (Atlanta: John Knox Press, 1977), 188.

Just as creation played an important role in Luther's understanding of the three estates, creation is also foundational for Bavinck and neo-Calvinism in general. Brian Mattson writes, "For Herman Bavinck, the Christian doctrine of creation provides a foundational account of reality that ultimately serves to irreducibly distinguish Christian theism from its anti-Christian alternatives. It therefore represents his most basic ontological alternative to dualistic ontologies."[52] Bavinck bases this in the Christian confession of the Apostles Creed: "I believe in God, the Father, Almighty, Creator of heaven and earth."[53] There is something unique to bearing witness to God's role as creator in the Creed. Mattson argues that creation serves as the central motif of Bavinck's theology.[54] As in many other areas of his theology, Bavinck takes a very Trinitarian approach to the doctrine of creation. He views the Trinitarian cooperation in creation as the Father being the first cause of creation, the Son as the personal agent of creation, and the Spirit as the personal immanent cause by which things live and move and have their being.[55]

The Reformed tradition draws a close relation between its doctrine of creation and its understanding of worldview. Albert Wolters writes that a worldview (from the German *Weltanschauung*) can be seen as, "the commonsense perspective on life and the world, the "system of values" or "ideology," which in one form or another is held by all normal adult human beings regardless of intelligence or education."[56] The Dutch Reformed tradition is tied closely to the use of worldview in part because of Abraham Kuyper's referring to Calvinism as all-embracing worldview in his 1898 Stone Lecture Series. This shifted the understanding of Calvinism from a theological point of view to a comprehensive system of thought that embraces all of life. In this respect Calvinism as a worldview claimed to be comprehensive as well as to possess immediate applicability.[57] In this series of lectures Kuyper writes:

> Thus it is shown that Calvinism has a sharply-defined starting-point of its own for the three fundamental relations of all human existence: viz., our relation to *God*, to *man* and to the *world*. For our relation *to God*: an immediate fellowship of man with the Eternal, independently of priest or church. For the relation of man *to man*: the recognition in each person of human worth, which is his by virtue of his creation after the Divine likeness, and therefore of the equality of all men before God and his

---

[52] Mattson, *Restored to Our Destiny*, 19.
[53] Ibid. RD, 2.416.
[54] Ibid., 20.
[55] Herman Bavinck, *In the Beginning: Foundations of Creation Theology*, ed. John Bolt, trans. John Vriend (Grand Rapids: Baker Books, 1999), 42.
[56] Albert Wolters, "Dutch Neo-Calvinism: Worldview: Philosophy and Rationality," 2. http://www.allofliferedeemed.co.uk/Wolters/AMWNeo_Cal.pdf. Originally appeared in *Rationality in the Calvinian Tradition*, ed. H. Hart, J. Van der Hoeven and Nicholas Wolterstorff (Toronto: University Press of America, 1983).
[57] Wolters, "Dutch Neo-Calvinism: Philosophy and Rationality," 4.

magistrate. And for our relation *to the world*: the recognition that in the whole world the curse is restrained by grace, that the life of the world is to be honored in its independence, and that we must, in every domain, discover the treasures and develop the potencies hidden by God in nature and in human life. This justifies us fully in our statement that Calvinism duly answers the three above named conditions, and thus is incontestably entitled to take its stand by the side of Paganism, Islamism, Romanism and Modernism, and to claim for itself the glory of possessing a well-defined principle and an all-embracing life-system."[58]

For Kuyper, Calvinism is a life-system, or worldview. In this worldview, Kuyper says that we "must" understand the workings of the world because God has gifted and mandated humans to do so. The cultural and creational mandate of Genesis 1:28 is then taken as a call for the Calvinist worldview to be applied to all aspects of creation, including that of learning. This verse states, And God blessed them. And God said to them, "Be fruitful and multiply and fill the earth and subdue it, and have dominion over the fish of the sea and over the birds of the heavens and over every living thing that moves on the earth."[59] Bavinck himself argues for a "creation based worldview."[60] He writes, "From this [creation based] perspective arises a very particular worldview. The word "creation" can denote either the act or the product of creation. From one's understanding of the act flows one's view of the product."[61] Creation, and a particular aspect of dominion over creation, stands at the heart of this Reformed worldview. It terms of education, being given the positive mandate to rule over creation should free one to have a positive cultural impact through understanding God's work in creation. In this worldview, the Christian lives by faith in the ordinances of God and works within God's creation for the glory of God. In much the same way that only the Christian can properly fulfill his or her vocation in the estates, so too can only a Christian properly fulfill the cultural mandate.

In the Lutheran tradition there is more of an emphasis on creation existing through the spoken word of God. Lutheran theologian Carl Braaten writes, "We hold with the classical dogmatic tradition that we have received a twofold revelation of God—through the law of creation (*lex creationis*) and through the gospel of Christ. There is revelation not only of God's redemptive love in Jesus Christ but also of God's law through the structures of creation."[62] God reveals

---

[58] Abraham Kuyper, *Calvinism: Six Stone Lectures* (Edinburgh: T&T Clark, 1899), 32–33.
[59] Gen. 1:28
[60] Herman Bavinck, *In the Beginning: Foundations of Creation Theology*, ed. John Bolt, trans. John Vriend (Grand Rapids: Baker Books, 1999), 56.
[61] Bavinck, *In the Beginning*, 56.
[62] Carl Braaten, *That All May Believe: A Theology of the Gospel and the Mission of the Church* (Grand Rapids: Eerdmans, 2008), 12–13.

himself through creation; this is why Luther was able to see a "church without walls"⁶³ in the prelapsarian garden.

There are several implications for how these traditions' understanding of pedagogy relates to classical education. Both the Lutheran and Reformed traditions see God's revelation in nature. The Lutheran emphasis is more upon recognizing Christ as revealed in creation, whereas the Dutch Reformed emphasis is upon understanding God's revelation in nature. The difference lies in recognizing who Christ is in creation versus seeking out knowledge that is inherently bound in creation. The lack of this cultural mandate in the Lutheran tradition also makes for a different emphasis in what the Christian should be doing. Rather than attempting to subdue creation, in the Lutheran tradition, "the purpose of their [the Christian's] earthly work is not to save the culture, but to serve their neighbor, functioning as channels for God's providential care for His creatures."⁶⁴

The Reformed credo of the cultural mandate very much effects how Reformed theology has viewed education and learning. Leith writes, "John Calvin emphasized the importance of learning not merely in order to study the Bible but also in order to study God's created order. The study of the liberal arts was for him an act of Christian obedience. One of the most significant of Calvin's achievements in Geneva was the establishment of the Academy in 1559, an institution which attracted students from all of Europe. Its character clearly states that the work of the Academy is a Christian concern."⁶⁵ The 'created order' attests to their being a built in order to creation that the neo-Calvinist has been divinely given the right to discover through the cultural mandate. Abraham Kuyper picks up on this theme in his Stone Lectures delivered at Princeton University. Kuyper takes a position in which Calvinism is the highest expression of the Christian faith. He refers to Calvinism as a "life system"⁶⁶ by which the Christian is able to understand the world around him or her. Kuyper intended his use of the English phrase "life system" to be an equivalent to the German *weltanschauung* that is normally translated as "worldview" in English.⁶⁷ Calvinism truly becomes a worldview in the methodology set forth by Kuyper.

---

⁶³ Luther, "Lectures on Genesis 1–5," LW 1: 103.
⁶⁴ Angus Menuge, "Citizens and Disciples," *Learning at the Foot of the Cross: A Lutheran Vision for Education*, eds. Joel D. Heck and Angus J. L. Menuge (Austin: Concordia University Press, 2011), 57.
⁶⁵ Leith, *An Introduction to the Reformed Tradition*, 210.
⁶⁶ Kuyper, *Calvinism*, 1.
⁶⁷ Peter S. Heslam *Creating a Christian Worldview: Abraham Kuyper's Lectures on Calvinism* (Grand Rapids: William B. Eerdmans Publishing Company, 1998), 88.

Pedagogy as Theological Praxis

The cultural mandate to subdue creation is combined with a view towards predestination and God's decree. The neo-Calvinist vision of subduing the earth combined with foreordination leads to an understanding that 1) This form of Calvinism should enter all spheres of life as being the system most fit to understand the world. 2) That there is an order built into the world that can be understood through the careful study of a subject. 3) Because Calvinism is best equipped to understand the workings of the world, Calvinism should have a definite impact upon culture and learning.

Neo-Calvinism also understands its place in creation under the concept of renewal of creation. Haas writes, "If sin is the primal catastrophe of cosmic proportions for creation, then redemption must be understood biblically as the work of restoration that encompasses the whole of the cosmos. Scripture speaks of redemption as 'the renewal of all things' (Matt. 19:28), the event whereby God will 'restore everything' (Acts 3:21). God has acted in and through Christ to "reconcile to himself all things" (Col. 1:20).[68]

Bavinck begins his chapter on creation in *Reformed Dogmatics* by writing, "The realization of the counsel of God begins with creation. Creation is the initial act and foundation of all divine revelation and therefore the foundation of all religious and ethical life as well."[69] Bavinck makes a trajectory beginning with creation that claims to be the foundation for revelation and ethics. Creation is the foundational act of revelation.

Bavinck also believes it is important to view creation as a Trinitarian act. He writes, "Holy Scripture, accordingly, teaches the Triune God is the author of creation. Scripture knows to intermediate beings. . . . Creating is a divine work, an act of infinite power and therefore is incommunicable in either nature or grace to any creature, whatever it may be. But Christian theology all the more unanimously attributed the work of creation to all three persons in the Trinity."[70] Creation is a triune act because no other being has the ability to create *ex nihilo* (which Bavinck earlier defends).[71]

For Bavinck, creation also has a teleological goal for which it is headed. He views the goal of creation as being more than an expression of God's goodness and love.[72] He writes that God's goodness and love is found in the act of creation, but it is insufficient to say that this requires the act of creation on the part of God because, "God is the all-good Being, perfect love, total blessedness

---

[68] Guenther Haas, "Creational Ethics is Public Ethics," *Journal for Christian Theological Research*, 12 (2007): 12.
[69] Bavinck, *RD*, 2. 407.
[70] Bavinck, *RD*, 2. 420–421.
[71] Ibid., *RD*, 2. 416–420.
[72] Ibid., *RD*, 2. 431.

within himself, and therefore does not need the world to bring his goodness or love to maturity, any more than he needs it to achieve self-consciousness and personality."[73] To the contrary, he defends a traditional Reformed position that, "Christian theology almost unanimously teaches that the glory of God is the final goal of all God's works."[74] Because God is his own end, his glory can be the only teleological goal: "He does not seek the creature [as an end it itself], but through the creature he seeks himself. He is and always remains his own end. His striving is always—also in and through his creatures—total self-enjoyment, perfect bliss."[75] Cornelius Plantinga, a contemporary heir of the Dutch Calvinist tradition, writes, "Creation is neither a necessity nor an accident. Instead, given God's interior life that overflows with regard for others, we might say creation is an act that was *fitting* for God."[76]

Thus, for Bavinck, creation is the foundational act of the benevolent Trinitarian God who has created for his own glory. This leads Bavinck to the position of having a "creation-based worldview." Bavinck's organic principle also implicitly guides his creational worldview. He writes that mechanistic and pantheistic worldviews fail to appreciate distinction in creation: "both fail to appreciate the richness and diversity of the world; erase the boundaries between heaven and earth, matter and spirit, soul and body, man and animal, intellect and will, time and eternity, Creator and creature, being and nonbeing; and dissolve all distinctions in a bath of deadly conformity."[77] Bavinck argues for an organic mixture of definite unity and diversity. He writes that there is "profuse diversity," but also "a superlative kind of unity."[78] He advocates for unity that maintains and appreciates diversity in its being: "In virtue of this unity the world can, metaphorically, be called an organism, in which all the parts are connected with each other and influence each other reciprocally. Heaven and earth, man and animal, soul and body, truth and life, art and science, religion and morality, state and church, family and society, and so on, though they are all distinct, are not separated. There is a wide range of connections between them; an organic, or if you will, an ethical bond holds them all together."[79] In this citation Bavinck points to distinction and unity in a multitude of spheres. He points to social, political, organic, and metaphysical spheres. The implication is also that there are numerous other points of unity and diversity to which he does not point. Bavinck suggests that seeing this link in creation demonstrates how his understanding of the Christian worldview,

---

[73] Ibid., *RD*, 2. 432.
[74] Ibid., *RD*, 2. 433.
[75] Ibid., *RD*, 2. 435.
[76] Cornelius Plantiga, Jr., *Engaging God's World: A Christian Vision of Faith, Learning, and Living* (Grand Rapids: Eerdmans, 2002), 23.
[77] Bavinck, *RD*, 2. 435.
[78] Ibid., *RD*, 2. 435–436.
[79] Ibid., *RD*, 2. 436.

"has overcome both the contempt of nature and its deification."[80] Bavinck believes his position takes a middle ground between these two extremes.

Stewardship and Creation

Related to the importance of the concept of creation in Reformed theology is that of stewardship. This section will demonstrate why stewardship has remained an important theme in the Reformed tradition, and how it is markedly different from the Lutheran account. Chapter one provided an analysis of the use of *oikonomia* and stewardship language in the Bible. Whereas Luther emphasized the dwelling in a household aspect of this word, the Reformed tradition has emphasized the household manager aspect. This is an important distinction because it represents a different emphasis in how man relates with the created world. In both the New Testament account as well as the LXX, cognates of *oikos* that imply stewardship tend to focus more on the act of naming the steward than upon the significance of stewarding. This places more emphasis upon the *action* being done as opposed to the *actor*.

Although the emphasis in the Reformed tradition is upon stewarding and its role in regards to the cultural mandate, in many ways there is a stronger link between the idea dwelling as a family and creation. Most of the noun cognates of *oikos* refer to the physical building or edifice in which one dwells,[81] but *oikoumene* refers to the inhabited earth.[82] In meaning 'inhabited earth,' *oikoumene* was used to signify land in contrast to that used by the barbarians. In the Roman period this word took on a political meaning, as that land which was under Roman rule was part of the *oikoumene*. Brown writes that in the New Testament, "The *oikoumene* is the inhabited world in the sense that all its population has to suffer under Satanic powers for religious, but mainly political reasons."[83] *Oikoumene* points towards Christ in that in the inhabited world becomes the kingdom of God. In Acts 17:6 the preaching of the apostles is seen as a political crime because they are "the men who have turned the *oikoumene* upside down."

Vincent Bacote demonstrates the link in Dutch neo-Calvinist theology between the doctrine of creation and the concept of stewardship.[84] Bacote

---

[80] Ibid., *RD,* 2. 438.
[81] T. Muraoka, *A Greek-English Lexicon of the Septuagint*, (Leuven: Peeters, 2009), 487–489.
[82] Colin Brown, ed., *The New International Dictionary of New Testament Theology*, vol. 1 (Exeter: Paternoster Press, 1975), 518–519.
[83] Ibid., 519.
[84] Vincent E. Bacote, *The Spirit in Public Theology: Appropriating the Legacy of Abraham Kuyper* (Grand Rapids: Baker Academic, 2005). In particular to the concept of stewardship, see chapter four entitled, "The Spirit and Creation Stewardship," 117–148.

argues that for the importance of understanding common grace when addressing creation and stewardship. He writes, "Is the work of the Spirit in common grace so dynamic in character that creation is considered to have not only latent potential but also numerous possibilities that may result from responding to common grace in various contexts?"[85] The implication of this question is that yes, there is latent potential in creation that can be discovered by humans. This process of discovery of what can be known in creation is part of the common grace given to all humans in the Reformed perspective. Bacote writes:

> The work of the Holy Spirit in creation is characterized by the central category of indwelling. The Spirit's inherence in creation had been constant from the inception of creation and has enabled not only the preservation and survival of life but also the development of life culturally and socially. Though sin is a reality, the Spirit's indwelling presence resists the dissolution of the biophysical order and orients the development of history towards its ultimate eschatological goal. As Kuyper argued, the Spirit leads creation to its destiny, the glory of God. Humans play a vital role in leading creation to its *telos*, and their efforts at social-architectural planning and development reveal the reciprocity inherent in common grace. At the same time, the results of society building reflect the imperfection that always results because of the limitations of those who would strive to improve the character of human life in the realms of society and culture. Though the ordinances of creation are discovered, refined, and maybe re-created, no society approximates the eschatological kingdom. Though the various attempts to develop society are relativized by human limitations, it may be possible to detect (provisionally) evidence of the Spirit's work in various cultures and nations, even those that are outside the covenant and not in the process of Christianization.[86]

One of the best recent attempts to show the relation of stewardship and learning is Ronald Vallet's *Stewards of the Gospel*.[87] Vallet's primary purpose in this book is to remove the modern connotation of stewardship being primarily linked with stewarding money, and place the emphasis upon Christians being entrusted with the gospel of Jesus. With this framework in mind, he attempts to show how being entrusted with so valuable of a gift relates to the subject of theological education. The danger for the Reformed position of emphasizing the steward is of course that emphasis will be taken away from the God who is proclaimed.

The Doctrine of Sin and Creation

The role of the fall and what the fall means for humanity is another important aspect of Calvinistic and neo-Calvinist theology. This section will provide a

---

[85] Ibid., 120–121.
[86] Ibid., 139–140.
[87] Ronald E. Vallet, *Stewards of the Gospel: Reforming Theological Education* (Grand Rapids: Eerdmans, 2011).

summary of the role sin plays in Bavinck's theology in relation to creation. This is important in regards to pedagogy because the fall gives Bavinck a negative view of the nature of the child learning. He counters philosophies of education in which the child is to find his or her own way in part because of his hamartiology that emphasizes the fact that unregenerate children cannot find their own way, especially apart from some type of religious training. Following knowledge of God as creator comes knowledge of God as redeemer, which is fundamental for a doctrine of sin.[88] The Reformed tradition has always emphasized original sin, which "renders human existence both tragic and miserable and takes on a life of its own. Most often the tradition regards sin as the human transgression of God's covenant, which represents God's active will for every human society and individual."[89]

Understanding creation in the Reformed tradition also allows one to understand the role of sin in creation and how sin affects God's interaction with the world: "Though the God we meet in revelation is in conflict with the world, this is so in such a way that it is clear that it is God's own world, and in fact that God clashes with it precisely because it is God's own creation. The rescue which God seeks is not a deliverance out of this existence, not a writing off of the world, but the deliverance of this world and of this existence."[90]

Bavinck takes a slightly less pessimistic view of human nature as compared to others in the Reformed tradition. He affirms the drastic results of the fall, but writes that he remains amazed at what humans are capable of post-fall. One could call this a positive doctrine of original of sin. Bavinck's work on sin occurs in volume 3 of *Reformed Dogmatics*.[91] In this section Bavinck addresses many of the traditional questions of Reformed theology in regards to sin such as: the origin of sin, effects of the fall, original sin, etc.

One way Bavinck differs from many of fellow Reformed writers is he does not mind asking honest questions about the historicity of their being a literal Adam and Eve who fell from grace. He views paradise as something humans are moving towards, not as something located in the distant past. He writes that if Irenaeus, Clement, Athanasius, and Anselm interpret Genesis 3 in whole or part allegorically then modern interpreters should be free to do so as well. He believes Genesis 3 remains inspired Scripture because this passage witnesses to the human experience and reality of a fallen state of being. He leaves this open to question, but also says that the fall of Adam and the resurrection of Christ are

---

[88] A. Dakin, *Calvinism* (London: Duckworth, 1949), 29.
[89] Merwyn S. Johnson, "Sin," *The Westminster Handbook to Reformed Theology*, ed. Donald K. McKim (Louisville: Westminster John Knox Press, 2001), 210.
[90] Hendrikus Berkhof, "God as Creator and the World as Createdness," *Major Themes in the Reformed Tradition*, ed. Donald K. McKim (Grand Rapids: Eerdmans, 1992), 79.
[91] Bavinck, *RD*, 3. 25–190.

the two events by which all Christian dogmatics are governed.[92] Bavinck wishes to hold to there being a literal fall while allowing for some of the specifics of the fall as recorded in Genesis 3 to be open to allegory. He writes:

> All in all, the science of nature and history to this day lacks the right to make a pronouncement on the truth of the state of integrity and the fall of the first humans. The witness pertaining to these things contained in Genesis, confirmed by the later appeal made to it by the prophets and apostles and Christ himself, and intertwined as a necessary constituent in the whole revelation of salvation, continues to maintain itself in people's conscience and meshes perfectly with the reality our daily experience informs us about.[93]

Tensions such as this have led some scholars to suggest that there are in a sense, "two Bavincks."[94] To say that there are two Bavincks is to draw attention to the tension between the spiritual and scholastic nature of Bavinck's corpus. John Bolt writes that this classification of two Bavincks has been made because there are seeming irreconcilable themes in tension in his work.[95] In one sense Bavinck was a historical scholar steeped in his tradition, and in another his work denotes a very modern man engaging with the thinkers of his time. The two Bavincks are that of:

> The fundamentalist scholastic and the good progressive modern man. . . . The two sides of Bavinck the theologian reflect a pull between the academic theologian (*wetenscappelijke theoloog*) and the churchly dogmatician (*kerkelijke dogmaticus*). The pull of the former led him to Leiden[96] and is reflected in his engagement with

---

[92] Ibid., *RD*, 3. 38.
[93] Bavinck, *RD*, 3. 39.
[94] Veenhof, *Revelatie en Inspiratie*, 108–111. John Bolt, "The Imitation of Christ Theme in the Cultural-Ethical Ideal of Herman Bavinck" (PhD diss., University of St. Michael's College, 1982), 38–78. John Bolt, "Grand Rapids Between Kampen and Amsterdam: Herman Bavinck's Reception and Influence in North America," *Calvin Theological Journal* 38:2 (Nov. 2003): 264–269.
[95] Bolt "Grand Rapids Between Kampen and Amsterdam," 265.
[96] This is a reference to Bavinck's undergraduate studies at the University of Leiden where he studied with many of the leading liberal theologians of his day. He went on to receive his doctor of theology from Leiden in 1880. For a biography of Bavinck's time at Leiden, see chapter three of Ron Gleason, *Herman Bavinck: Pastor, Churchman, Statesman, and Theologian* (Phillipsburg: P & R Publishing, 2010), 45–68, "The Separatist Enrolls at Leiden." Bavinck was raised in a theologically conservative family in which his father was a prominent pastor and theologian in Kampen. It came as a surprise to the family that Bavinck would choose to enroll at Leiden. Gleason makes notice of this tension: "This time [in Leiden] had to be a stark contrast to what Bavinck had been exposed to by his parents and in the small circle of Separatists. Leiden and Kampen were worlds apart. Bremmer rightly asks how Bavinck survived in the world of liberal, historical-critical theology and modern philosophy" (53). For more on Bavinck's internal struggles with this brand of liberalism as well as his spirituality see George

modern culture and science. It also explains Bavinck's passion for scholarly precision and fair mindedness even with those who were his religious or theological opponents.[97]

Bolt views this tension as a positive aspect of Bavinck's theological work. Bavinck lived during a time of change and the growth of knowledge, and as he aged he tried to deal honestly with the questions the world was raising with the theological tools with which he had been equipped.

Bavinck's desire to engage with the modern world had two results. First, Bavinck's engaging the Reformed tradition with modern consciousness drew him to Kuyper's neo-Calvinism, and especially to the Kuyperian emphasis upon common grace. This was in part why Bavinck choose to move from his teaching position in Kampen to the Free University of Amsterdam.[98] He viewed the opportunity at Amsterdam as one in which he could interact with other fields of study while remaining a systematic theologian. Second, Bavinck's desire to engage the world led him to deal with more practical matters near the end of his life. Bolt writes, "this [engaging in culture through neo-Calvinism] is the reason why Bavinck the theologian spent more of the last decade of his life exploring philosophy, psychology, pedagogy, the role of women in society and church, economics, war, and international relations than he did dogmatics."[99]

Bavinck's cultural engagement is less domineering than the type proposed by Kuyper. Kuyper approaches creation with the cultural mandate, and the implicit understanding that the type of cultural engagement he will do is the correct type. Bavinck takes a more subtle approach. He affirms that God is over the organic relation of the spheres of life, but he seems to openly and honestly search for the grain of truth that other fields and systems of thought may bring to the table. This type of approach typifies the differences between Kuyper and Bavinck on academic and cultural engagement. Beach writes:

> Kuyper was a man of broad vision and sparkling ideas, Bavinck was a man of sober disposition and clear concepts. Whereas Kuyper was more speculative, tracing out intuitively grasped thoughts, Bavinck was a more careful scholar and built on and from historical givens. While Kuyper is notable for his efforts to bring reform to the church and society, applying the principles of Calvinism to the social and political concerns of his time, even helping to orchestrate the first Christian political party in the Netherlands (the Antirevolutionary Party), Bavinck's strengths resided in

---

Harinck, "'Something That Must Remain, If the Truth Is to Be Sweet and Precious to Us': The Reformed Spirituality of Herman Bavinck," *Calvin Theological Journal* 38:2 (November, 2003): 250–255.
[97] Bolt, "Grand Rapids Between Kampen and Amsterdam," 267–268.
[98] Bolt, "Grand Rapids Between Kampen and Amsterdam," 268.
[99] Ibid.

examining some of the inadequacies of old answers and so demonstrating the need to press forward with new proposals.[100]

Now that Bavinck has established that there is a fall in the human experience that one can look back to, one of his more pertinent points is his understanding of corruption upon the human because of sin. He believed that Luther expressed himself too strongly in his descriptions of sin: "Though it was meant well, it was certainly open to serious misunderstanding when Luther called original sin 'the essence of humans.' . . . And also in the Formula of Concord stated, in Luther's own words, that in spiritual matters the mind, heart, and will were 'altogether corrupt and dead,' no more capable [of good] than 'a stone, a trunk, or mud.'"[101] Bavinck wants to maintain original sin as being a loss of original righteousness and corruption of nature while avoiding the images of incapability because of sin put forth by the Lutherans.[102] Bavinck also bases his understanding of original sin in the organic motif. The fall of the first humans has affected all humans because humans are of, "an organic unity, one race, one family."[103] The role of original sin plays a large part in Bavinck's doctrine of sin. He views original sin as, "a moral quality of the person who lacks the communion with God that one should and does possess by virtue of one's original nature."[104]

Sphere Sovereignty

Another important theme that is distinct in Dutch neo-Calvinist theology is sphere sovereignty. The basis for sphere sovereignty in neo-Calvinism is tightly linked to the importance of creation as outlined above. This section will examine the role sphere sovereignty plays in Dutch neo-Calvinist theology, and in the work of Bavinck in particular. Sphere sovereignty is perhaps the best known distinctive feature ,. of neo-Calvinist theology. Bavinck uses his doctrine of creation to generate a nuanced form of sphere sovereignty. Although he does not always use the language of sphere sovereignty explicitly, he states that there are distinct and diverse spheres that operate in harmony because of an organic ethical unity they share. Even though sphere sovereignty is not one of the major factors in Bavinck's theology, it remains important to examine sphere sovereignty because of its particularity to the larger picture of Dutch neo-Calvinist theology.

---

[100] J. Mark Beach, "Abraham Kuyper, Herman Bavinck, and 'The Conclusions of Utrecht 1905,'" *Mid-American Journal of Theology,* 19 (2008): 11.
[101] Bavinck, *RD*, 3. 98.
[102] Ibid., *RD*, 3. 99.
[103] Ibid., *RD*, 3. 102.
[104] Ibid., *RD*, 3. 117.

Pedagogy as Theological Praxis

The idea of sphere sovereignty was strongly set forth by Abraham Kuyper, but did not play quite as large of a role in the work of Bavinck. In fact, Bavinck does not directly use the phrase "sphere sovereignty" anywhere in *Reformed Dogmatics*. Bavinck takes a more refined, Trinitarian approach to creation and nature. For Kuyper, society was made up of various spheres such as government, the family, science, business, art, etc. Each of these spheres is not accountable to each other, but rather to God. Sphere sovereignty allowed Kuyper to say that each sphere was self-governing and hence it inherently contained a degree of self-governing moral accountability. Kuyper first introduced the concept of sphere sovereignty at the inaugural address of the opening of the Free University of Amsterdam in 1880. In this address Kuyper says that sovereignty is the right to rule, and "absolute sovereignty cannot reside in any creature but must coincide with God's majesty. . . . We acknowledge at the same time that this supreme Sovereign once and still delegates his authority to human beings, so that on earth one never directly encounters God Himself in visible things but always sees his sovereign authority exercised in human office."[105] An affirmation of sphere sovereignty at the opening of the Free University posed a number of advantages to Kuyper. For one, it gave Kuyper the ability to say that no other authority should be able to impose its will upon the learning present at the Free University as it stood as an individual sphere. It supposed that the authority that was given to the founders of the Free University were given by God rather than any external authority. This limited the extent to which the government could interfere with the life of the University, as the two operated in separate spheres. There is therefore both a unity and disunity to the concept of sphere sovereignty. The unity lies in the fact that all knowledge comes from God, and part of the neo-Calvinist project was to discover the work of God in all sphere of life to His glory. The proper knowledge gained in one sphere should be in tandem with the knowledge gained in another sphere. Sphere sovereignty allowed Kuyper to declare a social agenda that kept government "in its place" so to speak. Richard Muow writes, "The creation order, he [Kuyper] argued, displays a rich variety of societal spheres. Since all of these spheres have the same origin in 'the divine mandate,' political authority must respect the fact each of the other spheres has its own integrity."[106]

Another advantage of sphere sovereignty in theological method is that it does provide solid ground for why the Calvinist should be culturally engaged. In sphere sovereignty one is able to place any area of life, whether it be economic theory, familial relationships, ecclesiastical issues, political practices

---

[105] Abraham Kuyper, "Sphere Sovereignty," *Abraham Kuyper: A Centennial Reader*, ed. James Bratt (Grand Rapids: Eerdmans, 1998), 466.
[106] Richard Muow, "Some Reflections on Sphere Sovereignty," *Religion, Pluralism, and Public Life: Abraham Kuyper's Legacy for the Twenty-First Century*, ed. Luis E. Lugo (Grand Rapids: Eerdmans, 2000), 88.

and many others under the larger banner of Calvinist theology. One is also able to represent these spheres as interrelated and dependent on one another. Kent Van Til writes, "Political rights, family and economic values, and religious truths coordinate and complement, rather than oppose one another [in sphere sovereignty]."[107] Muow writes, "In the Kuyperian scheme, God invested the original creation with complex cultural potential, which human beings were expected to actualize."[108] This actualizing of creation potential represents one way in which the neo-Calvinist vision differs from Luther in regards to hamartiology. Though Calvinism is often characterized by its belief that total depravity has ravaged how the human interacts with the created order, the neo-Calvinist vision provides a more positive outlook in regards to how Christ's redemptive mission is played out. For Luther, the estate of *politia* was a result of the fall. For Kuyper the political sphere is fallen, but is redeemable. Not only is it redeemable, but it should be redeemed and engaged by the Calvinist worldview. He writes:

> Can we imagine that at one time God willed to rule things in a certain moral order, but that now, in Christ, He wills to rule it otherwise? As though He were not the Eternal, Unchangeable, Who, from the very hour of creation, even unto all eternity, had willed, wills, and shall will and maintain, one and the same firm moral world-order! Verily Christ has swept away the dust with which man's sinful limitations had covered up this world-order. . . . The world order remains just what it was from the beginning. It lays full claim, not only to the believer (as though less were required from the unbeliever), but to every human being and to all human relationships.[109]

Kuyper's insights are helpful here in that it is God who is the sovereign creator and ruler over creation.[110]

Kuyper relates the study of science to Calvinism in that through this study the glory of God is advanced that a better understanding of the workings of the world. "Faith in such a unity, stability and order of things, personally, as predestination, cosmically, as the counsel of God's decree, could not but awaken as with a loud voice, and vigorously foster love for science."[111] Kuyper removes any level of subjectivity as being present in understanding the work of God in the world. Even the faith placed in the system of Calvinism does not contain a degree of subjectivity: "Without a deep conviction of this unity, this stability and this order, science is unable to go beyond mere conjectures, and

---

[107] Kent A. Van Til, "Abraham Kuyper and Michael Walzer: The Justice of the Spheres," *Calvin Theological Journal* 40:2 (Nov., 2005): 269.
[108] Muow, "Some Reflections on Sphere Sovereignty," 94.
[109] Kuyper, *Calvinism*, 89–90.
[110] Elaine Storkey, "Sphere Sovereignty and the Anglo-American Tradition," *Religion, Pluralism, and Public Life: Abraham Kuyper's Legacy for the Twenty-First Century*, ed. Luis E. Lugo (Grand Rapids: Eerdmans, 2000), 190.
[111] Kuyper, *Calvinism*, 151.

only when there is faith in the organic interconnexion [sic] of the Universe, will there by also a possibility for science to ascend from the empirical investigation of the special phenomena to the general, and from the general to the law which rules over it, and from that law to the principle, which is dominant over all."[112] The type of Calvinism put forth by Kuyper is somewhat overbearing in its assumption of correctness. Though there is much cultural engagement on the part of Kuyper, it is usually tinged with his presumption of Calvinism being by far the superior system of thought. In Bavinck's work he is able to tone down some of the seeming arrogant attitude that comes with the neo-Calvinist system.

Though Kuyper offers Calvinism as an excellent avenue through which the Calvinist can become culturally engaged, one must admit that there are several possible flaws in its application. The disunity of sphere sovereignty is contained in the very nature of there being separate spheres of knowledge. It is impractical that the government as a sphere should not influence other spheres operating within its geographic boundaries. For instance, if the government of the Netherlands believes that the knowledge being taught at the Free University in the late 19th century were of a seditious nature to the local government, it is doubtful that the state would not in some way intervene. The analogy begins to break down when the spheres of knowledge begin to cross boundaries with each other. If the concept of sphere sovereignty were indeed acted upon by a given group of people, it seems that it would only work well in a quasi-utopian society that acknowledged the sovereignty of other spheres. Kuyper writes, "The cogwheels of all these spheres engage each other, and precisely through that interaction emerges the rich, multifaceted multiformity of human life. Hence also rises the danger that one sphere in life may encroach on its neighbor like a sticky wheel that shears off one cog after another until the whole operation is dispersed."[113] Kuyper acknowledges that it would be easy for a system involving sphere sovereignty to fall into disrepair, but does not offer specific guidelines for how such disrepair should be avoided.

Kuyper's delivering of a speech on sphere sovereignty at the founding of the Free University of Amsterdam is no coincidence. His lifelong desire had been to establish a place of Christian learning in which he could be sure that the state would not interfere in the affairs of his university. Haas writes that in sphere sovereignty, "Each one of the plurality of institutions of human society—family, church, state, school, business, labour union, art cooperative, voluntary association, and other social organizations—is granted its distinctive shape and sphere of sovereignty by God. No institution has sovereignty over other institutions so that it grants them the right to exist and function. Again, this is grounded in the creation order, in the nature of the very structure of creational

---

[112] Ibid.
[113] Abraham Kuyper, "Sphere Sovereignty," *Abraham Kuyper: A Centennial Reader*, ed. James D. Bratt (Grand Rapids: Eerdmans, 1998), 467–468.

social life."[114] This quote from Haas sounds a very familiar chord to Luther on the estates. Both the estates in Lutheran theology and sphere sovereignty in neo-Calvinism ground their understanding in creation. The relevant question here is how much these concepts are an outgrowth of theological positions, or whether they spring from exegetical claims.

One of the most substantial critiques of the social ramifications of sphere sovereignty in the twentieth century was that it presented a sense of Aryan racial superiority over Africans. One of the most direct contemporary critiques of Kuyper in regards to racial superiority has been put forth in a chapter by Peter Paris.[115] Paris writes:

> By the end of the nineteenth century, this Aryan doctrine of racial superiority had been linked with the emerging evolutionary theories of Social Darwinism. Christianity's general acceptance of the Hamitic curse, coupled with the application of Darwinian insights, enabled scholars of that day to rank human civilizations, with Western Europe at the top and Africa at the bottom. Thus, in his first Stone Lecture at Princeton Theological Seminary a century ago, Kuyper surprised nobody in his audience by placing his discussion of Calvinism in the framework of an evolutionary theory of cultural development. In fact, most academics of his time subscribed to such a theory.[116]

The underlying assumption of culture being advanced through neo-Calvinism is that the culture of which he is speaking is the Western culture. Paris goes on to argue that the cultural naivety displayed by Kuyper in his forming of sphere sovereignty is unacceptable in its Western-centric attitude. Paris writes that what Kuyper says in regards to a Western-centric mindset was no different in attitude from most other theologians or politicians of his time, but if such a policy were actually instituted, it could potentially have catastrophic consequences.[117] Though common grace played a large role of Kuyper's theology, it seems that common humanity and its cultural significance did not.

The most well known example of the negative impact of sphere sovereignty occurring was in the Dutch Reformed Church of South Africa. The Dutch Reformed Church had been established in South Africa for some time in the region of South Africa was originally a Dutch colony (referred to as Cape Colony). In 1869 John McCarter published a history entitled *The Dutch*

---

[114] Haas, "Creational Ethics is Public Ethics," 29.
[115] Peter J. Paris, "The African and African-American Understanding of Our Common Humanity: A Critique of Abraham Kuyper's Anthropology," *Religion, Pluralism, and Public Life: Abraham Kuyper's Legacy for the Twenty-First Century*, ed. Luis E. Lugo (Grand Rapids: Eerdmans, 2000), 263–280.
[116] Ibid., 268.
[117] Ibid., 271.

Pedagogy as Theological Praxis

Reformed Church in South Africa,[118] in which he provides an historical sketch of Dutch influence and establishment of the church in that region.

Transitioning to the next section on providence, it is also worth noting that Kuyper saw a link between sphere sovereignty and providence. Commenting on this linkage in which he wrote in the Stone Lectures Kuyper writes:

> How, now, can we prove that love for science in that higher science, which aims at unity in our cognizance of the entire cosmos, is effectually secured by means of our Calvinistic belief in God's fore-ordination? If you want to understand this you have to go back from predestination to God's decree in general. This is not a matter of choice; on the contrary, it *must* be done. Belief in predestination is nothing but the penetration of God's decree into your own personal life; or, if you prefer it, the personal heroism to apply the sovereignty of God's decreeing will to your own existence.[119]

Providence

Another important theme in Bavinck's theology that also holds a close relation to creation is that of providence. This section will analyze why providence is an important part of Bavinck's work. It is worthwhile to mention the connection Bavinck makes in the title, "Creation and Providence" and hence linking the two subjects. 'Providence' has traditionally been defined in the Reformed tradition as being a threefold work: "God's preservation of creation, God's cooperation with all created entities, and God's guidance of all things toward God's ultimate purposes and their highest good. What this doctrine emphasizes is that the triune God, in goodness and power, preserves, accompanies, and directs God's entire universe. No facet of God's work is excluded from divine care."[120] Benjamin Farley writes:

> The Reformed doctrine of the providence of God emphasizes that the triune God, in goodness and power, preserves, accompanies, and directs the universe. This work of preservation, accompaniment, and direction pertains to the entire universe—physical and human—and excludes no fact of God's work. The doctrine of providence constitutes a central tenet of Reformed theology and belongs to the essence of the biblical message. To that extent, it is held and expounded as a doctrine of the

---

[118] John McCarter, *The Dutch Reformed Church in South Africa* (Edinburgh: T&T Clark, 1869).
[119] Kuyper, *Calvinism*, 147–148.
[120] Benjamin Wirt Farley, "Providence," *The Westminster Handbook to Reformed Theology*, ed. Donald K. McKim (Louisville: Westminster John Knox Press, 2001), 187.

church's faith, based on divine revelation, and must be energetically preached as part of God's Word.[121]

The act of creation, "puts existence under God's ordering power and providence."[122] Bavinck writes that the purpose of creation does not lie in the creation itself, "for the establishment of the purpose precedes the means."[123] Further, "It is God's good pleasure to bring the excellences of His triune being into manifestation in His creatures, and so to prepare glory and honor for Himself in those creatures. For this glorification of Himself, too, God does not need the world, for it is not the creature who is independently and self-sufficiently exalting His honor; rather, it is He Himself who by means of the creature or without him glorifies His own name and revels in Himself."[124]

Bavinck often uses the phrase 'divine decree' to refer to an aspect of the sovereignty of God, and he defines God's decree as, "his eternal purpose whereby he has foreordained whatsoever comes to pass."[125] This is stated as 'divine decree' rather than 'divine decrees' because the singular (as used in the Westminster Confession) conveys, "The idea of the universe is in fact one single conception in the divine consciousness."[126] Bavinck takes a traditionally Reformed position in providence. Cornelius Venema writes that for Bavinck, "To exclude anything from the scope of God's eternal counsel would compromise God's independent existence and work as the Creator and Lord of all things. Whatever transpires in creation and in the whole subsequent course of providence and re-creation must be encompassed within the decree of God."[127]

Bavinck links the fact that God is creator *ex nihilo* to his providential role in creation. One of the central claims of a Reformed theology of creation is that God created the world, and in do doing declared his creation to be good.[128] Bavinck writes,

---

[121] Benjamin Wirt Farley, "The Providence of God in Reformed Perspective," *Major Themes in the Reformed Tradition*, ed. Donald K. McKim (Grand Rapids: Eerdmans, 1992), 87.
[122] Lisa Sowle Cahill, "Creation and Ethics," in *The Oxford Handbook of Theological Ethics*, eds. Gilbert Meilaender and William Werpehowski (Oxford: Oxford UP, 2005), 9.
[123] Herman Bavinck, *Our Reasonable Faith*, (Grand Rapids: Eerdmans, 1956), 169.
[124] Ibid.
[125] Herman Bavinck, *The Doctrine of God* (Edinburgh: The Banner of Truth Trust, 1979), 369.
[126] Ibid., 371.
[127] Cornelius Venema, "Covenant and Election in the Theology of Herman Bavinck," *Mid-America Journal of Theology* 19 (2008): 76.
[128] Cf. Gen. 1:10, 12, 18, 21, 25, 31. R. Michael Allen, *Reformed Theology* (London: T&T Clark, 2010), 158.

All of these considerations naturally and directly lead from Creation to Providence. After all, from the very moment that the world in its entirety or each of its creatures was called into being by the creative act of God, they immediately come under the surveillance of God's providence. There is no gradual transition here, nor any gulf or breach. For just as creature, because they are creatures, cannot come up out of themselves, so too they cannot for a moment exist through themselves. Providence goes hand in hand with creation: the two are companion pieces.[129]

Bavinck sees this link as important because it demonstrates that God did not withdraw from the world upon creation. The biblical account tells of a God who is active in his creation. Bavinck argues that seeing the role of providence in creation will effectively distance the doctrine of creation from falling into deism.[130]

Herman Bavinck within the Scope of Reformed Theology

Thus far this chapter has named some of the distinctive aspects of Dutch neo-Calvinist theology, including: creation and culture, common grace, the inspiration of Scripture and its relation to the organic, stewardship and creation, the doctrine of sin and creation, sphere sovereignty, and providence. This section will present how Herman Bavinck's theological insights fit within the larger scope of Reformed theology and how these distinctive aspects of Reformed thinking could impact his views on education. The Calvinist themes that will be discussed in this section are: the sovereignty of God, the understanding of "self," Trinitarian theology and the glory of God.

As previously stated, for Bavinck the key question for Reformed dogmatics is, "How is the glory of God advanced?"[131] Bavinck writes, "The Reformed person does not rest until he has traced all things retrospectively to the divine decree, tracking down the "wherefore" of things, and he has prospectively made all things subservient to the glory of God; the Lutheran is content with the

---

[129] Bavinck, *Our Reasonable Faith*, 177. Bavinck provides a number of Scriptural references for the links between creation and providence. He writes, "It [Scripture] calls the work of providence a life-giving and a preserving activity (Job. 33:4 and Neh. 9:6) a renewing (Ps. 104:30), a speaking (Ps. 33:9), a willing (Rev. 4:11), a working (John 5:17), an upholding of all things by the word of His power (Heb. 1:3), a caring (1 Pet. 5:7), and yes, even a creating (Ps. 104:30 and Isa. 45:7). What is implied in all these expressions is that after the creation of the world God did not leave the world to itself, looking down upon it from afar. The living God is not to be pushed to one side or into the background after the creation issues from His hand. The word providence means that God supplies the world with what it needs. It is an act of God's mind not only, but also of His will, a carrying out of His counsel. It is an activity by which from moment to moment He keeps the world in existence" (178).
[130] Bavinck, *Our Reasonable Faith*, 177.
[131] Bavinck, *RD* 1. 177.

"that" and enjoys the salvation in which he is by faith a participant. From this difference in principle, the dogmatic controversies between them (with respect to the image of God, original sin, the person of Christ, the order of salvation, the sacraments, church government, ethics, etc.) can be easily explained."[132] The glory of God and the providence by which one has been redeemed are the overarching themes by which Bavinck believes Reformed theology differs from Lutheran theology.

In his book, *Our Reasonable Faith* Bavinck includes a chapter entitled "Creation and Providence" which provides insight into his views on the role of providence in the larger picture of his theology. The idea of having a Trinitarian understanding of God is one that pervades Bavinck's theology. In this particular chapter he begins, "The practical significance of the doctrine of the trinity for the life of the Christian is evidence enough that the Holy Scripture does not want to give us an abstract concept of deity, but rather wants to put us into contact, all of us personally, with the living and true God."[133] This Trinitarian understanding of God in creation and providence leads Bavinck to emphasize the active and personal work of God in creation. It is through the Word and the power of the Spirit that creation takes place. In addition, the active role of God in creation should lead to a creaturely understanding of God being active in creation: "His eternal power and Godhead are thoughtfully discerned from the creatures, the things that were made. We do not learn to know and to glorify God in independence from His work, but rather in and through His works in nature and in grace."[134]

It must be asked why it is important to understand the role of creation in Bavinck's theology. For Bavinck, and Reformed theology in general, creation demonstrates the creative power of God, and his role as a God who is active in the life of the creature. "The act of creation is an act of condescension,"[135] in which God has freely chosen to associate himself with his creation. The goodness of creation flows from the goodness of the creator, and this is why sin has so drastically separated the creator from the created.

The subject of apologetics also plays an important role in neo-Calvinism. Bavinck differs from Abraham Kuyper and later followers of neo-Calvinism[136]

---

[132] Ibid.
[133] Bavinck, *Our Reasonable Faith*, 162.
[134] Ibid.
[135] Berkof, "God as Creator and the World as Createdness," 80.
[136] One of the most notable followers of this tradition in the mid-twentieth century was Cornelius Van Til (1895–1987). He uses Bavinck's work copiously in many of his works, but aligns himself more with Kuyper on apologetics. Harriet Harris writes, "Van Til presents an apologetic in which presuppositions rather than evidences and rational argument are basic to the defense of the faith. His method is commonly labeled

on the subject of Christian apologetics. Kuyper took a position of presuppositional apologetics (also known as evidentialism). Bavinck's friend and contemporary, Princeton theologian Benjamin Warfield criticized the lack of focus Bavinck placed upon apologetics in his theology. Warfield believes that Bavinck did not allow enough room for objective evidences of faith in his work. Van Den Belt writes, "Warfield does not understand the aversion of the Dutch theologians against apologetics and remarks that 'it is a standing matter of surprise to us that the school which Dr. Bavinck so brilliantly represents should be tempted to make so little of Apologetics.'"[137] The difference between the two thinkers is that for Warfield, "faith always rests on evidences, and the evidence that the Christian religion is true is not necessarily the same as the evidence that one is a Christian. He found that Bavinck reversed the natural order by assuming that saving faith is a necessary prerequisite of the certainty regarding the Christian religion. In his opinion, the conviction of the truth, on the contrary, preceded the commitment to Christ."[138] Princeton theologians such as Warfield and J. Gresham Machen viewed apologetics as an important part of their theological task because of the challenges presented by nineteenth century liberal. Therefore, when Warfield read the work of a brother in arms with a similar theological task to him own in Bavinck, he desired for Bavinck to have a greater emphasis upon the apologetic task in his work.

Bavinck argues that rational evidences for faith only reach the external aspect of facts, and hence do not reach the heart of the matter of faith. He writes that such a dependence primarily on rational evidences will lead at best only to a "historical faith."[139] Kuyper makes the case that there should not be a disconnect between faith and reason, but at the same time one's faith should not be an irrational faith.[140]

The importance in drawing this distinction in focus upon apologetics represents the difference in two streams of thought in the Reformed tradition. Warfield and Kuyper emphasize the work the spirit performs through the means of argument and human reasoning. Bavinck on the other hand insists that there is a foundational difference between arguments that lead to a historical faith and the work of the Spirit which leads to a saving faith.[141] Bavinck's account of apologetics is also related to his understanding of Scripture. For Bavinck, the Bible makes no attempt to provide evidence for the existence of God. Bavinck's

---

'presuppositionalist'. All Kuyperians reject evidentialist apologetics." Harriet A. Harris, *Fundamentalism and Evangelicals* (Oxford: Oxford UP, 1998), 206.

[137] Van Den Belt, *Authority of Scripture in Reformed Theology*, 232.

[138] Van den Belt "Herman Bavinck and Benjamin B. Warfield on Apologetics and the *Autopistia* of Scripture," 35–36.

[139] Van Den Belt, *Authority of Scripture in Reformed Theology*, 235.

[140] Ibid., 232.

[141] Van Den Belt, *Authority of Scripture in Reformed Theology*, 236.

starting place is that humans are innately theistic, and foundational arguments for the existence of God are not necessary. He writes that to deny the existence of God is a sign of folly and moral degradation (Ps. 14:2).[142] On Bavinck's understanding of defending the existence of God, Nicholas Wolterstorff writes:

> While of course acknowledging that many of our beliefs about God are formed by reasoning, Bavinck's point has been that there is in us an innate disposition to form beliefs about God *immediately*. The closest Bavinck ever comes to offering an explicit evaluation of immediately formed theistic beliefs is his comment that "it would be a 'wretched faith that first had to prove God's existence before it prayed to him.'" Yet, in Bavinck's discussion there is, unmistakably, an implicit evaluation: The fact that a belief about God is formed by one's innate disposition to form theistic beliefs immediately is a *merit* in the belief, not a demerit. Bavinck rejects Locke's thesis that to be entitled to believe something about God one has to form or hold that belief on the basis of good evidence. Bavinck was an antievidentialist concerning theistic belief.[143]

The importance of Bavinck's understanding of apologetics will come to bear in the next chapter when his neo-Calvinism is applied to education. In Bavinck's writings on education he is thoroughly theistic, but he does not usually begin trying to defend a theistic position in a secular world. Instead, he assumes the theistic position. For but one example of Bavinck's method on this point he writes at the beginning of his article "Calvin and Common Grace," "Christianity has from the beginning laid claim to be the one true religion. Already in the Old Testament the consciousness exists that Jehovah alone is Elohim and that the gods of the heathen are of naught and vanity; and in the New Testament the Father of Jesus Christ is the only true God, whom the Son reveals and declares, and access to whom and communion with whom the Son alone can mediate."[144]

Bavinck's Distinctive Theological Positions in Regards to Education

Though the distinctive aspects of Dutch neo-Calvinist theology will be further discussed in chapter 5, it is important to highlight at least a few core themes at this point in order to conclude the chapter and begin to relate Bavinck's theology to his pedagogy. Cornelius Jaarsma points to two themes that appear throughout Bavinck's educational writings: "In the first three chapters [of Bavinck's *Principles of Education*] he defends his organic philosophy, a theocentric view of life, by pointing out the inadequacies and weaknesses of an

---

[142] Nicholas Wolterstorff, "Herman Bavinck—Proto Reformed Epistemologist," *Calvin Theological Journal*, 45:1 (2010): 140.
[143] Ibid. The quotation in the paragraph is taken from K. F. A. Kahnis *Die lutherische Dogmatik: Historisch genetisch dargestellt,* 3 vols. (Leipzig: Dorffling & Franke, 1861–1868), 1.128.
[144] Bavinck, "Calvin and Common Grace," 437.

educational philosophy which makes man the center and norm."[145] The 'organic' plays an important role in Bavinck's pedagogical writings just as it does in his theological work. This represents the importance of the organic theme throughout Bavinck's corpus. The organic means that there is something actively occurring in the process of a child learning. The organic also means that the exact educational needs of children may shift as history progresses. Jaarsma later writes, "He [Bavinck] regards society as a marvelous organism having grown under the direction of God, and a blessing to many."[146] An organism continues to grow with the progression of time, and so should society's knowledge and application of that knowledge. This growth and change in society is a providential work under the guiding hand of God.

Second, a theocentric emphasis upon the glory of God rather than man (or child) runs throughout Bavinck's pedagogical works. Bavinck uses this Reformed theme to combat pedagogies of his contemporaries that placed the educational emphasis upon the child. Again, he does not need to prove that the child needs a theological foundation, but assumes this is the case.

It is also clear that common grace is an important factor in how Bavinck understood education. As previously quoted in his article "Calvin and Common Grace," Christianity was for Calvin the one true religion through which one could obtain proper knowledge of God. All humans may obtain general knowledge, but common grace should point towards the truth found in Christ.

As this chapter has provided a foundation by which to understand Bavinck's Dutch Reformed theology, the next chapter will provide an analysis of some of Bavinck's writings on pedagogy. Through this format the connection between chapters will become clearer as it is seen how Bavinck's theological reflection relates to his later pedagogical works. In addition, some differences will begin to appear in how Luther and Bavinck approach pedagogy.

---

[145] Cornelius Jaarsma, *The Educational Philosophy of Herman Bavinck* (Grand Rapids: Eerdmans, 1935), 150.
[146] Ibid., 182.

4. Herman Bavinck, Neo-Calvinism, and Education

As discussed in the previous chapter, practical subjects such as psychology, pedagogy, politics, the role of women in society and education occupied Bavinck's mind in the last decade of his life. Perhaps because of this late emphasis, immediate posthumous scholarship on Bavinck places more emphasis on his pedagogical insights than upon his systematic theology. Five works on his pedagogy appeared within sixteen years of his death.[1] It is striking that the first scholarly work on Bavinck's theology did not appear until 1953.[2]

This chapter will deploy the underlying concepts driving Bavinck's form of neo-Calvinism discussed in the previous chapter to analyze two works. The first

---

[1] S. Rombouts, *Prof. Dr. H. Bavinck, Gids Bij de Studie van Zijn Paedagogische Werken* (Hertogenbosch –Antwerpen: Malmberg, 1922); J Brederveld, *Hoofdlijnen der Paedagogiek van Dr. Herman Bavinck, met Critische Beschouwing* (Amsterdam: De Standaard, 1927); L van der Zweep, *De Paedagogiek van Bavinck* (Kampen: Kok, 1935); Cornelius Jaarsma, *The Educational Philosophy of Herman Bavinck* (Grand Rapids: Eerdmans, 1935); and L. van Klinken, *Bavincks Paedagogische Beginselen* (Meppel: Boom, 1937). The only one of the four Dutch works in this collection that has been translated into English is J. Brederveld, *Christian Education: A Summary of Bavinck's Pedagogical Principles* trans. Two Members of the Faculty of Calvin College (Grand Rapids: Smitter Book Company, 1928). This publication list attests to the fact that the influence of Bavinck's educational works was confined primarily to his native Netherlands and the Dutch Reformed community associated with Calvin College in Grand Rapids, Michigan. It should also be noted that the author of this thesis is unaware of any book length volumes or scholarly articles in the English language since 1936 dealing with Bavinck's understanding of education prior to the recent publication of Timothy Shaun Price, "Herman Bavinck and Abraham Kuyper on the Subject of Education as Seen in Two Public Addresses," *The Bavinck Review*, 2:1 (2011) 59–70. Bavinck's own works on education include: *Paedagogische Beginselen* (Kampen: Kok, 1904); *De Povoeding der Rijpere Jeugd* (Kampen: Kok, 1916); *De Nieuwe Opvoeding* (Kampen: Kok, 1917); *Handleiding bij het Onderwijs in den Christelijken Godsdienst* (Kampen: Kok, 1932). None of these works are currently available in English. For a literary bibliography of Bavinck's works currently available in English see, John Bolt, "Herman Bavinck Speaks English: A Bibliographic Essay," *Mid-American Journal of Theology* 19 (2008): 117–126. For a bibliography in monograph form of Bavinck's work in both Dutch and English see Eric D. Bristley, *Guide to the Writings of Herman Bavinck* (Grand Rapids: Reformation Heritage Books, 2008). Because of the lack of sources available in the English language on Bavinck's pedagogy, the primary source that will be discussed in this chapter is Brederveld's *Christian Education: A Summary of Bavinck's Pedagogical Principles*.

[2] A. A. Hoekema, *Herman Bavinck's Doctrine of the Covenant*, ThD diss., Princeton Theological Seminary, 1953).

is an essay by Bavinck entitled "*Klassieke Opvoeding* (Classical Education)."[3] The second is a paraphrase of Bavinck's *Paedagogische Beginselen* first published in 1904.[4] Brederveld's summary of *Paedagogische Beginselen* was first published in 1927, six years after Bavinck's death, and translated into English in 1928.[5]

Analysis of more than one of Bavinck's works has been chosen for several reasons. First, analyzing Bavinck's essay "Classical Education" will allow a point of conversation with Luther as both theologians are at times interacting with the classical tradition. Having this common theme allows one to see how their theological differences are applied to classical education. Although Luther and Bavinck were separated by close to four hundred years, both thinkers saw validity in the application of the liberal arts tradition. This point of contact allows for conversation between the two traditions on a point of commonality. This point of commonality can lead to practical analysis of how the two traditions have implemented classical education differently. Second, whereas "Classical Education" is largely a historical blueprint of the classical learning tradition, in *Pedagogical Principles* Bavinck focuses upon the application of his approach to pedagogy. These two works are able to complement each other and provide a larger picture of Bavinck's views on education. Also, *Pedagogical Principles* is the closest access the English reader has to Bavinck's volumes on education as much of his work remains heretofore untranslated into English. Prior to approaching these two works, discussion of the historical context will situate Bavinck's work on education. This will aid in understanding why the Dutch neo-Calvinist tradition often took a reactionary approach in some of the tradition's writings. In addition, Bavinck's pedagogical works discussed in this chapter are the primary pedagogical works of his that have been translated into English. It is through "Classical Education" and *Pedagogical Principles* that the English reader is able to begin grasp Bavinck's pedagogical writings.[6] Though it would be preferable to interact with the full extent of Bavinck's pedagogical works available in Dutch, the works discussed in this chapter are sufficient for this thesis for at least two reasons. Because this thesis focuses primarily upon

---

[3] Herman Bavinck, "Classical Education" *Essays on Religion, Science, and Society*, ed. John Bolt, trans. Harry Boonstra and Gerrit Sheeres (Grand Rapids: Baker Academic, 2008), 209–244. The essay "Classical Education," was originally published as "Klassieke opvoeding, I, II," in *Stemmen des tijds* 7:1 (1918): 46–65, 113–147.

[4] J Brederveld, *Hoofdlijnen der Paedagogiek van Dr. Herman Bavinck, met Critische Beschouwing* (Amsterdam: De Standaard, 1927).

[5] J. Brederveld, *Christian Education: A Summary and critical discussion of Bavinck's Pedagogical Principles*, trans. Two Members of the Faculty of Calvin College (Grand Rapids: Smitter Book Company, 1928).

[6] The Dutch Reformed Translation Society has opened many of Bavinck's works to the English-speaking world, but there are no current plans to translate Bavinck's works on pedagogy. John Bolt, personal conversation with author, Edinburgh, Scotland, September 2, 2010.

Lutheran and neo-Calvinist understanding of classical education, it is crucial to have in English an article Bavinck wrote specifically about classical education. This provides an important link in providing direct access to Bavinck's thoughts regarding classical education. Second, an examination of "Classical Education" is further buttressed by having one of Bavinck's primary pedagogical textbooks, *Pedagogical Principles*, available in English. To provide an account of Bavinck's work on the subject of pedagogy, it is best to proceed by taking a brief look at the historical context in which Bavinck was writing.

Herman Bavinck in Context

Prior to providing a historical sketch of Herman Bavinck's (1854–1921) time, it would be helpful to note a few details of his life which will primarily serve to demonstrate the conflict Bavinck saw throughout his life between theological liberalism and the Reformed faith, as well as the tension between doing systematic theology and a theological engagement with contemporary issues. Jaarsmsa wrote in 1935 that the years of Bavinck's life, "represent an age unparalleled in change, especially in scientific, industrial, social, and educational spheres. The scientific method applied on ever broader scale had proved productive in psychology as well as in physics and other exact sciences. Its application was now attempted in theological sciences as well."[7] It was into this battle with new ways of viewing the world and theology that Bavinck would soon enter.

Three cities in particular mark the periods of transition in Bavinck's life: Leiden, Kampen, and Amsterdam. Herman was born to Jan and Gesina Bavinck on 13 December, 1854 in Hoogeveen, the Netherlands. Bavinck's family did not belong to the major Dutch Reformed Church, but rather to a smaller and more theologically conservative Reformed church that had its founding in an 1834 succession from the main Dutch Reformed church. Herman's father Jan was a pastor, and also went on to pastor and teach in a seminary in Kampen, which was associated with the Bavinck family's denomination.[8] From 1874–1880 Bavinck studied at the University of Leiden, which at the time was viewed as the center of modern, liberal theology in the Netherlands. This move was a surprise to the family who expected Herman to remain in Kampen. Ron Gleason notes the importance of this decision by Herman: "His [Herman Bavinck's] church affiliation had numerous spoken and unspoken expectations both for young Herman as well as for Jan and Gesina and the Bavinck family, which was, after all, a pastor's family. It was expected that a pastor in the Separatist churches would lead by example and certainly would not put a child

---

[7] Jaarsma, *The Educational Philosophy of Herman Bavinck*, 35.
[8] Willem De Wit, *On the Way to the Living God: A Cathartic Reading of Herman Bavinck and An Invitation to Overcome the Plausibility Crisis of Christianity* (Amsterdam: VU Press, 2011), 17.

of the covenant in harm's way spiritually. Herman's decision to attend Leiden instead of the Theological Seminary in Kampen felt like a bomb in the Separatist churches and caused ripple effected that lasted for quite a long time."[9] Bavinck's choice to attend Leiden seemed to be out of a desire to extend himself theologically. He grew up in the so-called heartland of his family's conservative denomination, and he may have wanted to learn from those outside of his denomination. Even at a young age, he seemed well aware of the challenges that would lay ahead in attending the liberal university. He wrote in his diary on 23 September, 1874, "Shall I remain in the faith? God grant it."[10]

Herman excelled at Leiden completing his doctoral degree in theology and preparing a thesis on the Reformer Huldrych Zwingli (1484–1531). After his time there was done, Bavinck became a pastor in Franeker for one year before returning to Kampen as a professor of theology in 1883. Bavinck flourished and developed as a theologian during his time in Kampen. He remained in Kampen until 1902 when he succeeded Abraham Kuyper as Professor of Theology at the Free University of Amsterdam. Kuyper had attempted to persuade Bavinck to come to the Free University on many previous occasions. This was a long-standing invitation from Kuyper in that even as early as 1881 Kuyper had offered the young Bavinck a position at the Free University (which was founded in 1880).[11] By the time Bavinck had chosen to move to the Free University, he had established himself as a leading theologian of his time, having published the first volume of his four volume *Gereformeerde Dogmatiek* in 1895 and the final volume appearing in 1901.[12] It was in Amsterdam that Bavinck would remain throughout the rest of his teaching career.

Bavinck's transition in career from Kampen to Amsterdam also coincided with a transition in Bavinck's theological writing. In the bucolic setting of Kampen Bavinck spent most of his writing energy working through his *Gereformeerde Dogmatiek*, whereas in the bustling city setting of Amsterdam Bavinck focused more upon social issues. Gleason argues that this may have been partly due to the change in his interlocuters in Amsterdam. He writes:

> As Bavinck settled in to his new environment, he found that it fit and suited him well. Bavinck did not completely blend into the masses in cosmopolitan Amsterdam, but rather was catapulted onto the stage of life both within his church as well as in a

---

[9] Ron Gleason, *Herman Bavinck* (Phillipsburg: Presbyterian & Reformed Publishing, 2010), 45–46.
[10] Gleason, *Herman Bavinck*, 48.
[11] Ibid., 91.
[12] All four volumes were not available in English until their publishing by the Dutch Reformed Translation society presented them from 2003–2008. Herman Bavinck *Reformed Dogmatics*, ed. John Bolt, trans. John Vriend (Grand Rapids: Baker, 2003–2008).

broader setting. He maintained theological contacts with a broad spectrum of theologians, some of whom were his mirror opposite. In Amsterdam, Bavinck stood on "broader ground," which is not meant to insinuate that he relinquished his principles or core beliefs. He remained thoroughly and solidly Reformed, but his contacts were increasingly varied. Both at the Free University as well as in society in general, Bavinck was surrounded by a caliber of individual that he did not encounter daily in the town of Kampen. . . . The atmosphere in Amsterdam was also conducive to a prolific and prodigious production of writing. In a very real sense even though he was in a more challenging academic environment, he produced a number of less technical works.[13]

Willem DeWit notes some of the areas into which Bavinck's interests expanded: "Especially during the last two decades of his life, after the completion of the first edition of his dogmatics in 1901, Bavinck publishes many books and articles on education, aesthetics, ethics, family, philosophy of science, social relationships, position of women, etc."[14] Bavinck's personal letters attested that he was aware of this changing shift in what he wanted to write about. In 1904 Bavinck wrote to his friend Dosker, "As I grow older my mind turns more and more away from dogmatic to philosophical studies and from these to their application to the practical needs of life about me."[15] Bavinck's shift in surrounding most likely contributed to his shift in writing emphasis.

There have been several reasons put forward for why this transition in Bavinck's writings took place. De Wit himself argues that this shift is part of a "catholic Reformed ideal" that Bavinck began developing in the 1880's.[16] This ideal was that the Reformed worldview could be integrated into all areas of life. Others have more pessimistically viewed it as a withdrawal from dogmatics to escape from older Reformed theology and his own unresolved problems in his doctrine of Scripture.[17] Though this second postulation may have some merit, the development of a Reformed Christian worldview (as could be used interchangeably with "catholic Reformed ideal") was one that Bavinck continued to develop. Bavinck argued that the Reformed worldview was set in opposition to a secular, evolutionary worldview. The desire to form a Christian worldview was one that was adamantly shared by Kuyper, and Bavinck viewed his late shift in writing emphasis as an application of this worldview.

---

[13] Gleason, *Herman Bavinck*, 344.
[14] De Wit, *On the Way to the Living God*, 55.
[15] Jaarsma, *The Educational Philosophy of Herman Bavinck*, 24.
[16] De Wit, *On the Way to the Living God*, 55.
[17] DeWit, *On the Way to the Living God*, 55.

Pedagogy as Theological Praxis

The Historical Setting of the Netherlands in the 19th Century

It is also important to understand the context in which Bavinck was writing because much of what the Dutch neo-Calvinist thinkers were doing was a reaction against social, political, and theological liberalism. One of the primary struggles taking place in nineteenth century Netherlands was between the power of the monarchy and the elected officials. During the 1840s in The Netherlands the term "liberal" was often applied to those who argued for equal rights and opportunities to be given to people of all classes.[18] Kossman writes, "Only in the 1840's—twenty years after it was born in France and adopted by Belgium— did doctrinaire liberalism take shape in the Netherlands."[19] Kossman goes on to say that the primary difference between the doctrinaire liberalism taking root in the Netherlands is that it lacked the Romanticism and rising middle classes that were present in France and Belgium. Whereas in these latter two countries, "doctrinaire liberalism seemed to express itself naturally and spontaneously, the Dutch variant looks studied and affected."[20]

The term "liberal doctrinaire" was a pejorative term given to this group as a result of its members' book learning as well as the group's inability to speak for the common people. William II allowed for the formation of a new constitution by this group in 1848.[21] This:

> Created a genuine constitutional monarchy, spreading sovereignty between the monarch and the States-General. It divided the latter's legislative functions between the First or Upper Chamber, representing the provinces, and the Second or Lower Chamber, which was directly elected by the people. The effective agent of government would be a Cabinet formally commissioned by the monarch but after 1868 in practice responsible to the Second Chamber. Of particular moment for Kuyper's career, the new system made education a matter of national, not local policy.[22]

During this period Dutch political and ecclesial life was still working through the influence of the rise of modern humanism and the French Revolution of 1789. James Skillen writes, "The Protestant Reformation turned to the Scriptures as a supreme authority for life and faith. Modern humanism could not accept such a supra-personal, objective authority any more than it could accept the authority of the Roman Church. Humanism aligned itself with

---

[18] This is most likely taken from the root of the Latin *liber* meaning, "free."
[19] E.H. Kossman, *The Low Countries, 1780–1840* (Oxford: Clarendon, 1978), 188.
[20] Ibid., 189.
[21] James Bratt, "Introduction: Abraham Kuyper and His Work," *Abraham Kuyper: A Centennial Reader*, ed. James D. Bratt (Grand Rapids: Eerdmans, 1998), 6.
[22] Ibid., 6–7.

the principle of autonomy of the moral personality."[23] The casting off of any external authority led to an inevitable dichotomy between faith and public life.

A second factor that led to the political climate of early nineteenth century Holland was the French Revolution. The place of the church in life was being replaced by reason. Christian symbols were removed from churches, cemeteries and other public places. The Supreme Being was no longer seen as an almighty God, but as reason.[24] This act of abolition of the influence of the church upon the state and the sense of a higher authority over the common people spread waves of influence far past the borders of France.

The nineteenth century in Europe could be seen as a reaction against the more disturbing aspects of the French Revolution. In another sense it also carried the ideas of the French Revolution further. It therefore, "opened the door both to reaction and to liberalism, to conservatism and to socialism, to all manner of new theologies and to a revival of the old one, to secularism and evangelism, and to agnosticism idealism."[25] These competing ideologies would soon be at work in the governing powers in the Netherlands. This region had long been influenced by a Reformed worldview, but these influences began to wane with the coming to power of secularism. It was against this secularism the Dutch neo-Calvinists tradition would eventually react. In fact, Abraham Kuyper referred to the French Revolution as the point of departure that characterized his time. The revolution was, "the consummation and zenith, but at the same time the downfall and destruction, of the hopes and ideals of the eighteenth century."[26] Although the revolution believed that it had achieved its goal of reason apart from God, ultimately it failed in maintaining a sustainable system of government apart from any type of religious beliefs.

One of the leading figures during this time in favor of conservative political change was Groen van Prinsterer (1801–1876). In politics he was an orthodox Protestant, or what was often referred to as the "Anti-revolutionary" party. This was in response to the "revolution" party that was not only known to be anti-Christian and anti-biblical, but also anti-historical and anti-philosophical.[27] He believed that the ideal of a sovereign people rather than a sovereign God would

---

[23] James William Skillen, "The Development of Calvinistic Political Theory in the Netherlands, with Special Reference to the Thought of Herman Dooyeweerd" (PhD diss., Duke University, 1974), 112–113.
[24] John Bolt, *A Free Church, A Holy Nation: Abraham Kuyper's Public Theology* (Grand Rapids: Eerdmans, 2001), 9.
[25] L. Praamsma, *Let Christ Be King, Reflections on the Life and Times of Abraham Kuyper* (Ontario: Paideia, 1985), 9.
[26] Ibid.
[27] Skillen, *The Development of Calvinistic Political Theory in the Netherlands, with Special Reference to the Thought of Herman Dooyeweerd*, 217.

lead to decay in any society. Van Prinsterer therefore sought to understand the limits of human political authority that were under the authority of God. Because he believed a reaction against the French Revolution was necessary, he became one of the leading figures to return Dutch Calvinistic political theory to the forefront. Van Prinsterer represented the pendulum swing on the opposite side of revolutionary ideas, which is why his party was aptly named "anti-revolutionary." In another very real sense the Dutch Calvinistic ideas were anti-revolutionary in that they sought to return to a system of law and political theory that held to an understanding of God sovereign over the workings of man.

The importance of the continuity of beliefs between Van Prinsterer, Kuyper, and others such as Bavinck in the Dutch neo-Calvinist tradition on the subject of the results of the French Revolution cannot be overstated. Rodgers writes:

> In Kuyper's insistence upon the unbelief of the Revolution we have emphasized for us his essential agreement with Groen's analysis of that movement. Kuyper is therefore included among those Dutch Christian leaders in the nineteenth century who perceived in the Revolution the inauguration of a new religion whose principles were coming to dominate the life of the Dutch nation, a religion of reason, systematically opposed to the Christian religion and bent upon its eradication.[28]

Van Prinsterer's influence upon Kuyper is seen not only in the foundations of his beliefs about politics, but also in how he understood the relationship between education and society. Van Prinsterer believed that there was essentially no qualitative difference between the authority of the head of a nuclear family and that of the head of a state (i.e. king or prince). The state is different only in that it has a supremacy and independence, and hence sovereign authority. This thought would eventually be further fleshed out in Kuyper's theology of sphere sovereignty. This conception is seen in education in that Van Prinsterer insisted that it was the right of parents to decide upon the education of their child. The state is its own sovereign authority, but in this formulation the sphere of the family decides upon the education of the child. Van Prinsterer preferred for local communities and provinces to have the right to decide upon the education of its children rather than a central government entity.[29] He maintained that ultimately all sectors of government and education were under the sovereignty of God, but that each grouping of persons should be able to choose the type of education that was appropriate for its children.

---

[28] R.E.L. Rodgers, *The Incarnation of the Antithesis* (Edinburgh: Pentland, 1992), xv–xvi.
[29] Skillen, *The Development of Calvinistic Political Theory in the Netherlands, with Special Reference to the Thought of Herman Dooyeweerd*, 220–221.

The influence of these two streams of thought was evident both in the Dutch Reformed Church of Bavinck's and Kuyper's heritage, and in the political atmosphere of the time. The influence upon the Church led to ecumenicism being more important than doctrinal distinction. For instance, when the Synod of the Netherlands Reformed Church met in 1816 is was addressed by a high government official speaking on behalf of the king. He made it clear that the church was not to concern itself with theological debates. In fact, this speaker said that the synod was, "not called to decide doctrinal differences, but to administer the church."[30] This call to make one of the primary goals of the church administration and to leave doctrine of the church to the current status quo, effectively doctrinal beliefs "undefined and undiscussed."[31] How were the ministers of the Dutch Reformed Church to respond to the call for doctrine not to interfere with the administration of the church? The only possible responses are to allow for the state promulgation in the affairs of the church, or to form some type of political and religious rebellion against this act. Placing sphere sovereignty as an important doctrinal locus allowed for Kuyper and others to allow for less interference by the state in local matters of the church and society.[32]

Although Kuyper is better known for his political involvement because of his role as Prime Minister, Bavinck was also politically engaged. During the late nineteenth century and early twentieth century the Netherlands had an overtly Christian political party in the form of the Anti-Revolutionary party. There were Christian and quasi-Christian parties other than the Anti-Revolutionary party during this time, but none so powerful. In 1905 Kuyper entreated Bavinck to take over leadership of this party (which Bavinck performed from 1905–1907).[33] In 1911 he was appointed to the First Chamber of the Netherlands Parliament, and served in this capacity until 1919.[34] Although he did not actively campaign for the position, he gladly took the role of serving citizens as an elected official.[35] During his first few years in this

---

[30] Karel Blei, *The Netherlands Reformed Church 1571–2005* (Grand Rapids: Eerdmans, 2006), 57.
[31] Ibid., 58.
[32] Kuyper extended this removal of state intervention in the affairs of the church to the realm of education as well. Thus, at the opening of the Free University of Amsterdam he chooses to entitle his inaugural speech "Sphere Sovereignty." This was a not so hidden to elucidate why in his opinion the state had to say what was going to be taught and how it should be taught at his university. For an English translation of this speech, see Abraham Kuyper, "Sphere Sovereignty," *Abraham Kuyper: A Centennial Reader*, ed. James Bratt (Grand Rapids: Eerdmans, 1998) 461–490.
[33] Gleason has an excellent account of Kuyper's requests towards Bavinck to take on this role, and Bavinck's trepidation to taking on such a task. Gleason, *Herman Bavinck*, 375–380.
[34] This position was roughly equivalent to that of a United States senator.
[35] Gleason, *Herman Bavinck*, 369.

Pedagogy as Theological Praxis

position he took a back seat, but eventually became more actively involved in the proceedings. One of his most notable aims during this time was lobbying for the establishment of Christian schools that would operate outside of government funding.

Bavinck was also looked to as a moral and spiritual voice in this capacity. During his tenure, women were still not allowed to vote in the Netherlands. His reply to this question was, "that with the Bible open in his hand, there was no other reasonable Christian answer to the question of voting rights than to allow women the right to vote. . . . The thrust of his argument regarding secular voting privileges was based upon the Word of God."[36] Bavinck's political life occurred during a very unique time in which he could openly express biblical arguments to aid in forming positions on social questions. In regards to education, Gleason writes that Bavinck's political involvement aided in his move from primarily writing dogmatic theology to throwing his energy and attention to matters that dealt more with family and education.[37] Gleason also notes, "education had always been the love of his [Bavinck's] heart and that Bavinck had manifested that love in an unequivocal manner."[38]

This brief introduction to the political and social scene of nineteenth and early twentieth century Holland sets the stage for analyzing some of Bavinck's writings on the topic of education. The next several sections will analyze specific writings of Bavinck on education.

Bavinck's Work on Education

As mentioned in the introduction, Bavinck published four books between 1904–1917 on the subject of pedagogy in addition to several articles. Two of these articles, "Trends in Pedagogy" and "Classical Education" have recently been made available to the English-speaking world through the Dutch Reformed Translation Society.[39] "Trends in Pedagogy" will be briefly discussed for two reasons. First, in this essay Bavinck provides the reader with a working definition and place to ground pedagogy. As it is primarily pedagogy, not andragogy, that is discussed in Bavinck's work, it is helpful to have such a definition. Second, during the latter period in Bavinck's life when he was writing more about social issues he was attempting to actively engage with alternate worldviews, and he believed that these worldviews played out in the field of pedagogy. Gleason notes that when Bavinck wrote *The Education of*

---

[36] Ibid., 395.
[37] Gleason, *Herman Bavinck*, 396.
[38] Ibid., 397.
[39] Herman Bavinck, "Classical Education," *Essays on Religion, Science, and Society*, ed. John Bolt, trans. Harry Boonstra and Gerrit Sheeres (Grand Rapids: Baker Academic, 2008), 209–244.

Mature Youth (*De Opvoeding der rijpere Jeugd*) in 1916 he, "demonstrated that he was more than acutely aware of what was occurring in Germany and America in the area of education as well as what the Roman Catholic Church and the socialists were teaching their students. A year later he published *The New Education* (*De nieuwe opvoeding*), where he gave detailed analysis of and commentary on the results of the then new empirical and experimental pedagogics."[40] While attempting to write from a distinctly Christian position, it was evident that he well understood the positions he opposed.

Before immediately examining Bavinck's writings on education, it may be helpful to gain a broader picture of Bavinck's pedagogical thought. Cornelius Jaarsma lists thirteen distinctive aspects of Bavinck's educational theory that are worth including here. It should be noted that all of these are not a direct correlation to classical education, but this list is helpful in understanding what Bavinck is thinking about education.

1. Education is a conscious, purposeful, systematic life process of adjustment, orientation, and moulding of the individual.
2. Education is a purposeful process, having its goal in the perfecting of man in the image of God.
3. The origin of man is found in a direct creative act of God rather than in a process of biological evolution.
4. The individual is a product of heredity and environment and the growing self-determination in the interaction of the former.
5. Only a psychology recognizing the sensual-spiritual nature of man can be really fruitful in the study and practice of education.
6. Education is normative as well as experimental in character.
7. Religio-ethical education is the supreme function of the educative process. As such it should constitute the core of the entire curriculum.
8. Method is the teacher's systematic, planned order of procedure.
9. The way to self-control is through intelligent obedience. This is another way of saying that discipline is the way to freedom.
10. The role of the teacher is that of friendly, sympathetic guidance.
11. Church, culture, and state constitute the three great units of society; the family unit he regards basic to the whole structure. All these institutions find their center in the ultimate principles of reality and their goal in the kingdom of God.
12. Social changes must be evaluated ethically according to norms inherent in man's social relationships.
13. Education is a social function in the sense that the entire social order must assume its educational responsibility.[41]

---

[40] Gleason, *Herman Bavinck*, 414.
[41] Jaarsma, *The Educational Philosophy of Herman Bavinck*, 214–226.

Pedagogy as Theological Praxis

Trends in Pedagogy

Thus far in this chapter I have set out an outline of Bavinck's life, context, and work on pedagogy. The next section of this chapter will deal specifically with Bavinck's writings on education. One of the foundational questions for discussing Bavinck's understanding of pedagogy must be to first ask where he locates pedagogy within the field of knowledge. Bavinck provides a definition for his understanding of pedagogy: "Pedagogy is a philosophic subject and is closely related to theology or philosophy. It is true that recently there have been various attempts to loosen this bond and to make pedagogy a completely independent subject. These attempts, however, will not succeed because education always assumes an answer to questions about human origin, essence, and purpose; and this answer (if ever possible) cannot be supplied by any exact science, but only by religion or philosophy."[42] This definition is telling for how Bavinck understands education. Pedagogy cannot function independently because it claims to be able to lead to answers to some of life's most difficult questions. To answer a question such as, "What is man's purpose?" one can look to philosophy or theology, but pedagogy as a teaching field cannot offer an answer without being in tandem to a broader field of knowledge. The question of how pedagogy should be performed is ultimately a question of worldviews. In this essay Bavinck spends more time pointing to Christianity as the only adequate worldview to address differing positions than he does naming these competing worldviews.

Bavinck also links Christianity with how one practices pedagogy. He writes:

> One can thus understand that Christianity brought about a great change in the theory and practice of education. Christianity is not a pedagogy as such, no more than it is a social or political system or some kind of special science. Through regeneration, Christianity has made the person a citizen of the kingdom of heaven and has put him in a new, childlike relationship with God. At the same time, it had a most powerful influence on all of life in society and state, in science and art, and also on education and nurture. This influence is also shown in the fact that when Christianity through the ages split into various churches and confessions, each of these groups brought about its special and unique changes in the common educational ideal.[43]

Bavinck makes it clear that in the Western context, Christianity has had a large impact upon how pedagogy is performed. Historically, he sees Christianity as the overriding force shaping Western civilization. In the remainder of this essay Bavinck details some of the other pedagogies that were

---

[42] Herman Bavinck, "Trends in Pedagogy," *Essays on Religion, Science, and Society*, ed. John Bolt, trans. Harry Boonstra and Gerrit Sheeres (Grand Rapids: Baker Academic, 2008), 205.

[43] Bavinck, "Trends in Pedagogy," 205.

popular at the time of his writing. He divides modern pedagogy into four groups, and his primary critique remains that there are fundamental flaws with attempting pedagogy apart from any theological foundation. This will inevitably end with placing undue emphasis upon the child rather than God. Bavinck ends the critique by writing, "With a completely secular idea of the task of education, these differences are irreconcilable, because the purpose of the creature is never found in the creature itself, but from the nature of things, only in God, the Creator."[44]

"Classical Education"

A second relevant essay in the *Essays on Religion, Science and Society* collection is entitled "Classical Education." In this essay Bavinck traces what he terms "classical education" from its Roman roots to his present day situation. His purpose in writing this essay is twofold. First, by providing a history of classical education Bavinck is able to demonstrate the positive role it has had in Western civilization. Similar to the point made in "Trends in Pedagogy," he shows the role Christianity has played in taking the Greek liberal arts and reconstituting them for the purposes of Christian pedagogues. Second, towards the end of the essay he focuses upon the situation in his native Netherlands, and thereby shows the benefit classical education could have in his contemporary setting. Throughout *Reformed Dogmatics* Bavinck uses this same technique. He provides a historical context by which one is able to more clearly see the issue at hand.

One of the first questions that must be addressed in this essay is what exactly Bavinck means by classical education. He writes that the Latin word *classicus*, "assumes the general meaning of excellent and exemplary, and it becomes the designation for whatever is authoritative and serves as a model."[45] This essay is particularly relevant because Bavinck takes a more nuanced view of classical education as compared to Luther. This is in large part due to the vast array resources on the subject available to Bavinck in the early twentieth century that would have certainly not been available to Luther. When Luther writes about the liberal arts in "To the Councilmen," he is primarily stating the seven liberal arts as he was taught them and focusing upon the learning of biblical languages.

Early in this essay, Bavinck makes a case that there is an historical precedent for there being a specific type of education infused with Christianity. Education for the Jewish believer out of which Christianity arose would have been primarily through the traditions of the Hebrew Scriptures and people, and

---

[44] Ibid., 208.
[45] Bavinck, "Classical Education," 209.

also in the practice of a type of trade. Bavinck highlights how in one sense training for a trade in the Greco-Roman world would not have been particularly different for the Christian or the non-Christian. He writes, "Christians were in the world and were not able to leave the world. . . . They got married and were given in marriage. They had children and had to educate them for some kind of occupation. They themselves were involved in various jobs and had to work for their daily bread."[46] The average Christian in the Greco-Roman world did not have the luxury to spend hours every day in learning apart from one's vocation. The daily toil of work to earn one's "daily bread" was the average lot in life for nearly all humans. This is a very similar expression to what Luther makes in his expression of *oeconomia* in "To the Councilmen." He uses the toil of daily life to expresses that parents did not possess the requisite time that would be needed to train one's children. The fact that both Bavinck and Luther see the toil of life as a hindrance to education gives credence to its validity as a historical problem. This 'problem' is addressed in a slightly different way by Bavinck as compared to Luther. For Bavinck, he focuses upon the effects of the fall in hindering full human flourishing. Luther on the other hand focuses upon the vocational call of the believer. In this manner Luther redeems the seemingly menial task of vocation, whereas Bavinck focuses upon the future redemption to take place.

At this point in the essay Bavinck makes a turn in his argument. It is clear on the surface that the practical element of education in vocation must be secured before the theoretical aspect of learning theology and philosophy. Bavinck raises the point of how the Christian who wished to enter a learned profession should do so. Bavinck writes, "Where could they obtain such training apart from the pagan schools? After all, in the beginning the Christians themselves did not have their own institutions of education, except for the catechumenate, and for a long time in many places lacked such institutions."[47] He proposes the distinction between the place of the Christian in society and the importance that education and indoctrination play into that discussion. Bavinck argues that in the Christian tradition as soon as there was a question as to whether Christians should have engagement with secular/pagan philosophy there was a difference of opinion in the church. He references the examples of Tertullian and Tatian opposing an incorporating of theology and philosophy, and on the other side Clement and Origen advocating a synthesis of these two disciplines in certain discourses. Bavinck does not comment on his position on the topic as much as he works through the particulars of the two sides. In his overview of classical education he tries to present himself as a neutral voice in the conversation.

---

[46] Ibid., 210–211.
[47] Bavinck, "Classical Education," 211.

The closest he comes to arguing a position in this case is by stating that in practicality there can be no strict separation between Christianity and a particular cultural expression. He makes the point that the Hebrews under the leadership of Moses made free use of the objects of silver and gold that were used as aids in worship as prescribed by Yahweh. In the early church, painting in the catacombs, "reflected the style of antiquity, the architecture of the churches was arranged to the models of the basilica, and philosophy was used for the defense of the Christian faith."[48] Bavinck again makes the case that practice precedes theory. The church of the Greco-Roman world did not necessarily think about whether it was appropriate to mimic the pagan culture's understanding of architecture in their paintings in the moment. Rather, reflection upon the interaction with one's culture in activities such as this is made when there is appropriate time for reflection. Other examples, such as the use of the Greek and Latin language demonstrate that for Bavinck there can be no strict separation between the church and its interaction with culture. He made a similar case in "Trends in Pedagogy" in that Western culture cannot escape from the influence Christianity has had upon its shaping, nor should it necessarily attempt such escape.

Bavinck's argument here is clearly infused with elements of common grace and sphere sovereignty. He purposefully uses an analogy of the Hebraic use of the elements of silver and gold to be redirected for the purpose of the one holy God. In neo-Calvinism God is creator of these elements, and they are objects that can be redeemed as part of God's creation, rather than being a material matter fundamentally opposed to God. Dutch neo-Calvinism is able to incorporate classical education under its banner because of its understanding of common grace. Bacote writes, "Kuyper held that the Spirit, as a part of common grace, distributes gifts and talents of intellect and artistry to the regenerate and the unregenerate. As a result, it is possible to look upon the contributions of non-Christians in the arts and sciences and in the sociocultural arena with appreciation, though with a critical eye."[49] Classical education does not seem to be the only model of education which Bavinck favors, but the Dutch tradition can gladly borrow from "pagan" sources of the Greeks and Romans. Throughout Bavinck's work he balances the use of non-Christian sources with the understanding that only Christianity can ultimately be the foundation for one's education or worldview.

Bavinck uses this analogy of objects and architecture to be redeemed for the Christian faith for his understanding of pedagogy. This point will become more practically applicable in his exposition of *Pedagogical Principles*, but at the moment it is sufficient to say that Bavinck has no trouble using "secular"

---

[48] Bavinck, "Classical Education," 212.
[49] Vincent Bacote, *The Spirit in Public Theology: Appropriating the Legacy of Abraham Kuyper* (Grand Rapids: Baker Academic, 2005), 127.

models of psychology and pedagogy for his teaching model if they do not contradict his understanding of the Christian faith.

This point in his essay also serves as a place of interaction between Bavinck's understanding of the relation of the church and state, and Luther's understanding of *politia*. Bavinck writes:

> In the meantime [in terms of historical progression] the church steadily assumed a more positive attitude with regard to the world, especially since the days of Constantine. It absorbed as much culture as was necessary to subject and guide it, and the church raised itself to be an empire of culture, which soon governed all areas of life. Thus, on the one hand, the church acknowledged marriage, family, occupations, science, art, and so forth as natural gifts that could be appreciated and enjoyed. On the other hand, all these gifts were of a lower rank, inferior to and in the service of the supernatural order, which had descended to earth in the church and in its hierarchy, mysteries, and sacraments.[50]

Although Bavinck is primarily recounting the historical position of the church in relation to state and culture, one's selective retelling of history helps to reveal the point that is being made. His expression here of subjecting and guiding culture is clearly an expression of the cultural mandate of Gen. 1:28. For the neo-Calvinist, one is not only to subdue the creation, but should also influence its direction.

From this point Bavinck notes the important role that education has played in the church. The primary example he uses is that of monasticism. The monastic orders preserved much of the Western culture that would have been otherwise lost during the decline of the Roman Empire. Bavinck expresses this by saying, "In still another way the church gave opportunity to the ancient culture. In the violent times experienced by Europe during and after the mass migrations, an incredible amount of art and literature of antiquity disappeared. Thus one must appreciate even more the boon that a great number of manuscripts were collected, saved, read, and copied in the monasteries."[51] Whereas earlier in church history Bavinck is expressing a struggle with how the Christian should interact with the pagan world, it seems that now Bavinck is making a case that Christianity has become a preserver of culture. Once Christianity has found its place in a society, it is difficult to separate the sacred from the secular and its role in influencing culture.

Bavinck spends a large portion of this essay tracing the idea of classical education through the Middle Ages, the Reformation, and the Enlightenment. He details primarily the use of Latin as a universal tongue of learning, and how

---

[50] Bavinck, "Classical Education," 212.
[51] Ibid.

the revival of this language among scholastics resulted in a return to the study of the classics. It is in this discussion that Bavinck makes reference to the trivium. He writes:

> Aristotle and Aristotlean philosophy had been elevated in the Middle Ages, but humanism regarded them as the great spoilers of reason, of healthy human understanding (*ratio*), of language, of style, of the natural expression of thoughts into words (*oratio*). Logic therefore had to give way to rhetoric, Aristotle to Cicero, and Quintilianic, barbaric Latin of the Middle Ages to pure, classical Latin. When the humanists thus returned to the sources and became absorbed in the writings of the ancients, their eyes were opened to the beauty that was revealed in the literature and the arts.[52]

Bavinck views this rediscovery of knowledge as a watershed moment for both Christianity and Western Civilization. Whereas Bavinck earlier infused his concepts of common grace and cultural activity into this essay, he now notes the role of the organic in education and culture: "Many strove for a reconciliation between humanism and Christianity, and with Johannes Sturm[53] describes the purpose of education as *sapiens atque eloquence pietas*—as true piety linked organically with through knowledge and genuine culture."[54] This phrase literally translates simply as, "wise eloquence and piety." Rather than providing a wooden definition, Bavinck has chosen to add his own perspective on what it means. He adds the organic link and the concept of "genuine culture" to what was originally in the phrase. What does he mean by "genuine culture?" In one sense genuine portrays the same type of idea he is trying to get across with organic in that both appeal to a base concept.

A shift in his argument occurs when he explains the difference in learning between the classical period and the Enlightenment: "The ancients might have been the pioneers of learning, but they were not finishers; they must therefore not be followed, but rather outpaced and surpassed."[55] Again, this is the organic at work in Bavinck's views. Pedagogy today should not just be a return to what has been done in the past. History leads one to an organically flowing purpose. In Bavinck's view, if one wishes to teach the liberal arts, this should not be done by overlooking two thousand years of Christian history. History organically develops and should be looked to for how a particular subject should be practiced today.

---

[52] Bavinck, "Classical Education," 216–217.
[53] Johannes Strum (1507–1589) was an influential German educator, who is most closely associated with the gymnasium system of education.
[54] Bavinck, "Classical Education," 217.
[55] Bavinck, "Classical Education," 232.

Pedagogy as Theological Praxis

Another critical point Bavinck makes prior to the Enlightenment concerns the type of education people were receiving. He writes that the main type of knowledge that was being produced during this time period was that of learning a specific art or craft, and to be introduced to a guild. He writes:

> The old method of nurture and education has as its main purpose to have the student acquire a knowledge of the past and to induct him into one of the existing guilds for learning the art of craft. This method worked well in its time but is not suitable for today. It overloaded the memory, but critical thinking was underdeveloped; it created people learned but not wise, obedient but not independent; it prepared for school but not for life. Today we need a different education, one that is derived from nature that takes its position not in antiquity but in the present. Its purpose is to form a person to be an independent being, with his or her own thoughts and judgments, to be a useful, helpful member of society.[56]

Bavinck calls for a new type of education that produces the ability of independent thought. There is much value in training for a vocation, but Bavinck argues that this should not be the end of one's learning. He combines creation with the organic to form one's pedagogy. It is "derived from nature" but it is also focused upon the needs of the present.

Bavinck uses the path of the German educational system (which was also influential upon the Dutch system) to shift to his contemporary context in the Netherlands. He explains dominant systems of education in the Netherlands, each of which was involved to some extent with classical education. These were:

1. Gymnasium: This system had classical languages as its main subjects.
2. *Ober-Realschule*: This system was primarily for mathematical and natural science in addition to modern languages. It did not include the study of Latin or Greek.
3. *Realgymnasium*: Bavinck sees this institution as a middle ground between the previous two. It taught Latin as well as modern subjects.[57]

The background of these schools sets the context for Bavinck to discuss his local setting. The need for more than just an elementary education for the working class citizens led in 1863 to the establishment of the *hoogere burgerscholen*. Literally, this was the "higher-citizens schools," which found its place between vocational schools and gymnasiums. The mention of the *hoogere burgerscholen* is relevant because it strayed from its original purpose as a middle ground school to teach children who would enter into industrial vocations and began to compete with the gymnasium schools. One can

---

[56] Ibid., 233.
[57] Ibid., 234–236.

understand how such as progression would happen. A teacher with the student's best interest in mind would certainly try to do whatever he or she could to open the academic potential of the individual. Once the *hoogere burgerscholen* became an established entity, it could be seen as a threat rather than an institution established for second-class vocational students. Bavinck writes:

> When the *hoogere burgerscholen* gradually and without notice developed in a direction totally different from what was originally intended, they became competitors with the gymnasiums, and a struggle for equal rights between them has continued for the past forty years. From time to time appeals were made to the governments. . . . Prime Minister Kuyper answered that he could not accept such an amendment at that time because the crucial issue of classical education should not be decided in such an incidental manner. But he declared that he was not an absolute proponent of a classical education for all future students, and he would certainly not make it mandatory for all who desired to attend a university.[58]

The *hoogere burgerscholen* offered an alternative to the norm of classical education. The point Kuyper notes is that it is not the role of the government to universally decide whether classical education is appropriate for all students. This is a crucial point for understanding the role of classical education in society. Even if Kuyper does not have a vested interest in the *hoogere burgerscholen*, this argument works in his favor. By making the case that the state should not have a final say in what is or is not taught in the *hoogere burgerscholen*, he can also make the case that the government should not have a final say about what is or is not taught at the Free University of Amsterdam, or any other Christian school for that matter. With this in mind, neither Bavinck nor Luther argue for classical education as being the only model for education. Luther sees classical education as an ideal. Bavinck sees classical education as a tradition with a valid historical foundation, but not as the only model. There is an antithesis throughout Bavinck's writings. At times he argues vehemently against positions he sees as untenable for the Christian faith, while at other times he believes one should adapt to "modern times." Such is his stance on classical education.

Bavinck's Views of Classical Education

In this article Bavinck does not see classical education as a type of ontological norm for education that will always be the best model for education. In fact he says near the end of his article, "Classical antiquity is no longer the ideal of education for us, and it will never again be that."[59] He states this within a larger

---

[58] Ibid., 235. It should be noted that Kuyper was well trained in the classics. His masters thesis is written in Latin. A new edition has recently been released: Abraham Kuyper, *Abraham Kuyper's Commentatio (1860) The Young Kuyper about Calvin, a Lasco, and the Church* 2 vols. vol. 24 of Brill's Series in Church History (Leiden Brill, 2005).
[59] Bavinck, "Classical Education," 241.

criticism of classical education. His primary criticism of the classics is that in his context they are usually taught apart from any historical point of reference. Bavinck writes, "If at the gymnasium or university one spends weeks and months reading Homer, Plato, Sophocles, and others without any serious attempt to introduce the student to the person and the time of the authors, and the content and the philosophical, aesthetic, cultural, historical value of their works, then one cannot expect that the student will feel interest or love for classical antiquity."[60] Formation in experience is important for Bavinck. The grammatical-critical method had long been the primary method of education in Bavinck's context. It should also be noted that it is not the trivium and quadrivium that Bavinck is criticizing. It seems that his contemporary system had favored grammatical arts almost in opposition to the sciences. This criticism is also closely related to that of studying the liberal arts apart from any type of Christian worldview. Again, for Bavinck this would be a meaningless pursuit.

Despite his criticisms Bavinck maintains that classical learning should have a place in the Netherlands' educational system. In fact (in a similar fashion to Luther) Bavinck believes the current moment would be an excellent opportunity to reform and continue the teaching of the classics. He writes:

> But the great cultural and historical value of that antiquity has never been realized as well as today. The influence of Israel and also of Hellas and Latium on our culture is much more clear to us now than in previous centuries; these are and will remain our spiritual forbears. The study of antiquity is therefore not only of formal and practical value: for the development of thinking, understanding Greek and Latin terms in our scholarship, understanding citations and allusions in our literature, and so forth. Its lasting value also lies in the fact that the foundations of modern culture were laid in antiquity. The roots of all our arts and learning—and also, though in a lesser degree, the sciences that study nature—are to be found in the soil of antiquity. It is amazing how the Greeks created all those forms of beauty in which our aesthetic feeling still finds expression and satisfaction today; in their learning they realized and posited all the problems of the world and of life with which we still wrestle in our heads and hearts. They were able to achieve that, on the one hand, because they rose above folk religion and struggled for the independence of art and learning; but on the other hand, they did not loosen art and learning from those religious and ethical factors that belong to man's essence. In the midst of distressing reality, they kept the faith in a world of ideas and norms. And that idealism is also indispensable for us today; it cannot be replaced or compensated for by the history of civilization or new literature.[61]

Bavinck sees a definite relation between his contemporary context and that of the ancients. They lived during a time of "distressing reality" but were able

---

[60] Bavinck, "Classical Education," 241.
[61] Bavinck, "Classical Education," 241–242.

to keep "the faith in a world of ideas and norms."⁶² Bavinck himself was struggling in this time period with how to adapt to the changing, modern world. The ancients offered one way to deal with such a situation.

A second related reason Bavinck offers for maintaining classical education is that of "national and international concern."⁶³ This article is written in the context of the first Great War. Bavinck views the common ideas shared with other nations about pedagogy as one of a shared heritage. Bavinck writes, "the maintaining of Latin is a national concern because with it we maintain something that has always been our honor and our fame. . . . The current world war estranges nations from each other—nations that belong to each other according to history, religion, and culture, but it appears that all unity and cooperation will be submerged under enmity and hate for a long, long time, perhaps forever."⁶⁴ Bavinck argues that the war has promoted nationalism and chauvinism. Whereas the Europeans nations have a shared commonality, this has been placed in the background in favor of nationalism. He sees classical education as but one common bond that the nations of Europe share.

Bavinck ends the article on a theological note. Overall, this piece is not particularly theological. It is primarily an overview of the history of classical education with some thoughts about what classical education has to offer contemporary society. The theological turn at the end is almost an addendum to the letter. It is most likely prompted by a desire to make a theological argument towards ending the current hostility taking place in Europe. He writes:

> If there is one thing that is essential in these grave times, it is that Christian nations be reconciled to each other, close ranks, and take to heart the call to conserve the treasure that has been entrusted to them in religion and culture. This is true for religion, for the Christian religion. Recently Professor [Rudolf] Eucken from Jena pointed out correctly that the Bible—which until now has formed a common foundation for religion and art—is increasingly discarded by both. How will these nations ever again become a power for mankind if they do not possess an inner unity in Scripture and do not draw from one communal well?⁶⁵

Bavinck reminds the reader of a shared morality and history. In this case he uses the shared values of Christianity and the classical education tradition to call for university among the people of Europe.

---

⁶² Ibid., 242.
⁶³ Ibid.
⁶⁴ Ibid., 242.
⁶⁵ Ibid., 242–243. The work Bavinck is referring to in this quotation is Rudolf Eucken, *Die geistesgeschichtliche Bedeutung der Bibel* (Leipzig: Kroner, 1917).

Bavinck's purpose in writing this article was to trace how classical education became an embedded part of Dutch culture, and to ask whether this is a system that needs to be changed. Bavinck offers some prescription to this question near the end. Classical education cannot be practiced in the larger culture without acknowledging and responding to the changes taking place in one's contemporary setting. This article was written during the third stage of Bavinck's theological development in which he spent an increasing amount of his time responding to modern questions as a public theologian. Although Bavinck is not particularly 'theological' in this article, his method is much the same as in *Reformed Dogmatics*, published twenty-three years prior. History provides one with a lens into the organic development of a doctrine or topic. In this case, the organic development of classical education as not only an entrenched, but also valid aspect of Western culture is viewed in light of its historical lineage. Again, this historical development does not validate classical education as being the best model for all peoples at all times, but it does provide credence to the continuance of some form of classical education. The case is made that classical education has been a force for social and religious good throughout most of Christian history. This tracing is not just a recitation of facts, but Bavinck believes there is an evolutionary character to the organic development of a particular thought. The concept of classical education continues to grow and be added to throughout human history. At one of his more positive points in the article when discussing the role of classical education in neo-humanism and Romanticism Bavinck writes, "They [classical inspired works published at this time] altogether form one organic whole, are inspired by one thought, propelled by one divine force, and striving after one goal—the forming of the human race into genuine, free humanity. According to Lessing, what appears to be education from our perspective is from God's perspective the revelation that he grants successively to mankind, thus leading them to the realm of the true, the good and the beautiful, the human kingdom fused with God's kingdom."[66]

At the beginning of the essay he also subtly makes the point that there is nothing wrong with the Christian taking the classical model from their Greek and Roman forbears. Just as early Christians drew inspiration for fields such as philosophy and art, so too is classical education a tradition that has its basis in Greco-Roman culture, but has been repurposed by the Christian tradition.

With this background in mind, the next piece that will be addressed in Bavinck's writings is that of *Pedagogical Principles*. *Pedagogical Principles* was Bavinck's first book published on education, published in 1904. This article has been placed in conjunction with *Pedagogical Principles* because of the vast difference in emphasis offered between the two pieces.

---

[66] Bavinck, "Classical Education," 220–221.

Pedagogical Principles

Perhaps the best place to begin an analysis of *Pedagogical Principles* is to ask why Bavinck wrote a book such as this. This period at the end of his career in which he wrote about pedagogy, psychology and other contemporary issues of his time are often seen as the third stage in his writing. In his first stage as a young professor at Kampen he produced what he is best known for today, the four-volume *Gereformeerde Dogmatick*. In his second stage he produced *Christelijke Wetenschap*, and *Christelijke Wereld en Leuensbeschouwing*, which was expanded at for his Stone Lecture Series given at Princeton, and later published as *The Philosophy of Revelation*.[67] Following this period Bavinck entered a third stage where he focused upon what he saw as the social concerns of the contemporary world.

Brederveld argues that there are two primary factors behind Bavinck's interest in pedagogy. The first he sees as Bavinck's, "concern for man, and which causes him to seek the field of study most congenial to this concern."[68] This so-called concern for man is driven by man's inner struggle for spiritual good. In many ways Bavinck is an idealist in the practical application of his theology. He hardly ever approaches an issue without tracing its historical formation and justification. He uses this historical path to represent how the issue should be approached in the present day. Brederveld writes, "He [Bavinck] longs to know that which is unchangeable and far beyond all human caprice, that which is immovable amidst the shifting opinions. But that which is objective is never for Bavinck merely external; it is something which can and must be taken up into his own life. And this is the reason why he is not primarily interested in external nature and the natural sciences, why he inclines rather towards humanism than toward realism, though believing that above both stands Christian pedagogy."[69] Though Brederveld's introduction is mostly a glowing picture of Bavinck's thought and work, he does make an important point that for Bavinck external practice is of no value without internal renewal.

The realism to which Bavinck is opposed is based upon "pragmatism," which is primarily associated with William James, Charles Sanders Pierce and John Dewey in terms of education. Because Bavinck is engaging with pragmatism, it would be helpful to provide a definition of pragmatism. William James writes:

> A glance at the history of the idea [of pragmatism] will show you still better what pragmatism means. The term is derived from the same Greek word *pragma*, meaning

---

[67] Herman Bavinck, *The Philosophy of Revelation: The Stone Lectures for 1908–1909 Princeton Theological Seminary* (London: Longmans, Green, and Co., 1909).
[68] Brederveld, *Christian Education*, 10.
[69] Brederveld, *Christian Education*, 12.

action, from which our words 'practice' and 'practical' come. It was first introduced into philosophy by Mr. Charles Peirce in 1878. In an article entitled 'How to Make Our Ideas Clear,' in the 'Popular Science Monthly' for January of that year. Mr. Pierce, after pointing out that our beliefs are really rules for action, said that, to develop a thought's meaning, we need only determine what conduct it is fitted to produce: that conduct is for us its sole significance. And the tangible fact at the root of all our thought-distinctions, however subtle, is that there is no one of them so fine as to consist in anything but a possible difference of practice. To attain perfect clearness in our thoughts of an object, may involve—what sensations we are to expect from it, and what reactions we must prepare. Our conception of these effects, whether immediate or remote, is then for us the whole of our conception of the object, so far as that conception has positive significance at all.[70]

John Dewey is the best representative to put in conversation with Bavinck, because he combined the ideals of James and Pierce. Pierce was a logician, James an education and humanist, and Dewey in effect embraced both points of view.[71]

Philosopher and educator John Dewey is most closely associated with the pragmatism (and hence Realism) to which Bavinck refers. Bavinck is keen to interact with his peers, as is the case here. When *Paedagogische Beginselen* was published in 1904, Dewey had just begun to make his indelible mark upon the American system of education. His first major work on education, *The School and Society*[72] was published in 1899, and was followed in 1902 by *The Child and the Curriculum*. *The School and Society* was a groundbreaking achievement, and was soon translated into almost every European language as well as Chinese and Arabic.[73]

Bavinck was responding to the pedagogical trends of his day, if not directly reading Dewey. It was during this time Dewey was also teaching at the University of Chicago (1894-1904) and developing his philosophy of pragmatism as an empirically based theory of knowledge. For Dewey, to be pragmatic means, "looking upon the *consequences* of any proposition as a necessary test of its validity, provided, of course, that those consequences are not just imagined but are the results of actions taken in accordance with the proposition itself. Thus, to take the simplest of instances, if someone declares, "The cat is on the mat," her statement sounds like an answer to the question, "Where is the cat?" For that statement to be true, it should result, if acted upon,

---

[70] William James, *Pragmatism in Focus*, ed. Doris Olin (London: Routledge, 1992), 39.
[71] Philip W. Jackson, "John Dewey," *A Companion to Pragmatism*, eds. John R. Schook and Joseph Margolis (Oxford: Blackwell Publishing, 2006), 61.
[72] This work is also occasionally cited as *The School and Social Progress*.
[73] Brian Holmes, "The Reflective Man: Dewey," *The Educated Man: Studies in the History of Educational Thought*, eds., Paul Nash, Andreas M. Kazamias, and Henry J. Perkinson (London: John Wiley & Sons, 1965), 304.

in finding the lost animal."[74] Within pragmatism the example above would take the cat as being on the mat to have no definite meaning unless one were in search of the cat. For Dewey, pragmatism is a rule for "*all* thinking, *all* reflective consideration to *consequences* for the final meaning and test."[75]

Why did Bavinck feel the need to respond to "realism", and what was his primary critique of this system? Bavinck and Dewey both well understood that philosophical underpinnings would guide one's approach to education. Dewey writes, "If we are willing to conceive education as the process of forming fundamental dispositions, intellectual and emotional, toward nature and fellow-men, philosophy may even be defined as the general theory of education."[76] In an essay entitled "The Need for a Philosophy of Education" Dewey writes, "But the philosophy of education must go beyond any idea of education that is formed by way of contrast, reaction and protest. For it is an attempt to discover what education is and how it takes place. Only when we identify education with schooling does it seem to be a simple thing to tell what education actually is, and yet a clear idea of what it is gives us our only criterion for judging and directing what goes on in schools."[77] Dewey and Bavinck both understood that the philosophical underpinnings of a system of thought will guide how pedagogy is practiced, and they had two very different views as to how this should be done.

Two of pragmatism's ideals that Bavinck attacks in *Paedagogische Beginselen* are idealism and a focus upon the individual. Dewey notes this stress, "Pragmatism and instrumental experimentalism . . . brought into prominence the importance of the individual. It is he who is the carrier of creative thought, the author of action, and of its application."[78] Although Bavinck is interacting with an early Dewey, the early Dewey also had this focus upon the individual as seen in the opening lines of the first essay of *The School and Society*: "We are apt to look at the school from an individualistic standpoint, as something between teacher and pupil, or between teacher and parent. That which interests us most is naturally the progress made by the individual child of our acquaintance, his normal physical development, his advance in ability to read, write, and figure, his growth in the knowledge of geography and history, improvement in manners, habits of promptness, order, and industry—it is from such standards as these we judge the work of the

---

[74] Jackson, "John Dewey," 59.
[75] Ibid., 60.
[76] John Dewey, *The Collected Works of John Dewey*, ed. Jo Ann Boydston (Carbondale: Southern Illinois University Press, 1967–1990).
[77] John Dewey, *John Dewey on Education: Selected Writings*, ed. Reginald D. Archambault (New York: The Modern Library, 1964), 3.
[78] Jackson, "John Dewey," 61.

school."[79] One sees both the pragmatic emphasis as well as the focus upon the individual in these lines.

Again, Bavinck's problem with realism/pragmatism is based in its philosophical foundation. He wants to orient pedagogy with a foundational understanding of focus upon the glory of God and the formation of a Christian worldview rather than focus upon the individual. In his summation of Bavinck's rejections of pragmatism, Jaarsma writes, "Truth is preexistent and is true prior to man's discovery of it. Ideas are true when they correctly represent the facts. Truth is the correspondence of thinking and being and not dependent upon workability as pragmatism asserts. Pragmatism mistakes a perfectly legitimate test of truth for truth itself."[80]

It should also be noted that Dewey maintained a disdain for what is traditionally viewed as a liberal arts education. Whereas the classical tradition emphasizes tradition, Dewey seemed opposed to the idea of there being a canon or "classic" texts to be taught in an education curriculum.[81] Korcok notes that Dewey's, "contempt for the classical liberal arts was obvious as he spoke of those who were "victims" of the old liberal arts."[82]

The second factor Brederveld notes in regards to Bavinck's interest in pedagogy is his embracing of the Reformed confession of the Christian faith. While Brederveld writes at length about Bavinck's "concern for man" principle, he offers but one sentence on Reformed theology being an important factor for Bavinck's pedagogy. Bavinck's "concern for man" is not the same as the individualistic approach of Dewey. This again points to the *"Weltanschauung"* Bavinck is attempting to develop.

Pedagogy and Neo-Calvinism

The purpose of this section will be to provide an overview of some of the key concepts Bavinck is discussing in regards to pedagogy, as well as how his understanding of pedagogy is influenced by his neo-Calvinist background.

---

[79] John Dewey, *Selected Educational Writings*, ed. F. W. Garforth (London: Heinemann, 1966), 80–81.
[80] Cornelius Jaarsma, *The Educational Philosophy of Herman Bavinck: A Textbook in Education* (Grand Rapids: Baker, 1935), 213.
[81] William M. Shea, "John Dewey and the Crisis of Education," *American Journal of Education* 97:3 (May, 1989): 297.
[82] Thomas Korcok, *Lutheran Education: From Wittenberg to the Future* (Saint Louis: Concordia University Press, 2011), 256. John Dewey, "The Problem of the Liberal Arts College," *American Scholar* 13 (October 1944): 392.

Pedagogy, in contrast to andragogy, refers specifically to the education of the young. In Bavinck's introduction to *Pedagogical Principles* he lists three matters he wishes to discuss in this volume: the need of education, the forming of a definition of education, and pedagogy as the science of education.[83]

Bavinck's definition of education in *Pedagogical Principles* is worth quoting at length:

> Education when taken in its broadest sense is effected by the environment of the child. Influences of various kinds and from all quarters crowd in on him and contribute to the moulding of him. The process is for the greater part unconscious and unintentional, but by the same token leaves an impression all the deeper. Nature and society form the environment; from them stream forth influences to which the child is subjected; and though, as was said most of these influences are unpremeditated, without them as general background education in the narrower sense, intentional education, could not exist. All the factors and agents with which creation abounds are means for education; ultimately, then, education understood thus broadly has its origin in God.[84]

Pedagogy, like so many other spheres of knowledge, finds it place in creation as the work of God. The use of creation as paradigmatic for understanding life is foundational to both Bavinck and Luther. Education is also an inherently theological activity. For Bavinck, education cannot be at its core anything but a theological activity because in takes place in a realm that is created and sustained by God. As highlighted earlier, Bavinck's *prima facie* assumption is that there is a God who is active in the world, and as such has no need to defend the plausibility of such action. Bavinck also highlights that much of what he considered 'education' is simply knowledge that is gained through experience.

For Bavinck education has its origin in God, and the science of education is pedagogy. When practical application is made of pedagogy, it becomes an art.[85] As mentioned in Brederveld's introduction, Bavinck's "concern for man" was one of the driving principles behind his writings on pedagogy. This concern is for both internal change and external action. Bavinck writes, "pedagogy enables us with more profound consciousness to engage in one of the most glorious types of activity God has entrusted to human beings. And to live consciously is the privilege and glory of man."[86] Bavinck's understanding of the organic also plays into his definition of pedagogy. He acknowledges that education has many aspects: theological, philosophical, psychological, etc. In this manner

---

[83] Brederveld, *Christian Education*, 17.
[84] Ibid., 18.
[85] Brederveld, *Christian Education*, 26.
[86] Ibid., 20.

Bavinck approaches the question of the one and the many. Bavinck writes, "It is, we may at once grant, the nature of science to strive for unity; its objective is all existence as a unified and co-operating plurality. But it is pertinent here to remind ourselves that science does not deny the distinctions, the plurality, within this unity, and that whatever its ultimate theoretical aim, science actually begins in every case with what are only fragments, and finds it necessary to divide labors, to specialize."[87]

One of the unique aspects of *Pedagogical Principles* is that it has the approach of a scientific textbook on pedagogy, but is infused throughout with Christian aspects and ideals. For Bavinck, it would not be possible to separate the art of teaching from a Christian worldview. In Bavinck's understanding, the Reformed vision of reality is best equipped to understand the world, and therefore best equipped to understand pedagogy. Bavinck writes:

> The harmony found in the Christian ideal is so far best expressed in and maintained by the Reformed church and its confession. The Reformed world view adorns all reality, even the most commonplace, with the nobility of God. Man, first of all, is God's creature and never finds the purpose of his existence in himself. This fact is basic and therefore in nurturing man into a man of God it should be our criterion. A corollary of this lofty conception of man and of the educational ideal is that in the midst of the world man is obliged to a service of his God and to be furnished unto all good works.[88]

Bavinck's primary disagreement with the pedagogy of his day was understanding the human as the ideal starting point: "Modern pedagogy then finds the aim of education in man and in man alone; everything higher than he is being ignored, and all order and every norm is to be derived from his own nature."[89] Neo-Calvinism (and most expressions of Christianity) offer a much different starting place in grounding one's interaction with the world in understanding God as creator and redeemer. One's starting point will clearly guide statements made about pedagogy. The interaction of *ecclesia*, *oeconomia*, and *politia* clearly had an impact upon Luther's understanding of pedagogy. Similarly, Bavinck's foundational understanding of God as creator leads him to begin pedagogy with theology. Bavinck's premise that pedagogy must begin with theology places him in a position in which to critique alternate worldviews, such as that being put forward by Dewey.

Bavinck separates himself not only from secular visions of education, but also from other expressions of Christianity:

---

[87] Ibid., 27.
[88] Brederveld, *Christian Education*, 41.
[89] Ibid., 39.

In the first place, Christianity informs us that man is 'God's image, His offspring, His son.' This characterization is mean in its absolute sense. The very absoluteness differentiates the Reformed confession from both the Roman Catholics and the Lutherans. Man is thus related to God both in his special disposition as individual and as a member of every organization found among men. Whoever rejects this answer to the question of the origin and essence of man has no answer, and consequently his education is without basis.[90]

Bavinck's creation of an antithesis between a Reformed worldview and one not based upon creation and man in God's image is familiar, but exactly what he is juxtaposing in the first part of this quote is unlike most of Bavinck's writings in that it is not particularly clear. It is not clear what is meant by the absoluteness of being in God's image. A Catholic or Lutheran would certainly affirm man as being *imago Dei* as well. The main point here is that differentiation of the Reformed confession is an important aspect of Bavinck's theology. He believes that the Reformed worldview has something unique to offer Christianity, and therefore attempts to show how it is different from other theologies and worldviews.

Bavinck also addresses common grace, but does so in a way to make his position unique. From the Dutch neo-Calvinist tradition, Bavinck placed much emphasis upon common grace, whereas Kuyper for instance placed more emphasis upon sphere sovereignty. After Bavinck has critiqued Catholic, Lutheran, and non-Christian positions on pedagogy, he wants to leave them with a parting note in which he says that other positions do contain an element of truth. He writes:

> In the first place, there is common grace making human life possible. It expresses itself in outward blessings but also in inward blessings, such as maintaining in man reason and intellect, conscious, natural love and a sense of truth, religious and moral concepts, sensibility to shame and honor, fear of disgrace and punishment. And every pedagogy—even though in theory denying it—owes its very existence to the common grace of God.[91]

In this case Bavinck is working in the realm of absolutes. He sets his position as being truth, even if those of an opposing position deny this truth. This position could be seen as invitation to other positions on pedagogy, but it is ultimate in that it assumes the Reformed vision has the most to offer.

The question "What is man?" is an important one for Bavinck and for pedagogy. His asking of the question and also "What does it mean to be human?" represents a much deeper thinking through pedagogy than what is

---

[90] Brederveld, *Christian Education*, 47.
[91] Ibid., 48.

usually done.[92] Bavinck's framing of this question is reminiscent of the psalmist writing, "What is man that you are mindful of him, or the son of man that you think of him?"

Classical Education in *Pedagogical Principles*

The purpose of *Pedagogical Principles* is to offer some ideas on what the conceptual framework of pedagogy should look like from an informed, Christian position. Bavinck does not offer a complete pedagogical method in this book, but rather offers counterpoints to some of the prevailing ideas of pedagogy in his day. Offering "principles" rightly draws attention to his purpose in this book of offering general principles to be applied in a broad context.

Because Bavinck is using a broad brush when approaching education, classical education in not his primary theme, but it does come up on occasion throughout the work. Just as he does in his article *Classical Education*, Bavinck provides some historical context for classical education. He writes:

> Parallel to humanism, which first revealed itself plainly about the time of the Reformation, and almost simultaneously there arose another force in the philosophic realm, which may be named realism. While the distinctiveness of humanism was a looking backward to the classics of the Romans and especially to those of the Greeks, realism sought its bearings in the present. Humanism concentrated its efforts in the interpreting of books, monuments, and other relics of antiquity, and in seeking after erudition and eloquence.[93]

Whereas humanism looked to the past for its sources, realism looked to the present and future study of nature for its answers. Again, Bavinck's primary critique of realism is he believes that it, more than humanism, looks to man as its primary point of departure. Humanism can also certainly look to man as its place of moral grounding if it is separated from a theological framework. Bavinck goes out of his way on several occasions to critique the realism system of education. In Bavinck's terms, realism thought itself to be the "proud master of the future."[94] Because of this focus on man as the point of departure, the child becomes the focal point of education. Should the child be the center of education? It would certainly seem valid to conjecture that the child is the one who has the most to gain from education. It is the child who takes it upon himself or herself to learn, train, and gain the experience of education. The broader context of Bavinck's castigation of the child being the center of education aids in shedding light upon what he is trying to say:

---

[92] Brederveld, *Christian Education*, 57.
[93] Ibid., 37.
[94] Brederveld, *Christian Education*, 37.

And once born, [under realism] the child should immediately become the centre of education. Not the parents, not the teachers, not the subject matter, not the state or society, but the child alone is centre and norm for the entire scheme of education. The art of educating the child in reality consists in not educating him; the task of education is to insure the child's perfect freedom by exercising a policy of "hands off". Nature also here must help herself; she may not be suppressed but may at best only be led. The so-called defects of children merely seem to be such; they are but the reverse of their good qualities. Hence we are to cease all talk of exhortation, discipline, force punishment, and subjection to obedience. Both home and school must teach the child to live his own, personal, and individual life.[95]

Bavinck states the opposition's point in such a manner to make it sound untenable. In his understanding, educational realism results in a throwing away of any educational tradition in an attempt to meet the desires of the child, whatever they may be. In one sense a child is at the center of education, because it is the child who is being education. Alternatively, in a very real sense, there are deeper things at play than just the child. In Bavinck's neo-Calvinist formulation, the education of the child should lead to the glory of God through the cultural influence of the Christian by means of education. There is a balance between Bavinck's earlier statement that in the Reformed vision, man is made in the image of God in an absolute sense, and making man (or child) an idol or God. For Bavinck, realism removes the child from any type of organic relationship with one's family and society.

For Bavinck, placing man at the center of education also raises problems for understanding the relation of the individual and the state. In practicality, this is the same issue Luther sought to address. Luther's primary argument from a non-religious point of view for the state supporting education was that doing so would produce good citizens capable of taking up public service. Bavinck's critique of their being no organic relation to society in realism is also similar to Luther. Throughout "To the Councilmen" Luther forms an intricate connection between *ecclesia*, *oceonomia*, and *politia*. Bavinck argues that were this radical platform followed the child would feel no obligation to the state, or for that matter anyone outside of himself or herself. He writes, "If man is the final aim in education, and if no other factors help decide this aim, it is, for example, impossible to determine whether education should be directed towards the development of the individual, or to the welfare of society. . . . If it be impossible to reach an agreement, either society will be sacrificed to the individual or the individual to society."[96] There is always a balance of finding where the Christian fits in society, and in this case it is finding the place of the well-educated Christian. Both Bavinck and Luther are trying to avoid extremes in their position. For Luther, his task was to avoid what he saw as the extremes

---

[95] Ibid., 38.
[96] Brederveld, *Christian Education*, 39.

of scholasticism on the one hand and a rejection of all education on the other. For Bavinck, he is attempting to avoid realism which would lead to a position of separation of the child from anything outside of himself or herself.

Luther and Bavinck are in agreement concerning the difference that a Christian orientation makes in education, although Bavinck takes a more conservative stance than even Luther. Luther argued that an education in the Bible and classics is valuable, "even if one had not a soul," because it makes for good citizens in society. Bavinck would most likely take this position as well, but he goes a step further by arguing that the teaching of the Scriptures offers the only firm foundation of absolute truth by which one can teach any particular subject. Because man's sense of perception and knowledge are corrupted by the fall, "God revealed [to] us the right norms in His law and in His gospel showed us the way to remove the sad antinomy in our human existence. And again from this salient all our relationships to our fellow man can be regulated."[97] Bavinck writes, "Therefore, we demand a place of honor in our schools for the Bible, the Christian religion, and dogma."[98] As stated at the beginning of this section, one of Bavinck's deepest interests was Bavinck's "concern for man." This concerned is deeply integrated with the sad state of human affairs Bavinck sees apart from the gospel. For Bavinck pedagogy, as with any other discipline, has no firm grounding and is in many ways meaningless apart from the ultimate truth of the gospel.

A Model of Education for Bavinck

From the material that has been thus far discussed, it is clear that a form of classical education is not the only model for which Bavinck is arguing. More important for him are the underlying principles of one's system of education. For him, having a Reformed worldview in which God as creator, rather than man, is at the center of pedagogy and provides pedagogy with its guiding principle. Bavinck writes, "Christianity attracted to itself from every sphere the good, the true, and the beautiful, and in that process was more concerned to preserve the unity of life view than to acquire a variety of material."[99] In this framework Christianity grounds itself in truth, and makes application of that truth in one's worldview. Bavinck's *Pedagogical Principles* is ultimately a textbook for pedagogical principles for *Christian* education. Bavinck goes to great lengths in this book to argue that God, not the child, should be the focal point in education. To cite but one more example of this thesis:

---

[97] Brederveld, *Christian Education*, 99.
[98] Ibid., 103. Bavinck goes on to explain what he means by dogma as that which is objective truth in religion.
[99] Brederveld, *Christian Education*, 88.

It is of fundamental importance to consider one's starting-point in determining the aim of education. Whoever views man in the totality of his relations is capable of arriving at the proper appreciation and differentiation. The result will be that a Christian cannot but view the relation of man and God as central—a relation which education ought most of all to take to heart, also in determining the subject matter.[100]

What is the practical application of such a position? Primarily, in the neo-Calvinist context such a belief should create a theologically informed citizenry that attempts to transform culture in all spheres of life.

Thus far this thesis has made an argument that Martin Luther and Herman Bavinck have unique tools to offer Christian theology in regards to the practice of pedagogy. In particular, several emphases of the Lutheran and neo-Calvinist positions have been offered that demonstrate how the Luther or neo-Calvinist educator would perhaps approach pedagogy differently. In addition, a case has been made that the classical education tradition has much to offer the practice of Christian teaching, and both Luther and Bavinck recognized this. A concluding chapter will examine contemporary practices of classical education using the lenses provided by Lutheran and Reformed traditions, and suggest what a return to the sources of Luther and Bavinck could add to these respective traditions.

---

[100] Brederveld, *Christian Education*, 120.

Pedagogy as Theological Praxis

Conclusion: Luther, Bavinck, and Liberal Arts in Practice

This thesis has analyzed the formation of Luther's and Bavinck's theological method while placing particular emphasis upon their writings on education. The conclusion will show how Luther and Bavinck can be interlocutors on the subject of pedagogy and suggest how their thoughts can be relevant to the practical question of how a child should be educated. In particular, this conclusion will provide commentary on some present-day practices of classical education pedagogy in the Lutheran and Reformed traditions, as well as offer insight for what returning to some of the thoughts of Luther and Bavinck regarding classical education could add to the tradition.

As has been discussed, Luther and Bavinck both had an idea of classical education in mind in their formulation of pedagogy. This was much more explicit in Luther, but Bavinck also appreciated what the classical tradition had to offer. For both theologians, classical education was not the only applicable model of education, but one they saw as having a historical precedent and also one that aligned with the Christian tradition. Many contemporary practitioners of classical education appreciate its historical alignment with the Western Christian tradition. Christian classical education is a popular option in both Lutheran and Reformed circles. Prior to further engaging the Lutheran and Reformed traditions in regards to classical education, a brief synopsis will be provided of Luther's and Bavinck's contributions to pedagogy as detailed in the four chapters of this thesis.

As examined in chapter one, the three estates were an important part of Luther's theology. *Ecclesia* involves man's relation to God, *oeconomia* involves the human's relation to other humans and the world around him or her, and *politia* involves the human's relation to the state. *Ecclesia* and *oeconomia* are prelapsarian estates in which man has been given the ability to freely participate. *Politia* is a postlapsarian estate, and Luther is ambiguous towards its place in creation. In some of his writings it is a necessary evil that restrains humans from falling into worse kinds of evil. At other times Luther views the state as a God ordained entity for which the Christian should be thankful.

In regards to education, the estates play an important role in Luther's letter, "To the Councilmen of all Cities in Germany that they Establish and Maintain

Christian Schools."[1] In particular, Luther incorporates the concept of vocation into education, and places it within a theological framework. God has provided humans with a vocation through which they may worship God and love and serve their fellow man. Luther also stresses the importance of biblical languages in his pedagogy. This leads him to a position where he views classical education as best suited to provide a student with the type of education that can lead one to a knowledge of God as well as benefit society. Luther makes his case to the councilmen that Christians who know the Bible and have received the type of education for which he is advocating are best equipped to serve in the *politia*. Luther also advocates for educational opportunities to be universally provided for boys and girls, as education will benefit both sexes.

Whereas Luther is taking the existing structure of classical education and altering it to a Christian form of classical education that meets his needs, Bavinck's pedagogy he puts forward ideas of what a Christian education should look like while also reacting against other forms of pedagogy. In particular, he reacts against a kind of pragmatism which places primary emphasis upon the child.

Bavinck's pedagogy is also heavily influenced by the Dutch neo-Calvinist tradition. In particular, the doctrine of creation is influential in the broader picture of his theology. The cultural mandate of Genesis 1:28 leads the neo-Calvinist to a position in which the Christian is best equipped to influence all spheres of life in God's created order. Therefore, in Bavinck's advocacy of pedagogy he is also arguing for a theological foundation so that the Christian may be equipped to defend the faith and influence culture. Ultimately, the Lutheran position is one that focuses upon God as gift-giver and understands man as gift-receiver in *ecclesia*, whereas the focus of the neo-Calvinist position is one in which man is created to go into the world and influence it to the glory of God. The next section will examine some of the correlations between classical education and the Reformed tradition.

Classical Education and the Reformed Tradition

A revival of classical education in evangelical circles in North America has influenced a variety of Christian traditions. Classical education has not only effected grade-school education, but has also led to the establishment of Christian undergraduate programs based upon the liberal arts tradition as well as classical Christian grade schools.[2] Although it is not always explicitly stated,

---

[1] Martin Luther, "To the Councilmen of All Cities in Germany that they Establish and Maintain Christian Schools," LW 46: 341–378.
[2] Since the thrust of both Bavinck's and Luther's work on education examined in this thesis focuses upon grade school pedagogy, that will also be the focus of this section. The following United States universities offer degree programs using a classical

many contemporary proponents rely on the Dutch neo-Calvinist tradition examined particularly in chapter three in forming their views concerning why one should offer a Christian classical education. Many who follow this stream have relied much more heavily upon the writings of Kuyper as compared to Bavinck. As chapter four made clear, Bavinck has much to offer Reformed theology in terms of pedagogy, but it is Kuyper who is usually looked to in terms of educational reform. I offer a variety of considerations as to why this is the case. 1) Kuyper's account of a Reformed Christian "worldview" has become an extremely popular concept taken up by many American evangelicals. Bavinck also thought in terms of a worldview, but Kuyper popularized the idea. To use the term "worldview" to describe one's beliefs about reality is no longer limited to those explicitly in the Reformed tradition, but is popular in many circles. This discussion began primarily through the writings of Francis Schaeffer,[3] and many evangelical traditions today would think it second nature to speak of forming a Christian worldview. Bavinck and Kuyper believed that a Reformed worldview could encapsulate all areas of life, and therefore strove for an academically robust and defensible form of Christianity. 2) While Bavinck's work was not particularly popular among Americans outside of the Calvin College setting due to much of his work being unavailable in English, much more of Kuyper's work was available throughout the twentieth century. Kuyper's 1898 Stone Lectures, delivered at Princeton University, in which he laid out his vision of a Calvinist worldview was widely available to the English speaking public. These Stone Lectures, published simply as *Calvinism* or *Lectures on Calvinism*,[4] served as an introduction to Kuyper's other work as it became available in English. Although Bavinck also delivered a Stone Lecture series a decade later in 1908 and 1909 under the title *Philosophy of Revelation*,[5] it did not possess the lay-level, innovating fire that Kuyper's lectures delivered. Even today, Kuyper's *Calvinism* is a seminal text that is perhaps the most quoted work in Kuyper studies, whereas Bavinck's *Philosophy of Revelation* is usually a secondary text after his more popular *Reformed Dogmatics* (in which a complete volume has only been made available in English in the past decade). 3) Kuyper's rejection of "secular"

---

education and/or a Great Texts approach: George Wythe University, Cedar City, UT; St. John's College, campuses in Annapolis MD and Santa Fe, NM; Thomas Aquinas College, Santa Paula, CA; New Saint Andrews College, Moscow, ID; The Torrey Honors Institute at Biola University, La Mirada, CA; Patrick Henry College, Purcellville, VA; Gutenberg College, Eugene OR; The College at Southeastern, Wake Forest, NC; Shimer College, Chicago IL; The Honors College at Baylor University, Waco TX; Imago Dei College, Oak Glen, CA; St. Mary's College of California, Morago, CA; Wyoming Catholic College, Lander, WY; The King's College, NY, NY.

[3] Francis Schaeffer, *The Complete Works of Francis Schaeffer: A Christian Worldview*, 5 vols. (Wheaton: Crossway, 1985).

[4] Abraham Kuyper, *Lectures on Calvinism* (Grand Rapids: Eerdmans, 1943).

[5] Herman Bavinck, *The Philosophy of Revelation: The Stone Lectures for 1908–1909, Princeton Theological Seminary* (London: Longmans, Green and Co., 1909).

modes of thinking as outlined in chapter three in favor of Christian versus secular scholarship was much more palatable for twentieth century evangelicals who were attempting to offer an alternative to secular education. Kuyper was able to draw an antithesis between Christian and non-Christian scholarship. In his *Encyclopedia of Sacred Theology*,[6] he took this even further by separating Christian and non-Christian science. As the fundamentalist movement became more concerned with separation from secular thinking rather than academic engagement with it,[7] this antithesis of Christian and non-Christian thinking became a popular idea. Although Bavinck was quite clear that he believed the Reformed faith was best suited to understand the world, he did not tend to do so in a divisive manner. Throughout his career Bavinck interacted with the modern world in an open and honest fashion, beginning in his university days at Leiden.[8] For the moment at least the more sectarian vision of Kuyper has won the day.

Despite these successes, many of Kuyper's views about science and education are deficient, as has been indicated in chapter three. In particular, his antithesis between Christian and secular science formed an unnecessary dichotomy within a unified view of knowledge. Through this separation, he eliminated the organic integration of knowledge for which he was originally striving. For these reasons, one of the purposes of this section will also be to offer an analysis and critique of ways in which Reformed liberal arts education is viewed today, as well as offer what Bavinck's vision of education can give to the contemporary liberal arts debate. Before engaging further in this discussion, it would prove helpful to ask why one would think that a Christian classical education would be the appropriate route for one's child.

There are a variety of reasons why some Christians believe a classical education will best suit their children, and some of these have been discussed throughout the thesis. As noted in the introduction, Douglas Wilson viewed the

---

[6] Abraham Kuyper, *Encyclopedia of Sacred Theology* (London: Hodder and Stoughton, 1899).

[7] Early fundamentalists such as J. Gresham Machen affirmed a distinction between Christian and secular culture, but were more academically rigorous than what became American fundamentalism. For a solid introduction to the beliefs in the fundamentals which eventually led to American Christian fundamentalism see, R. A. Torrey, ed. *The Fundamentals*, 2 vols. (Grand Rapids: Baker, 2003). This was originally published in four volumes in 1909.

[8] Willem DeWit, *On the Way to the Living God: A Cathartic Reading of Herman Bavinck and An Invitation to Overcome the Plausibility Crisis of Christianity* (Amsterdam: VU University Press, 2011). The book is a major recent volume in Bavinck studies that demonstrates this struggle of faith that Bavinck wrestled with throughout his career beginning in his university career at Leiden. Particularly insightful are DeWit's English translations of correspondence Bavinck kept with his theologically liberal leaning, life-long friend Snouck Hurgronje.

declining and de-Christianizing of the American public school as primary reasons for advocating classical education. Both of these impulses are also driven by a preparation for engagement with culture. Most forms of evangelical Christianity have moved beyond a complete separation of culture, and now focus more upon education providing a means by which a son or daughter can be prepared for life outside the home upon graduation. This shift can perhaps best be seen in the proliferation of degrees available from American schools that had traditionally been seen strictly a "Bible college." One can now earn a degree in nursing, law, business and various other subjects from a university traditionally associated with conservative forms of evangelical Christianity in North America. This trend in part attests to a Christian foundation for learning being validated by the academics that teach at such institutions and the students who choose to attend such schools.

The Association of Christian Classical Schools is a primary source for understanding the role Christian classical education is currently playing in the North American context. Quoting the ACCS mission statement at length will be helpful in understanding their purpose:

The primary mission of this association is to promote, establish, and equip schools committed to a classical approach to education in the light of a Christian worldview grounded in the Old and New Testament Scriptures. The mission of the association is both to promote the classical approach, and provide accountability for member schools to ensure that our cultural heritage is not lost again. This mission will be accomplished through the work of the Association of Classical and Christian Schools. Through these various means, ACCS seeks to set an educational standard for a unified and directed approach to classical and Christian learning.

Our mission is also to equip schools in teaching such subjects through the methodology known as the Trivium (grammar, logic, and rhetoric), the educational foundation of our Western culture. We believe that God will bless this approach as He has in the past, as long as it follows the principles set forth in his Word.

We recognize that Christ was born in the reign of Caesar Augustus, and that Christianity took root and grew to maturity in the West. For this reason, we believe that we must teach certain subjects so that they are understood and appreciated. This includes ancient history, languages, and culture, studied in the light of biblical Christianity and its impact on western culture. We recognize our cultural heritage as a gift from God, but in seeking to restore that heritage we by no means are intending to idolize it. Therefore, we ground all that we seek to do upon the revelation of God, both in creation and in Scripture, with the former being interpreted by the latter. The triune God of Scripture has created an ordered universe, which can only be fully known through an orderly submission to His revelation of Himself in Scripture. As

Christian schools, we are seeking to equip member schools to integrate all their teaching around the revealed Word of God.[9]

A variety of important points come to light in this mission statement. ACCS is an interdenominational organization that accepts affiliation of any schools promoting a Christian form of classical education. The mission statement begins with classical education as a given, and then applies a theological structure upon pedagogy. To the writers of the mission statement, this is an obvious combination. Each of the paragraphs of this mission statement also tries to ground its position in tradition. It sees it as a historical providence that Christianity grew in the midst of Western civilization. Since most Christian classical schools tend to be conservative theologically and take a theological stance in which it is the role of the Christian to be a light in a dark culture, it would seem odd that Christian classical schools would so openly adopt a non-Judeo-Christian tradition as the foundation of Christian pedagogy. The justification for this can be traced related to the Dutch neo-Calvinist understanding of common grace, by which secular forms of thinking contain truth that can be beneficial to the Christian.

Though it may not be realized, the tradition of Dutch neo-Calvinism is often used in reconciling the tension between a Christian worldview and secular knowledge for many practitioners of classical Christian education. In one of the more articulate contemporary works on Christian classical education,[10] Littlejohn and Evans allude to Kuyper's Dutch Neo-Calvinsim on several occasions. Littlejohn and Evans use neo-Calvinism's understanding of common grace as the answer to why it is an acceptable Christian practice to use the ancient liberal arts as foundational to Christian education. The authors write, "The inheritance from the ancients of the arts, along with philosophical truths, were understood to be the result of God's common grace by which he allowed the discovery (not the invention) of truth by the regenerate and nonregenerate image-bearer alike."[11] Although the term "common grace" is theologically anachronistic to the point the authors are trying to make, their goal is to state that all humans can know universal truth. Under the banner of common grace one is able to provide justification for the use of the ancients in pedagogy. In many ways this argument is similar to that made by Clement in *Stromata*[12] as discussed in the introduction. Whereas Clement argued that grace was given to the Jews in order to prepare for the coming of Christ, Littlejohn and Evans

---

[9] Association of Classical Christian Schools Mission Statement. Retrieved from: www.accsedu.org/Mission_Statement.ihtml?id=36663 [Accessed December 7, 2012]
[10] Robert Littlejohn and Charles T. Evans, *Wisdom and Eloquence: A Christian Paradigm for Classical Learning* (Wheaton: Crossway, 2006).
[11] Ibid., 33.
[12] Clement of Alexandria, *Stromateis: Books One to Three*, trans. John Ferguson (Washington, D.C.: The Catholic University of America Press, 1991).

make the case that it is by God's providence that the knowledge gained by the Greeks and Romans has been passed on to the Christian tradition.

In addition to the Greeks and Romans as sources of inspiration in the classical tradition, Littlejohn and Evans also point to one of the most cited works of the church fathers in support of classical education: Augustine's *On Christian Doctrine*.[13] They write:

> Augustine explained in his landmark work *On Christian Doctrine* that the linguistic arts unlocked the treasures of truth contained in the Scriptures. He saw grammar as being the key to understanding the languages of the texts, dialectic the means to their hermeneutical interpretation, and rhetoric the guide for dialogue, leading to the cyclical deepening of understanding of the wisdom and beauty of the Creator's self-revelation. The mathematical arts, likewise, drew the human soul heavenward and attuned the mind to fathoming the deep things of God, including order and immutability.[14]

Here Littlejohn and Evans go a step further: earlier classical education was a sign of God's common grace, and now it has become a means by which God has made himself known in the Scriptures through the study of the trivium. Augustine does see a use in the liberal arts for understanding the Scriptures. For instance, in his explanation of the use of dialectics (logic) Augustine writes, "The science of reasoning is of very great service in searching into and unraveling all sorts of questions that come up in Scripture, only in the use of it we must guard against the love of wrangling, and the childish vanity of trapping an adversary."[15] Thomas Korcok provides an excellent summation of Augustine's position on the liberal arts:

> Augustine believed that the purpose of education was to direct the student to disengage himself from less noble goals and turn inward to pursue the truth that lies within. He believed that divine illumination could be attributed to the indwelling of Christ. In, *On the School Master*, Augustine said, 'Our real Teacher is he who is listened to, who is said to dwell in the inner man, namely Christ, that is the unchangeable power and the eternal wisdom of God. To this wisdom every rational souls gives heed.' This understanding of the indwelling of truth is a key concept in Augustine's view of the liberal arts within a Christian educational framework. As a student was educated in the arts, Christ was at work in that student revealing wisdom and truth. Early on, Augustine had an optimistic view that, if the liberal arts were properly used, they could lead a person to a knowledge of things eternal, and of the true wisdom that was manifest in Christ Jesus. As Augustine matured as a theologian, he began to take a more limited view of what the liberal arts could accomplish. The epistles of Paul, particularly the Letter to the Romans, convinced

---

[13] Augustine, *On Christian Doctrine*, vol. 2 of The Nicene and Post-Nicene Fathers, ed. Philip Schaff (Grand Rapids: Eerdmans, 1977), 513–597.
[14] Littlejohn and Evans, *Wisdom and Eloquence*, 33.
[15] Augustine, *On Christian Doctrine*, 550.

Augustine that a saving knowledge of God could only come through Christ as He revealed himself in the Scriptures. By the time he completed *On Christian Doctrine* in 426, he came to realize that the gap between the infinite and righteous God on the one hand, and finite sinful man on the other, was too great to be bridged by the liberal arts.[16]

Luther and Bavinck would both see the significance in this position. The liberal arts are valuable in themselves, but cannot lead to salvific knowledge of Christ apart from revelation. Ultimately, a well-rounded liberal arts education should not be the goal of Christian classical education. Rather, Christian classical education should aid the Christian on a journey in understanding the truth that God has revealed concerning himself in the Scriptures and in the world.

Further, Littlejohn and Evans specifically point to the concept of worldview as formed by Kuyper and popularized by Francis Schaeffer in the latter half of the twentieth century as foundational for how one should approach learning and education.[17] The authors quote Kuyper's most famous statement taken from his Princeton lectures which climaxes in a brief summation of his doctrines of creation, common grace, sphere sovereignty and worldview:

> So what can educators do to shape or *overcome* a child's developing worldview. Well, when enculturation is purposeful or *active*, we call it *formation*, and we, as educators, need to be about the work of spiritual, cultural, and intellectual formation. Again, formation goes beyond teaching. It includes both *paideia* (formal instruction) and the *nouthesia* of Ephesians 6: 4. It is through formation that we can help reduce our students' susceptibility to the dualism that plagues so many Christians, causing us to separate our religious life from our everyday life. Such formation occurs when children learn (every day) how Christianity, the Bible, and God himself are integral to *everything*. As Kuyper said: 'God looks out across the whole of creation and says, 'there is not one thumb's breadth of it that is not Mine''—not the physical world; not the spiritual world; not history, science or spelling; not literature, art, or math; not governments, cultures, or societies. It is all his, and we must help our students internalize this enduring truth.[18]

Several crucial points come to light in this quotation. First, Littlejohn and Evans view this version of sphere sovereignty as a universal truth that adds precedent to the Christian's use of the ancient educational tradition. Second is the articulation of worldview. Bavinck saw experience as a form of education. Littlejohn and Evans recognize that a worldview is being formed in a child

---

[16] Thomas Korcok, *Lutheran Education: From Wittenberg to the Future* (Saint Louis: Concordia Publishing House, 2011), 12.
[17] Littlejohn and Evans, *Wisdom and Eloquence*, 43.
[18] Littlejohn and Evans, *Wisdom and Eloquence*, 44–45.

whether it is intentional or not. The goal of the parent is to teach the child in such a manner that will be formative for the child.

A third way Littlejohn and Evans use common grace is in their expression for what audience classical education would be appropriate. As some relation to Christianity has been assumed thus far when discussing the Christian's use of classical education, the question would naturally arise as to whether the Christian espousing classical education would view classical education as appropriate pedagogy for all humans. Littlejohn and Evans use common grace as a way to universalize classical education to both the follower of Christ and the non-believer: "Though we believe that the true knowledge of God and his ways is only accessible through faith, God's grace and mercy extend to all in some way (by God's common grace). Those who do not express personal faith in Christ are still able to reap the communal benefits of the gospel. . . . A related question is, for what kind of student is a liberal arts education designed? Our answer is simple: virtually any and all."[19] The authors would still certainly maintain that the nature of Christian classical education is not salvific knowledge. At the same time, exposure to truth as expressed in a Christian worldview could lead the student to desire further knowledge of the Trinitarian God and his created world that is the focus of study.

The authors provide an open picture of education for those who are of a family of faith as well as those who are not. This is a very different picture from forms of isolationist Christianity. The revival of Christian classical learning could also be seen as a reaction against the more isolating forms of fundamentalism that arose in the early twentieth century. It was previously mentioned how the early twentieth century reaction to the modern world that became fundamentalism resulted in an anti-intellectual reaction to secular thinking. In Mark Noll's excellent work, *The Scandal of the Evangelical Mind*, he makes the case that fundamentalism caused American evangelicals in the early twentieth century to retreat from open academic dialogue with differing views.[20] Noll acknowledges that while Christian fundamentalism held to some doctrines central to the Christian faith,[21] it produced at least three byproducts of its anti-intellectual culture:

---

[19] Ibid., 68–69.
[20] Mark Noll, *The Scandal of the Evangelical Mind* (Grand Rapids: Eerdmans, 1994). Though fundamentalism is discussed throughout the book, particular attention should be paid to 114–139.
[21] It is important to bifurcate the concept of "fundamentalism" into two groups. There were those who represented ideological fundamentalism in the late nineteenth and early twentieth century such as dispensationalists and those who argued for adhering to the "fundamentals" of the faith. The first group held to a literalist interpretation of the Bible that often led to separation from the larger culture. The five fundamentals were: the inspiration and inerrancy of the Bible, the virgin birth of Christ, the belief in Christ's

Pedagogy as Theological Praxis

1. It provided momentum to general anti-intellectualism through its reaction against naturalist philosophy and liberal forms of Christianity.
2. It firmed the commitments that conservative evangelicals had to some features of nineteenth-century evangelical-American synthesis that were already problematic (such as dispensationalism).
3. Its major emphasis stymied the exercise of Christian thinking about the world.[22]

As evangelicals have become aware of errors made from approximately the turn of the twentieth century through the end of World War II by the fostering of anti-intellectualism, there has been a revival of an intellectually robust expression of evangelical Christianity. In the Reformed expression this has in part been revived through the cultural mandate concept as expressed by Kuyper. In this tradition it is the duty of the Christian to understand the workings of the world to the glory of God. Kuyper's antithesis of Christian versus anti-Christian thinking was largely given up in favor of other emphases in Dutch neo-Calvinist theology, such as common grace and the cultural mandate.

The attempt at a more robust form of Christianity that Noll describes has a close relation to the revival of Bavinck studies. Part of the recovery of returning to an intellectual tradition is seeing what the past has to offer current practices. Through the work of the Dutch Reformed Translation Society, a mostly untapped source by the Anglophone community of evangelical heritage is being made available, particularly through the translating of Herman Bavinck's work. Bavinck offered an intellectually robust form of Christianity that desired to interact openly and honestly with the world around it through using the tools afforded by the Reformed faith. This is important because Bavinck did not deploy an antithesis between sacred and secular thinking, as did Kuyper. This allows for a more organic means of interaction with truth and knowledge as God has placed it in the world.

An excellent recent example of this sort of Christianity that wishes to return to an intellectually robust form of Christianity is the book series edited by David Dockery entitled "Reclaiming the Christian Intellectual Tradition." The series title itself reveals that the editor and writers believe that there is some type of tradition that should again be laid claim to by intellectually robust Christians. Dockery writes that the purpose of the series is to, "prepare a generation of Christians to think Christianly, to engage the academy and the culture, and to serve church and society. We believe that both the breadth and depth of the Christian intellectual tradition need to be reclaimed, revitalized,

---

death as the atonement for sin, the bodily resurrection of Jesus, and a literal interpretation of Christ's miracles.

[22] Noll, *The Scandal of the Evangelical Mind*, 115.

Conclusion: Luther, Bavinck and Liberal Arts in Practice

renewed, and revived for us to carry forward this work."[23] In particular, Gene Fant's book in this series, *The Liberal Arts: A Student's Guide*,[24] makes the case for why a student would (or should) be interested in studying the liberal arts in an undergraduate curriculum. Although this series, and this book in particular, take a broader evangelical position rather than a particularly Lutheran or Reformed position, there are several points in this book that express how American evangelicals are thinking about the topic of the liberal arts in regards to one's education. Fant argues that at the heart of a Christian liberal arts education should be the freedom (*libera*) that is given through learning. This is a theme that has persisted throughout the classical tradition in which education can free one to perform a variety of tasks for the good of self and the good of society at large. Although this idea of freedom is linked in both religious and secular expressions of classical education, Fant adds a religious aspect to the idea in his quoting from the Westminster Catechism in support of his position: "What is the chief and highest end of man? Man's chief and highest end is to glorify God, and enjoy him forever."[25] Fant writes, "The same [question of the catechism as quoted above] may be asked of any human endeavor, including education. The primary purpose of education is the glorification of God. The glorification of God typically finds an overflow in the edification of his people, whether the people of faith or humanity as a created race."[26] In this framework, learning of any type should serve as a means to glorify God, and Fant applies this specifically to the practice of the liberal arts. Fant's move in application of this aspect of the Westminster Catechism is certainly taking a lead from the work of Kuyper and Bavinck in applying a Reformed worldview to all areas of life.

One may gather that the classical tradition and the neo-Calvinist tradition are therefore taken to naturally fit well together. In the cultural mandate the human is called to use his or her abilities to excel in whatever path God has called him or her. The classical education tradition has a definite emphasis upon producing critically thinking and competent students. As stated earlier, Bavinck also recognized the importance that cultural expression plays in relation to Christianity. The classical tradition has been able to effectively adapt itself to a variety of cultures, which is certainly one of its benefits.

---

[23] David Dockery, "Introduction," Gene C. Fant Jr., *The Liberal Arts: A Student's Guide*, Reclaiming the Christian Intellectual Tradition (Wheaton: Crossway, 2012), 14.
[24] Gene C. Fant Jr., *The Liberal Arts: A Student's Guide*, Reclaiming the Christian Intellectual Tradition (Wheaton: Crossway, 2012).
[25] Westminster Larger Catechism, http://www.reformed.org/documents/index.html?mainframe=http://www.reformed.org/documents/larger1.html [Accessed December 7, 2012].
[26] Fant, *The Liberal Arts: A Student's Guide*, 19.

In regards to Dutch neo-Calvinist expressions of education, perhaps the most well-known neo-Calvinist educational institution in the United States is that of Calvin College in Grand Rapids, Michigan. This school is associated with the Christian Reformed Church, which holds ties with the Dutch Reformed church in the Netherlands. In 1920 the college became a four-year liberal arts college to follow the pattern set by Abraham Kuyper at the Free University of Amsterdam. Calvin College has also long been the center of Bavinck studies in the Anglophone world. While this college has not emphasized classical education, it has emphasized producing individuals who could attempt to fulfill Kuyper's words, "There is not a square inch in the whole domain of our human existence over which Christ, who is Sovereign over all, does not cry: 'Mine!'"[27] In this statement he promotes Christian engagement in all spheres of knowledge. A desire such as this to transform culture combined with a practical system of education found in classical education form a good match for the classical tradition. Lutheran theologian Robert Benne notes how Calvin College has historically bucked the trend of many other colleges of its time by maintaining its Christian intellectual heritage. He writes:

> Calvin College, for example, never succumbed to the replacement of the Christian account with the American or Enlightenment. Indeed, it had enough confidence in the Reformed version of the Christian account to continue to use it as the organizing vision of its life and mission. It also had enough philosophical sophistication to be suspicious of exclusive Enlightenment claims. It did not do obeisance to them. On the contrary, the college did 'worldview analysis' of the presuppositions involved in many secular approaches to knowledge. . . . Even as Calvin College took seriously the intellectual dimension of the Reformed tradition, it also attended to the spiritual and moral dimensions of that stream of the larger Christian tradition. As a Reformed institution, the college believed in the transformation of its students and its social surroundings, as well as the knowledge it offered them. There is, according to Calvin, a definable Christian 'way of life' that can be communicated to its students through many sorts of practices. These efforts at transformation permeate the institutional life of the college. No area of life is 'unclaimed for Christ,' to put it in the words of the college's progenitor, Abraham Kuyper.[28]

Benne notes that what primarily set Calvin apart in the twentieth century was its ability to hold on to its evangelical heritage for both the intellectual and spiritual development of its students. This is a vital aspect of theological education in the Reformed tradition. A Christian account of classical education must be able to spark the mind towards intellectual curiosity while also providing means by which the spiritual life of the one being taught may be nurtured as well.

---

[27] Abraham Kuyper, "Sphere Sovereignty," 466.
[28] Robert Benne, *Reasonable Ethics: A Christian Approach to Social, Economic, and Political Concerns* (Saint Louis: Concordia Publishing House, 2005), 221–222.

Conclusion: Luther, Bavinck and Liberal Arts in Practice

As mentioned earlier, it has been primarily Kuyper, not Bavinck who has been looked to as a source for of inspiration for pedagogy. It would therefore be appropriate to conclude this section with offering some ways in which Bavinck's work can aid the Reformed pedagogue. As has already been discussed through interaction with Mark Noll's work, there has been a revival of sorts in evangelical circles that has attempted to return to some of the intellectual prowess formerly associated with evangelical Christianity. Bavinck has much to offer this tradition. Bavinck combined an academic mind that sought to be a scholar in his field with a robust theology that emphasized renewal of the inner man. Such an approach is one that is desired by many in the classical education movement, and seeing how this is done by Bavinck can aid the movement. In many ways this is the tradition left by Calvin College in their use of Bavinck. Bavinck's focus upon the organic can also be helpful. Medieval proponents of classical education emphasized the interrelation of the liberal arts. In the same manner, Bavinck's use of the organic can add to the student's understand of different fields of knowledge all flow from the same creator. In his review of Bavinck's philosophy of education, Jaarsma writes, "If the object of knowledge is organic, it has inherent as well as instrumental value. The facts of history and the facts of science constitute more than so much information to be used in the effective control of one's environment. They have value in themselves, are treasures to be possessed as well as tools to be used. Enrichment of the human spirit in the possession of the truth is as significant as the enrichment of life in the operation of thinking in action."[29] An organic understanding of knowledge allows one to see the value of the one and the many in regards to education. The organic also represents how Christian thought can be foundational as well as integrated throughout a curriculum. Jaarsma writes, "Bavinck in harmony with his entire organic philosophy looks upon the entire curriculum as an organic whole in which religious education has the central place."[30] Religious education for Bavinck is the foundation through which other forms of education flow.

Contemporary Lutheranism and Classical Education

Now that a structure of Reformed education has been made with emphasis upon the work of Bavinck, this section will provide application for Lutheran classical education. The Association of Classical and Christian Schools was mentioned earlier, but there is also a cognate organization for Lutheran Schools called the "Consortium for Classical and Lutheran Education." This organization looks to Luther's "To The Councilmen" as a starting place for understanding how Lutheran classical education should be practiced today. John Hill, Pastor and Headmaster of Mount Hope Lutheran Church and School provides a brief

---

[29] Cornelius Jaarsma, *The Educational Philosophy of Herman Bavinck: A Textbook in Education* (Grand Rapids: Eerdmans, 1935), 204.
[30] Ibid., 159.

exposition of "To the Councilmen." His primary emphasis is upon Luther's call for reform of the educational system, his recommendation of the seven liberal arts, and his use of the Bible as the primary text of study.[31] The CCLE believes that what makes a Lutheran classical education Lutheran is the theological orientation of the teachers. One of the hallmarks of Lutheran classical education is that Lutheran classical schools will often be connected to a local parish or ecclesiastical structure, whereas the majority of classical Christian schools in the US are not linked to a particular church or denomination. Other than an emphasis upon being catechal and confessional, there is little that separates CCLE's statements on faith and the role of the educator from those of the AACS.[32]

Robert Benne, who was earlier referenced for his pointing to Calvin College as an example of a robust Reformed intellectual heritage, also draws a distinction between how Lutheran and Reformed expressions of education differ:

> Contrary to the Reformed approach, a Lutheran college does not give an automatic privilege to the Christian worldview, which in the end can 'trump' the other ways of knowing. Contrary to the Catholic approach, which sees all knowledge rising to a synthesis organized by Catholic wisdom, the Lutheran approach lives with more messiness. But it respects those models of Christian humanism and finds itself closer to them than to the modern secular tendency to marginalize and sequester into irrelevancy the Christian view of life and reality.[33]

Benne's point is that the Lutheran vision of education offers a unique emphasis while also sharing much in common with other expressions of Christian education.

Many emphases of Luther's thought have also become second nature to educational thinkers today. For instance, most educators would not question the idea of mandatory education for children, yet this was a radical idea that Luther proposed.[34] The theological concept of the priesthood of all believers also

---

[31] Retrieved from www.ccle.org/index.php/rightsidenav/lutherquotes [Accessed December 7, 2012].

[32] See The Consortium for Classical and Lutheran Education, "Marks of a Lutheran and Classical School (CCLE Position Statement)," *The Classical Education Quarterly* 1:2 (June 2007): 10–11.

[33] Benne, *Reasonable Ethics*, 237.

[34] It must also be noted that a strict view of the *politia*, rather than the *oeconomia*, being the primary vehicle through which education is practiced can have negative consequences. For instance, it is currently illegal for German natives to homeschool in Germany. If one believes that the home is the best place to educate a child, then there are no means by which to perform this type of pedagogy. Parents could potentially choose this route for a variety of reasons (fear of secular worldview influence, belief in

influenced Luther's push to have all classes of citizens, as well as both men and women receive an education.[35]

Just as Luther does in "To the Councilmen," Lutheran classical educators openly accept the classical model as being appropriate to the Christian faith. Lutherans have done much better than other traditions in maintaining classical education as a viable pedagogical form. Anthony Splittgerber provides a short explanation as to why this is the case: "Its (classical education) core philosophies are highly compatible with Christian teachings; consequently, many Christian schools have embraced classical education, even though classical education is not just for Christian schools."[36] Many Lutheran classical education proponents are aware of Luther's promotion of classical education, and therefore have a historical precedent by which to promote it today.

From this analysis, as well as that from Veith and others, the Lutheran tradition seems to remain aware of the role Luther has played in advocating for education as well as his advocacy of classical education. In regards to the estates, Veith is one of the few who has made a definite connection between what the estates can offer to classical education. Therefore, one could propose some ways in which an emphasis upon and awareness of the estates could enhance the Lutheran vision of classical education.

One of the primary ways in which an emphasis upon the estates can aid Lutheran education is that it begins by pointing to one of the primary emphases of Luther's theology, namely, that mankind is a recipient from God and is dependent upon his grace. In many ways the Lutheran tradition has been able to maintain the connection between *ecclesia* and education.

Lutheran classical education also usually has a much stronger tie to the church than do other expressions of Christian classical education. Littlejohn and Evans adopt an open model in regards to receiving those not necessarily of the Christian faith into their schools. The reason for this is 1) Common grace—God is able to work through the circumstances of what is being taught to perhaps

---

inadequacy of public oversight, desire for more influence in the educational track of the child, etc.). This situation cannot be completely blamed on Luther's later push for education to be primarily the responsibility of the state rather than the parent, but it certainly does not help. Some Germans have been prosecuted for choosing civil disobedience and practicing home schooling. See for instance, http://news.bbc.co.uk/1/hi/education/8576769.stm. [Accessed December 10, 2012].

[35] Marilyn J. Harran, "The Contemporary Applicability of Luther's Pedagogy: Education and Vocation," *Concordia Journal* October (1990): 319.

[36] Anthony B. Splittgerber, "A Research Study: Effects of Classical Education on Achievement in Lutheran Schools," *Classical Lutheran Education Journal* 5 (Sept. 2011): 17.

lead to faith. If one is claiming to teach truth in classical education, then it would benefit those who are Christian or otherwise. 2) An understanding that all truth is of God, and therefore there is not a better situation in which the student should learn.

In contrast, Lutheran education, classical or otherwise, is generally seen as a specifically ecclesial activity. Most Lutheran schools are open to those who are not from a Christian (or Lutheran) background from attending their schools, but there is an explicit connection between church and pedagogy that is not necessarily found in Reformed expressions. The church teaches the truth of God and his world. Pedagogy therefore becomes an activity of the church. There is often a less direct connection between church and pedagogy in the Reformed tradition. The reason may lie in that the Reformed outlook sees itself as infiltrating or recovering lost ground when it approaches classical education, whereas the Lutheran tradition is more comfortable identifying itself with the tradition. This could be in part because Luther himself advocated a classical education in "To the Councilmen." With education being closely tied to *ecclesia*, Lutheran pedagogy is also able to easily incorporate catechesis. Luther's *Small Catechism* was written in 1529 in order for fathers to be able to train their children in the doctrines and beliefs of the church. Hoffman writes, "The *Small Catechism* was, of course, written for laymen and was an abridged version with Scripture references of the *Large Catechism* which was primarily written for clergymen, teachers, and parents. The *Large Catechism* typifies the emphasis Luther placed on the importance of knowledge and understanding of the articles of faith. Luther believed strongly in the biblical directives, given us in Gen. 12:8 and 13:18, that the head of the family was to conduct worship in the home of the faith."[37]

The estates can also aid in one's vision of education in that the estates leads one to understand the value of one's vocation or calling. This value is not found in one's vocation being better than another, but in honoring God in whatever calling one may enter. Marilyn Harran writes, "Education includes both liberation and direction. Through education one realizes one's vocation, learns how best to perform it, and thereby acts as servant in the kingdom of God. In short, education is the means in the short run of realizing one's vocation and in the long run of contributing to the kingdom of God."[38] When the practice of Christian education is tied to an ecclesial structure that is practicing catechesis there is less concern of heterodox theological belief entering the classroom. A

---

[37] Patti Hoffman, "The Where of Education," *Learning at the Foot of the Cross: A Lutheran Vision for Education*, eds. Joel D. Heck and Angus J. L. Menuge (Austin: Concordia University Press, 2011), 160–161.
[38] Harran, "The Contemporary Applicability of Luther's Pedagogy: Education and Vocation," 321.

parent can assume that what is being taught in the classroom is similar to that of the home when this structure exists.

Korcok raises the question of whether catechesis is actually a form of indoctrination, which would undermine the very idea of a liberal arts education. His argument against the catechism in a liberal arts pedagogy being a form of mindless indoctrination is that in reality the catechism should be the opposite: a defense against indoctrination.[39] One of the most profound characteristics of the Reformation was its rejection of accepting Church authority without question. The catechism provides a means by which to understand the basic beliefs of one's tradition and their Scriptural foundation. Korcok writes, "Lutheran catechesis is best described as a life-long nurturing process that endeavors to enable individuals to grow in their identity as Confessional Lutherans."[40] He also notes that the catechism should be closely tied to the whole of the liberal arts education: "In Evangelical pedagogy, the catechical program never stands alone. It is always taught in tandem with the liberal arts, particularly those of the trivium."[41] In this relation he argues that the grammatical arts provide the student with the basics of communication and language, logic with the ability to produce independent thought, and rhetoric with the ability to speak well about the critical thoughts that have been processed.[42] Each of these liberal arts can benefit the mind in the learning and exposition of the catechism.

The spectrum of those who are serving as advocates of reform in pedagogy is much wider in the Reformed tradition in part because there has been no singular figure that has been the primary advocate of education to which the tradition can continually return. As has been previously demonstrated, even within the Dutch Reformed tradition the work of a theological giant such as Bavinck on education has been largely forgotten.

Because of Lutheran education's traditional ties to the liberal arts tradition, this should continue to be an emphasis of Lutheran education. Lutheran education emphasizes the learning of the Scriptures and the tie to *ecclesia* as being an essential part of the educational process. This emphasis should continue as it gives education a much needed emphasis of a liberal arts niche.

The estates are also an important part of Lutheran education because they provide an integrated picture of what education should be. Patti Hoffman writes:

---

[39] Korcok, *Lutheran Education: From Wittenberg to the Future*, 262.
[40] Ibid., 261.
[41] Ibid., 263.
[42] Ibid., 263–264.

> The Lutheran school does not strive to replace parents but rather to partner with parents in the education of their children. The triangular partnership between home, school, and church provides for the education of the whole child. It is still not only the right but the privilege of parents to be the first and most influential educators of their children. It is also the privilege and the responsibility of every member of each Lutheran congregation to make provisions for the education of the children of the congregation. . . . It is the responsibility of every member of the congregation, whether or not that member has children, to provide for the education of the children.[43]

Lutheran education offers a unique integrated picture in which the *ecclesia*, *oeconomia*, and *politia* are all involved in the educational process. Hoffman also emphasizes this education as a privilege and gift of God. Education is a good gift given by God, and the follower of Jesus has the opportunity to respond to, and make the most of that gift.

Another specific emphasis in Luther's educational exhortation in "To the Councilmen" is the learning of the biblical languages. This is a key point for Luther because it points to one of the primary purposes of education: the learning of the Bible. The Reformation freed the laity to study the Scriptures, and for Luther an education should enable one to do so well. An education should enable one to properly fulfill roles in home and society, but this cannot be done as it should be without knowledge of God as revealed in the Scriptures. God reveals himself through speaking creation into existence in the estates, but in a fallen world such fellowship with God is hindered without knowledge of God through the Scriptures. One of the primary foci of classical education is the ability to learn, grasp and apply language. In the learning of the biblical languages for the purpose of understanding the truths of God revealed in the Bible, one is applying the knowledge of the trivium to the Scripture. In grammar, one learns syntax and the basic grammatical rules of a language. In logic one learns how the biblical language fits together in a coherent whole. In rhetoric one is able to teach others the knowledge gained through study of the Bible. It is no wonder Luther thought the classical model appropriate in the application of studying the Bible. Susan Mobley puts it well: "Lutheran education retains the Scriptures at its heart, but also teaches students about the world in which they live.[44]

---

[43] Hoffman, "The Where of Education," 163.
[44] Susan Mobley, "Historical Foundations in the Lutheran Reformation," *Learning at the Foot of the Cross: A Lutheran Vision for Education*, eds. Joel D. Heck and Angus J. L. Menuge (Austin: Concordia University Press, 2011), 21.

Lutheran Classical Education and the Three Estates

None of CCLE's material specifically lists the estates as a source by which one may use to understand Lutheran education. They do list other well-known themes of Lutheran theology such as law and gospel, a theology of the cross, etc. There is the same emphasis of the creating of a worldview in CCLE that one finds elsewhere.

The current de-emphasis upon the estates in Lutheran theology accounts for why it is seldom seen in Lutheran literature on classical education. In their article, "Learning at the Foot of the Cross" Joel Heck and Angus Menuge make a passing reference to the estates and education. Similar to the CCLE statement on education, Heck and Menuge seem to be doing so in the context of listing Lutheran distinctives and why they are important for Lutheran classical education. They write:

> We must understand the nature of taking up our cross, the reality of suffering in a world of sin and the sometimes paradoxical truths of God's nature and His ways of dealing with humankind. We need to filter themes such as leadership, success and service through the lens of Scripture. We need to explore the nature of human beings and develop the whole person for service to the world and to the church. We need to integrate the means of grace (the Word and Sacraments) into our broader education as we develop children of God. We should strive to apply the difficult doctrine of the two kingdoms, two strategies God uses with the same final goal of salvation. Lutheran education should also prepare us for the three estates of family, church and state, emphasizing that it is our vocations in the family, so often neglected in education today, which are foundational for the well-being of church and state.[45]

Susan Mobley implicitly notes that there is a historical link between education and the estates. She writes, "In the view of sixteenth-century Lutherans, then, the schools were a vital part of the Church's mission to preserve and to spread the Gospel. The purpose of Lutheran education, though, was preparing students to serve the Church, the state, the community and their own families. Lutheran education stressed the study of the Scriptures and emphasized certain subjects that helped students to develop skills that would equip them for active service. What the Lutheran educational reformers of the 16th century did was to combine the liberal arts of the medieval scholastics with the humanistic program of the Renaissance."[46]

---

[45] Joel D. Heck and Angus J.L. Menuge, "Learning at the Foot of the Cross," *The Lutheran Witness* (February 2012): http://witness.lcms.org/pages/wPage.asp?ContentID=1208&IssueID=63 [accessed December 7, 2012].

[46] Mobley, "Historical Foundations in the Lutheran Reformation," 20.

Leonard Smith writes that the hallmark of Lutheran education is its ecclesial locus. He writes, "To understand Lutheran education, it is helpful to remember that Martin Luther—like St. Augustine—accepted infant baptism. Since there was no religious test for membership, and since it included everyone in a territory, the Lutheran Church (in the terminology of Ernst Troeltsch) was a church and not a sect. A second general point regarding Lutheran education is that Luther envisioned the church as a communion of true believers who regularly heard the word of God and who regularly, freely, and worthily received the sacrament of the altar."[47] Whereas the Reformed vision of education emphasizes the role of common grace in forming a liberal arts educational scheme, this Lutheran educational vision begins with emphasizing the role of *ecclesia* in education. Baptism brings humans made in the image of God into the body of Christ. Smith's claim that Lutheran education begins with accepting paedobaptism is to say that Lutheran education should have a distinctly ecclesial focus. In "To the Councilmen," one of Luther's primary aims is to convey the need for the learning of biblical of languages in the studying of the Bible. This claim of the Lutheran church as responsible for a territory also explains why it is able to readily appeal to the local secular authorities to promote the training of people in the biblical languages.

There is no necessary correlation between the estates and a specifically classical education. The estates are instituted by God, whereas classical education is but one form of teaching. Even if there is no direct correlation between classical education and the estates, there are several reasons why classical education can be useful to Lutheran theology, and also what the estates can add to a Lutheran vision of classical education. In "To the Councilmen," Luther called for the councilmen to encourage and reform education among the people of Germany because this would produce Christian citizens who love God, and these citizens who function properly in ecclesia, oeconomia and politia. He laid stress upon the type of citizens this would produce in politia as an educated citizenry will better the affairs of the state. Luther advocated for a classical education model that blended humanism with the theological education traditionally taught in the schools associated with the church because he saw the inherent value that a liberal arts classical education could provide in the wake of the potential Renaissance of learning he saw in the recovery of the biblical languages in Christian humanism. The councilmen would have surely seen the value in producing citizens who were able to serve well in a public role because of a liberal arts training that would produce theologically adept citizens who were also could have the opportunity to excel in various other disciplines that best suited the student. There is also a correlation between teaching that points to the Trinitarian portrayal of God and the place God has given to one in

---

[47] Leonard S. Smith, *Martin Luther's Two Ways of Viewing Life and the Educational Foundation of a Lutheran Ethos* (Eugene: Pickwick Publications, 2011), 35.

creation. Luther appropriately thought that the practice of classical education could prepare one for service in family and society.

One of the few pieces written on the relation of Lutheran education and the three estates is in a recent chapter by Gene Veith entitled, "Vocation in Education: Preparing for Our Callings in the Three Estates."[48] Veith's primary purpose in this chapter is to ground Luther's use of the estates in regards to education in his doctrine of vocation.[49] Veith separates the Lutheran doctrine of vocation from its Reformed expression: "Whereas the Reformed vision emphasizes what we are to do in our different callings—and even the Lutheran version deals with the "duties" of the various callings—the most important facet of Luther's understanding is that the different vocations are means through which God works." This vision of vocation does not simply refer to the job one may perform as a means of income. Vocations are primarily something that an individual is called to rather than the contemporary understanding of vocation as something chosen by the individual. Veith writes, "In vocation, God stations us in particular offices and relationships for service. God works through us, blessing others through our work."[50]

Veith uses Luther's doctrine of vocation to demonstrate that for Luther there was no distinction making holy orders and vocations more spiritual than secular vocations. In regards to education, this insight opens what may be studied and for what purpose. Any vocation that is not by its nature immoral could be transformed into a holy calling.

Veith's linking of Luther's understanding of vocation and education to the estates ultimately serves to validate so-called secular careers as perfectly valid forms of service in vocation. This also reorients vocation away from pragmatism and towards serving in vocation for the worship of God. Veith writes:

A school that takes vocation seriously will have a different ethos. It will honor differences among the students, recognizing that each individual's unique talents, interests, and personality are gifts of God and intrinsic to His calling. The school will help students discover these gifts. This will involve giving students many opportunities to try things, to follow up on interests, to go off on tangents. The true vocational school, however, will resist the temptations of

---

[48] Gene Edward Veith, "Vocation in Education: Preparing for Our Callings in the Three Estates," *Learning at the Foot of the Cross: A Lutheran Vision for Education*, eds. Joel D. Heck and Angus J.L. Menuge (Austin: Concordia University Press, 2011).

[49] Luther's use of vocation is an ongoing interest of Veith's. For a longer popular level work of Luther's use of vocation by Veith see, *God at Work: Your Christian Vocation in All of Life* (Wheaton: Crossway, 2002).

[50] Veith, "Vocation in Education: Preparing for Our Callings in the Three Estates," 100.

false pragmatism and servile education, as if the purpose of the school were to train wage-slaves for the economy or to create conformist drones for the mass culture. Rather, an education for God's calling focuses on the cultivation of human beings and the formation of Christians.[51]

Invoking the language of *vocatio* in regards to one's job can change it from a task to be performed for wages into a holy calling of God. It is a modern irony that when thinking of "vocational" schools one usually associates this with the concept of blue collar lower wage work rather than such work as being a calling done in service to God and one's society.

As stressed throughout this thesis, Lutheran education is able to explain why it is acceptable for a student to enter one vocation and not another, and also why one vocation is not necessarily of higher eternal value than another. Angus Menuge writes, "Although all Christians are equal in the sight of God (Gal. 3:28), our differing gifts mean that students will not be equal in their abilities to study various disciplines, and it does not help to disguise this fact by imposing an ideology of egalitarianism, which encourages unrealistic expectations."[52] Lutheran education does not try to masquerade as if all children are equally endowed mentally, but it does encourage the student to use what abilities have been given to him or her by God to use in a vocational calling. This should encourage one towards a robust education, not cause one to shirk away from it.

The idea of vocation is not limited to Lutheran theology, but it is usually not as well developed in other circles. For instance, in *The Liberal Arts* Fant states that there is an important connection between vocation and liberal learning. Fant's primary purpose in making this distinction is to fight the pragmatic temptation of education simply being a means of preparing one for an occupation. Though the fight against pragmaticism is helpful (as was done by Bavinck), Fant's theological rationale is somewhat less developed in regards to vocation as compared to the Lutheran vision. Fant writes:

> In current usage, 'vocational training' is equivalent to 'practical education,' but this is not historically the case. Most Christians have a clear sense of the importance of the term *calling* for their faith. Since I work with college students, I hear this question a great deal: 'What is God's calling on my life?' The Latin equivalent to *calling* came through the term *vocare*, 'to call,' which is root of the English *vocation*. A truly vocational education is one that understands the role of God's call on our lives, whether we are professional Christians or clergy or lay persons who view the work of our hands as a direct gift of God. From Samuel's 'here I am'

---

[51] Ibid.
[52] Angus Menuge, "Citizens and Disciples," *Learning at the Foot of the Cross: A Lutheran Vision for Education*, eds. Joel D. Heck and Angus J.L. Menuge (Austin: Concordia University Press, 2011), 55.

responses (1 Samuel 3) to Peter's and Andrew's answer to Christ's invitation to follow him (Matt. 4:17–19), the biblical record makes it clear that all Christ followers are to view their lives as dependent on a sensitivity to God's will.[53]

When considering the estates, this "sensitivity to God's will" can be stated more directly as submission to the call of God and the claim of Christ upon one's life. The estates focus on one's role in obedient worship as well as one's function in family and state.

The liberal arts education has usually been thought of as a means to free one intellectually to achieve one's goals in the world. As discussed in the first chapter, Oswald Bayer's work, *Freedom in Response* provides a strong link between ethics and the estates. He writes in the introduction, "The fundamental premise of these essays on theological ethics is that human freedom is the result of God's promise: 'I am your God. And therefore you are my people.'"[54] The estates call one to recognize the Triune God as the one who ultimately provides freedom in the granting of life and the unsolicited calling of a particular people. Freedom in the liberal arts is granted a higher purpose when this freedom is given a theological impetus. Bayer further writes, "They [the essays in this book] see the point of theology and its associated ethics as being defined by *promise*. At the same time, the concept of freedom functions as a vital concept to convey that principle of promise. Viewed from the standpoint of its history and its semantic range, *freedom* is most eminently suited to give rise to a fruitful debate about the truth of Christian faith and life."[55] Classical education and the liberal arts has the potential to free one to a variety of tasks, but this freedom should be grounded in the promise of God. In regards to the estates and classical education, this freedom displays itself in worship of God, in the educating of family, and in service to society.

Moving Forward: What Can be Learned from this Analysis

Whether from a Lutheran, Reformed, or other expression of Protestant Christianity, a concern for education and pedagogy has always been inherently tied to its structure. John Witte writes:

> The Protestant reformers early preoccupation with pedagogical reform was driven by both theological and practical concerns. The new evangelical theology assumed at least a minimal level of education in the community. The doctrines of *sola Scriptura* and lay participation in the vernacular liturgy assumed literacy and popular facility with Bibles, catechisms, and liturgical documents. The doctrines of the priesthood of all believers and the calling of all persons to a God-given vocation depended on the

---

[53] Fant, *The Liberal Arts: A Student's Guide*, 96.
[54] Bayer, *Freedom in Response*, 1.
[55] Ibid., 11.

> ready access of everyone to the educational program that suited their particular calling and character. The doctrine of the civil, theological, and educational uses of the law in the earthly kingdom presumed widespread understanding of both the moral laws of conscience and the civil laws of the state. Germany's traditional pedagogical beliefs and structures, the reformers believed, could not readily accommodate this new theology. Moreover, swift educational reform was critical to resolving some of the most pressing practical problems to beset the Lutheran Reformation in its early years. Evangelical church leaders desperately needed right-minded pastors and teachers to staff the new evangelical churches and charities. . . . Questions of education, therefore, demanded the reformers' immediate attention.[56]

Witte is able to draw out the importance that education, and particularly putting structures in place by which education could be practiced, played in the Reformation. Although Witte's focus is upon Germany, any place in which an evangelical change is taking place that focuses upon Scripture and a clergy and laity that is theologically knowledgeable will need to understand what role education will play in that movement. The need for Christians concerned about education did not stop with the Reformation. The desire for congregants who are knowledgeable has continued to influence educational reforms. Witte also rightly points out that the leaders of a movement need to be aware of needs for effective change to take place. Awareness of the need for change is what has sparked many today to opt for classical education.

Both the Lutheran and Reformed expressions of classical education have much to offer in regards to pedagogy in the twenty first century. In particular, Lutheran education already has a strong tradition of classical education as well as looking into one's own tradition for guidance in the present. Most critically thinking expressions of Christianity would prefer to have a laity that possesses some form of education, but the Lutheran expression has proven itself capable of fulfilling this educational task. The tie to an ecclesial structure is also an important strength of Lutheran education. Spiritual development that is taking place within the structure of a school is able to converge over to the church. This is perhaps one benefit of having a Lutheran school in a Church building in that students have some sense that the knowledge they are receiving in the school is related to that of the church. Korcok writes:

> I would contend that the melding of the liberal arts, particularly the lower three arts of the trivium, with an Evangelical catechetical program results in a pedagogical model that not only addresses the concerns of liberal education but goes beyond what the liberal education aspires to accomplish. Liberal education's chief concern is with liberating the mind. The Evangelical liberal arts pedagogy is concerned with the cultivation of the free man—the one who has been set spiritually free in Christ. It seeks to prepare citizens for faithful service in the spiritual and earthly realm, but a

---

[56] John Witte, "The Civic Seminary: Sources of Modern Public Education in the Lutheran Reformation of Germany," *Journal of Law and Religion* 12:1 (1995): 177.

happy side effect is that it also produces that which liberal education strives for: creative minds that are capable of critically examining the world in which they live.[57]

The advocacy for which Korcok pushes is a liberal arts program with an, "Evangelical catechetical program." In this manner liberal arts teaching is melded with Christian belief. Korcok also has continuity with the past: Luther makes it clear in "To the Councilmen" that his form of education will produce good citizens for society. Evangelical liberals arts has the goal in mind to produce followers of Jesus who are able to understand and act upon their role in God's world.

As has been elaborated, the topic of vocation also adds much value to Lutheran education. The Reformed vision is able to conceive of vocation in the sense that God has ordained human to certain tasks in life, but the Lutheran conception of vocation adds much more in terms of the mere living of life as a practical application of *ecclesia*. In worship and service to God one fulfills the calling given to him or her by God. This idea of vocation must be tempered with the opportunities that education can afford.

As has been discussed throughout, the Reformed tradition also has several important emphases in its work as well. In particular, there are several expressions of Bavinck's that could shed new light on the Reformed practice of classical education. Reformed theology has long been in the practice of apologetics. One distinct aspect that Bavinck adds to his theology and his pedagogy is his ability to take a historical view of his work. Bavinck places himself in the stream of theological practice, taking a broad picture of where he has been placed. Bavinck tries to take a very practical stance in his pedagogy. Common grace and an emphasis upon finding and acknowledging God's working in the world can lead to a Reformed Christianity that is able to actively and intelligently engage its culture.

The Lutheran and Reformed expressions of theological pedagogy have distinct gifts given by God that can further the manner in which it is used in contemporary pedagogy. The Lutheran tradition has a stronger historical connection to classical education in that Luther himself argued for its continuing establishment, but both traditions have at some point intersected with classical education. Another obvious value of a Lutheran or Reformed education is the moral grounding that is able to provide to its students. Bavinck saw this as one prominent reason why an education apart from any theological grounding would not function as it should. Luther made his case explicit. His focus upon the learning of biblical languages was in order that people would be

---

[57] Korcok, *Lutheran Education*, 267.

able to read their Bibles, and hence to know the God of the Scriptures who has called humans to moral mandates.

If one wishes to ground pedagogy in tradition, one of the benefits of the liberal arts tradition is its ability to conform to a variety of historical and cultural contexts. For instance, in their book *Teaching the Trivium*,[58] Harvey and Laurie Bluedorn argue specifically for a liberal arts education to be conducted within the context of the home. In some sense this is the return of Luther's ideal of education returning primarily to the *oeconomia*. As demonstrated by the Bluedorns throughout this extensive book, classical education is something that can (and in their opinion should) be practiced in the home. On the other hand, Christian schools continue to sprout throughout the North America that appreciate the academic rigor combined with the Christian heritage that is found in the classical tradition.

Related to the concept of education as a means of moral formation, both the Lutheran and Reformed streams emphasize a God-centered, theologically driven approach to education. This is foundational for perceiving why the task of education is important. Christian education offers a unique option in a crowded landscape of thought. For the Dutch Reformed, education is done to the glory of God, and for the Lutheran education is practiced in response to God in the freedom given through the cross.

It is important to point out that as Lutheran and other denominational expressions of classical education share much in common, they should attempt to rally around this point of commonality. On a secondary level, this point of commonality is the value classical education can offer to a pedagogical structure that focuses more upon cost benefit analysis and preparing students for ends that will make the most money rather than providing students with an education that will give them the freedom to God-given tasks. Reformed and Lutheran expressions can hold this in common. Contemporary higher education often focuses on career preparation without providing tools by which to evaluate the particular profession in which one is engaged, or to prepare one to be a flourishing human being. This drifting also affects educators who have been given no tools by which to evaluate why education is a social good.[59] When Christians share such a common goal it will prove beneficial for them to share ideas and work toward promoting what they believe to be a good thing. At the same time, the primary goal of Christian classical education should be in aiding young men and women in conforming to Christ. Promoters of Christian

---

[58] Harvey and Laurie Bluedorn. *Teaching the Trivium: Christian Homeschooling in a Classical Style* (Muscatine, Iowa: Trivium Pursuit, 2001).

[59] Harran, "The Contemporary Applicability of Luther's Pedagogy: Education and Vocation," 328.

Conclusion: Luther, Bavinck and Liberal Arts in Practice

classical education should have this as a primary end that can be supplemented by their thoughts on classical education.

Neither of these two traditions think that a liberal arts education is the final word on how education should be practiced, but classical education practitioners in both camps believe that it is perhaps the best solution currently available in Western education, and this conclusion has demonstrated how both have valuable material to offer pedagogical practice.

Performing a comparison between these two lines of theological inquiry also highlights how the classical education tradition could be adaptable for a variety of contexts. Luther began with a theological framework based around learning and applying the Bible, and from that foundation worked towards forming a liberal arts education. Bavinck began with a thoroughly Reformed worldview, and viewed pedagogical practice, and for that matter a classical education pedagogical practice as one ethical application of his theology. This comparison of Luther and Bavinck also represents that a discussion surrounding education should occur in one's theological tradition. Modern day practitioners of this style of pedagogy are heirs of a rich tradition of liberal arts education. As has been discovered through this line of inquiry, a return to sources such as Luther and Bavinck, as well as a realization of what is particular to one's tradition can make one better equipped to form a viable classical pedagogy for the present day. At their root, both Reformed and Lutheran classical education have a theological, Christocentric foundation driving what is being done. As long as this continues, the practice of classical education within a theological construct can be a fruitful activity. Ultimately, in the practice of classical education it should be Christ and the gospel that are made precedent, for "it is the Gospel, not the liberal arts, that restores a person to full humanity."[60]

---

[60] Korcok, *Lutheran Education*, 253.

References

Abbott, T. K. *Ephesians and Colossians*. The International Critical Commentary. Edinburgh: T&T Clark, 1897.

Abelson, Paul. *The Seven Liberal Arts, A Study in Medieval Culture*. New York: Russell & Russell, 1965.

Allen George. *Higher Education in the Making: Pragmatism, Whitehead, and the Canon*. Albany: State University of New York, 2004.

Allen, R. Michael. *Reformed Theology*. London: T&T Clark, 2010.

Althaus, Paul. *Die Theologie Martin Luthers*. Gutersloh: Gutersloher Verlagshaus Gerd Mohn, 1963.

———. *The Theology of Martin Luther*. Translated by Robert Schultz. Philadelphia: Fortress Press, 1966.

———. *The Ethics of Martin Luther*. Translated by Robert C. Schultz. Philadelphia: Fortress Press, 1972.

Aristotle. *APISTOTEDOUS TA PODITIKA: The Politics of Aristotle*. 2nd ed. English Notes by Richard Cosgrove. London: Longams, Green, and Co., 1874.

———. *Politicorvm Libri Octo*. Edited by Francis Susemihl. Lipsiae: In Aedibus B.G. Tevbneri, 1872.

———. *The Politics*. Edited by Stephen Everson. Cambridge: Cambridge University Press, 1988.

———. *The Politics of Aristotle*. Edited by Ernest Baker. Oxford: Clarendon Press, 1946.

———. *The Politics of Aristotle*. Edited by J.E.C. Welldon. London: MacMillan, 1901.

Augustine. *City of God*. Vol. 2 of The Nicene and Post-Nicene Fathers. Edited by Philip Schaff. Grand Rapids: Eerdmans, 1977.

Bacote, Vincent. *The Spirit in Public Theology: Appropriating the Legacy of Abraham Kuyper*. Grand Rapids: Baker Academic, 2005.

Ballor, Jordan J. "Christ in Creation: Bonhoeffer's Orders of Preservation and Natural Theology." *The Journal of Religion* 86:1 (January 2006): 1–22.

Barnes, Timothy David. *Tertullian: A Historical and Literary Study*. Oxford: Clarendon Press, 1971.

Barker, Ernest. *The Political Thought of Plato and Aristotle*. London: G. P. Putnam's Sons, 1906.

Barnes, Jonathan, ed. *The Cambridge Companion to Aristotle*. Cambridge: Cambridge University Press, 1995.

Balz, Horst and Gerhard Schneider, eds. Vol. 1 of *Exegetical Dictionary of the New Testament*. Edinburgh: T & T Clark, 2006.

Barber, Melanie, Stephen Taylor, and Gabriel Sewell, eds. *From the Reformation to the Permissive Society: A Miscellany in Celebration of the 400th Anniversary of Lambeth Palace Library*. Woodbridge: Boydell and Brewer Press, 2010.

Barth, Markus. *Ephesians 1–3*. The Anchor Bible. Garden City: Doubleday & Company, 1974.

Barthomelew, Craig. *Living at the Crossroads: An Introduction to Christian Worldview*. Grand Rapids: Baker Academic, 2008.

Bavinck, Herman. "Calvin and Common Grace." *Princeton Theological Review* (1909): 437–465.

———. "Classical Education. In *Essays on Religion, Science and Society*. Edited by John Bolt. Translated by Harry Boonstra and Gerrit Sheeres, 209–244. Grand Rapids: Eerdmans, 2008.

———. *De Nieuwe Opvoeding*. Kampen: Kok, 1917.

———. *De Povoeding der Rijpere Jeugd*. Kampen: Kok, 1916.

———. *The Doctrine of God*. Edinburgh: The Banner of Truth Trust, 1979.

———. *Handleiding bij het Onderwijs in den Christelijken Godsdienst*. Kampen: Kok, 1932.

———. *In the Beginning: Foundations of Creation Theology*. Edited by John Bolt. Translated by John Vriend. Grand Rapids: Baker Books, 1999.

———. Klassieke opvoeding, I, II." *Stemmen des Tijds*. 7:1 (1918): 46–65, 113–147.

———. *Our Reasonable Faith*. Grand Rapids: Eerdmans, 1956.

———. *Paedagogische Beginselen*. Kampen: Kok, 1904.

———. *The Philosophy of Revelation: The Stone Lectures for 1908–1909, Princeton Theological Seminary*. London: Longmans, Green and Co., 1909.

———. *Reformed Dogmatics: Vol. 1: Prolegomena*. Edited by John Bolt. Translated by John Vriend. Grand Rapids: Baker, 2003.

———. *Reformed Dogmatics: Vol. 2: God and Creation.* Edited by John Bolt. Translated by John Vriend. Grand Rapids: Baker, 2004.

———. *Reformed Dogmatics: Vol. 3: Sin and Salvation in Christ.* Edited by John Bolt. Translated by John Vriend. Grand Rapids: Baker, 2006.

———. *Reformed Dogmatics: Vol. 4: Holy Spirit, Church, and New Creation.* Edited by John Bolt. Translated by John Vriend. Grand Rapids: Baker, 2008.

———. "Trends in Pedagogy. In *Essays on Religion, Science and Society.* Edited by John Bolt. Translated by Harry Boonstra and Gerrit Sheeres, 205–208. Grand Rapids: Eerdmans, 2008.

Bayer, Oswald. *Freedom in Response. Oxford Studies in Theological Ethics.* Oxford: Oxford University Press, 2007.

———. *Martin Luther's Theology.* Translated by Thomas H. Trapp. Cambridge: Eerdmans, 2008.

Baylor, Michael G. *Action and Person: Conscience in Late Scholasticism and the Young Luther.* Vol. 20 of Studies in Medieval and Reformation Thought. Leiden: Brill, 1977.

Beach, J. Mark. "Abraham Kuyper, Herman Bavinck, and 'The Conclusions of Utrecht 1905.'" *Mid-American Journal of Theology* 19 (2008): 11–68.

Benne, Robert. *Reasonable Ethics: A Christian Approach to Social, Economic, and Political Concerns.* Saint Louis: Concordia Publishing House, 2005.

Berkhof, Hendrikus. "God as Creator and the World as Createdness." *Major Themes in the Reformed Tradition.* ed. Donald K. McKim, 79–86. Grand Rapids: Eerdmans, 1992.

Blei, Karel. *The Netherlands Reformed Church 1571–2005.* Grand Rapids: Eerdmans, 2006.

Blomberg, Craig. *Matthew.* Vol. 22 of New American Commentary. Nashville: Broadman Press, 1992.

Bluedorn, Harvey and Lauri Bluedorn. *Teaching the Trivium: Christian Homeschooling in a Classical Style.* Mucatine, Iowa: Trivium Pursuit, 2001.

Boehmer, Heinrich. *Luther and the Reformation.* Translated by E.S.G. Potter. London: G. Bell and Sons, Ltd., 1930.

Bolt, John. *A Free Church, A Holy Nation: Abraham Kuyper's Public Theology.* Grand Rapids: Eerdmans, 2001.

———. "Grand Rapids Between Kampen and Amsterdam: Herman Bavinck's Reception and Influence in North America." *Calvin Theological Journal* 38:2 (November 2003): 263–280.

———. "Herman Bavinck Speaks English: A Bibliographic Essay." *Mid-American Journal of Theology* 19 (2008): 117–126.

———. "The Imitation of Christ Theme in the Cultural-Ethical Ideal of Herman Bavinck." PhD Diss., University of St. Michael's College, 1982.

Bonhoeffer, Dietrich. *Creation and Fall: A Theological Exposition of Genesis 1–3*, Dietrich Vol. 3 of Bonhoeffer Works. Minneapolis: Fortress Press, 1997.

———. *Discipleship*. Minneapolis: Fortress Press, 2003.

Bornkamm, Heinrich. *Luther in Mid-Career 1521–1530*. Edited by Karin Bornkamm. Translated by E. Theodore Bachmann. London: Darton & Todd, 1983.

Bowen, James. *A History of Western Education*. Vol. 1. London: Methuen & Co., 1972.

———. *A History of Western Education*. Vol. 2. London: Methuen & Co., 1975.

———. *A History of Western Education*. Vol. 3. London: Methuen & Co., 1981.

Braaten, Carl E. *Principles of Lutheran Theology*. 2nd ed. Minneapolis: Fortress Press, 2007.

———. *That All May Believe: A Theology of the Gospel and the Mission of the Church*. Grand Rapids: Eerdmans, 2008.

Bratt, James. "Introduction: Abraham Kuyper and His Work." In *Abraham Kuyper: A Centennial Reader*. Edited by James D. Bratt, 1–18. Grand Rapids: Eerdmans, 1998.

Brederveld, J. *Christian Education: A Summary of Bavinck's Pedagogical Principles*. Translated by Two Members of the Calvin College Faculty. Grand Rapids: Smitter Book Company, 1928.

———. *Hoofdlijnen der Paedagogiek van Dr. Herman Bavinck, met Critische Beschouwing*. Amsterdam: De Standaard, 1927.

Bristley, Eric D. *Guide to the Writings of Herman Bavinck*. Grand Rapids: Reformation Heritage Books, 2008.

Brock, Brian. "On Generating Categories in Theological Ethics: Barth, Genesis and the *Standelehre*." *Tyndale Bulletin* 60:1 (2010): 45–67.

References

———. "Why the Estates? Han's Ulrich's Recovery of an Unpopular Notion." *Studies in Theological Ethics* 20:2 (2007): 179–202.

Brown, Colin, ed. *The New International Dictionary of New Testament Theology.* Vol. 1. Exeter: Paternoster, 1975.

Cahill, Lisa Sowle. "Creation and Ethics." In *The Oxford Handbook of Theological Ethics.* Edited by Gilbert Meilaender and William Werpehowski, 7–24. Oxford: Oxford University Press, 2005.

Calvin, Jean. *Institutes of the Christian Religion.* The Library of Christian Classics. Edited by John T. McNeill. Translated by Ford Lewis Battles. Philadelphia: Westminster Press, 1960.

Carlson, Edgar M. "Luther's Conception of Government." *Church History* 15:4 (1946): 257–270.

Carlson, Robert G. "English and the Liberal Arts Tradition in the High School," *The English Journal* 44:6 (September 1955): 323–329.

Clement of Alexandria. *Stromateis: Books One to Three.* Translated by John Ferguson. Washington, D.C.: The Catholic University of American Press, 1991.

The Consortium for Classical and Lutheran Education. "Marks of a Lutheran and Classical School (CCLE Position Statement)," *The Classical Education Quarterly* 1:2 (June 2007): 10–11.

Corbeill, Anthony. "Education in the Roman Republic: Creating Traditions." *Education in Greek and Roman Antiquity.* Edited by Yun Lee Too, 261–287. Leiden: Brill, 2001.

Dakin, A. *Calvinism.* London: Duckworth, 1949.

Dante. *The Divine Comedy Part II: Purgatory.* Translated by Dorothy Sayers. London: Penguin Classics, 1955.

———. *The Divine Comedy Part III: Paradise.* Translated by Dorothy Sayers. London: Penguin Classics, 1955.

Dewey, John. *The Collected Works of John Dewey.* Edited by Jo Ann Boydston. Carbondale: Southern Illinois University Press, 1967–1990.

———. *John Dewey on Education: Selected Writings.* Edited by Reginald D. Archambault. New York: The Modern Library, 1964.

———. *Selected Educational Writings.* Edited by F. W. Garforth. London: Heinemann, 1966.

De Wit, Willem. *On the Way to the Living God: A Cathartic Reading of Herman Bavinck and An Invitation to Overcome the Plausibility Crisis of Christianity.* Amsterdam: VU Press, 2011.

Didley, Will. *Understanding German Idealism*. Stocksfield: Acumen, 2008.

Dunn, James D. G. *The Epistles to Colossians and to Philemon*. The International Greek Text Commentary. Carlisle: Paternoster, 1996.

Ebeling, Gerhard. *Luther: An Introduction to His Thought*. Translated by R.A. Wilson. London: William Collins & Sons, 1970.

Eglinton, James. "Bavinck's Organic Motif: Questions Seeking Answers." *Calvin Theological Journal* 45:1 (2010): 51–71.

———. *Trinity and Organism: Towards a New Reading of Herman Bavinck's Organic Motif*. London: T&T Clark, 2012.

Eucken, Rudolf. *Die Geistesgeschichtliche Bedeutung der Bibel*. Leipzig: Kroner, 1917.

Fant, Gene C. Jr. *The Liberal Arts: A Student Guide*. Reclaiming the Christian Intellectual Tradition. Wheaton: Crossway, 2012.

Farley, Benjamin Wirt. "Providence of God." In *The Westminster Handbook to Reformed Theology*. Edited by Donald K. McKim, 185–187. Louisville: Westminster John Knox Press, 2001.

———. "The Providence of God in Reformed Perspective." In *Major Themes in the Reformed Tradition*. Edited by Donald K. McKim, 87–93. Grand Rapids: Eerdmans, 1992.

Feil, Ernst. *The Theology of Dietrich Bonhoeffer*. Translated by Martin Rumscheidt. Philadelphia: Fortress Press, 1985.

Findlay, G. G. *Apostles, Romans, and First Corinthians*. The Expositor's Greek Testament. Edited by W. Robertson Nicoll. Grand Rapids: Eerdmans, 1983.

Fine, Gail, ed. *Plato*. Oxford Readings in Philosophy. Oxford: Oxford University Press, 2000.

Forell, George Wolfgang. "Justification and Eschatology in Luther's Thought." *Church History* 38:2 (1969): 164–174.

France, R.T. *The Gospel of Matthew*. New International Commentary on the New Testament. Grand Rapids: Eerdmans, 2007.

Friedrich, Gerhard, ed. *Theological Dictionary of the New Testament*. Translated and edited by Geoffrey W. Bromiley. Vol. 5. Grand Rapids: Eerdmans, 1967.

Gaffin, Richard B. *God's Word in Servant-Form: Abraham Kuyper and Herman Bavinck on the Doctrine of Scripture*. Jackson, MS: Reformed Academic Press, 2008.

Gerstner, John H. *Wrongly Dividing the Word of Truth: A Critique of Dispensationalism.* Orlando: Soli Deo Gloria Ministries, 2000.

Gleason, Ron. *Herman Bavinck: Pastor, Churchman, Statesman, and Theologian.* Phillipsburg: P & R Publishing, 2010.

Goldrick, James E. *God's Renaissance Man: The Life and Work of Abraham Kuyper.* Darlington: Evangelical Press, 2000.

Gritsch, Eric W. "Luther as Bible Translator." In *The Cambridge Companion to Martin Luther.* Edited by Donald K. McKim, 62–72. Cambridge: Cambridge University Press, 2003.

Gryson, Roger, ed. *Biblica Sacra.* Stuttgart: Biblgesellschaft, 1969.

Haas, Guenther. "Creational Ethics is Public Ethics." *Journal for Christian Theological Research* 12 (2007): 1–36.

Hagner, Donald A. *Matthew 14–28.* Vol. 33B of Word Biblical Commentary. Dallas: Word Books, 1995.

Harinck, George. "Herman Bavinck and Gerhard Vos," *Calvin Theological Journal* 45:1 (April 2010): 18–31.

———. "'Something That Must Remain, If the Truth Is to Be Sweet and Precious to Us': The Reformed Spirituality of Herman Bavinck." *Calvin Theological Journal* 38:2 (November 2003): 248–262.

Harran, Marilyn J. "The Contemporary Applicability of Luther's Pedagogy: Education and Vocation," *Concordia Journal* (October 1990): 319–332.

———. *Martin Luther: Learning for Life.* Saint Louis: Concordia Publishing House, 1997.

Harris, Harriet A. *Fundamentalism and Evangelicals.* Oxford: Oxford University Press, 1998.

Hart, H., J. van der Hoeven and Nicholas Wolterstorff. *Rationality in the Calvinian Tradition.* Toronto: University Press of America, 1983.

Hart, Randall. *Increasing Academic Achievement with the Trivium of Classical Education: Its Historical Development, Decline in the Last Century, and Resurgence in Recent Decades.* Lincoln: iUniverse, 2006.

Hawthorne, Gerald F. *Philippians.* Vol. 43 of Word Biblical Commentary. Waco: Word Books, 1983.

Heck, Joel D. and Angus J. L. Menuge, "Learning at the Foot of the Cross," *The Lutheran Witness* (February 2012). http://witness.lcms.org/pages/wPage.asp?ContentID=1208&IssueID=63 [accessed December 7, 2012].

Heckel, Johannes. *A Juristic Disquisition on Law in the Theology of Martin Luther*. Translated and edited by Gottfried G. Krodel. Grand Rapids: Eerdmans, 2010.

Heideman, E. P. *The Relation of Revelation and Reason in E. Brunner and H. Bavinck*. Assen: Van Gorcum, 1959.

Hein, Steven. "Why Classical Education? A Case for Resurrecting the Old Education." *The Classical Quarterly* 1:1 (March 2007): 1–5.

Heslam, Peter S. *Creating a Christian Worldview: Abraham Kuyper's Lectures on Calvinism*. Grand Rapids: William B. Eerdmans Publishing Company, 1998.

Hoekema, A. A. *Herman Bavinck's Doctrine of the Covenant*. ThD diss., Princeton Theological Seminary, 1953.

Hoffman, Patti. "The Where of Education." In *Learning at the Foot of the Cross: A Lutheran Vision for Education*. Edited by Joel D. Heck and Angus J. L. Menuge, 157–168. Austin: Concordia University Press, 2011.

Holm Kristian. "Justification and Reciprocity." In *Word—Gift—Being*. Edited by Bo Kristian Holm and Peter Widmann, 87–116. Tubingen: Mohr Siebeck, 2009.

Holmes, Brian. "The Reflective Man: Dewey." *The Educated Man: Studies in the History of Educational Thought*. Edited by Paul Nash, Andreas M. Kazamias, and Henry J. Perkinson, 305–336. London: John Wiley & Sons, 1965.

Hopfl, Harro, ed. *Luther and Calvin on Secular Authority*. Translated by Harro Hopfl. Cambridge Texts in the History of Political Thought. Cambridge: Cambridge University Press, 1991.

Hsia, Po-Chia. *A Companion to the Reformation World*. Blackwell Companion to the Reformation World. Oxford: Blackwell Publishing, 2004.

Huntsman, Jeffrey, F. "Grammar." In *The Seven Liberal Arts in the Middle Ages*. Edited by David L. Wagner, 58–95. Bloomington: Indiana University Press, 1983.

Jaarsma, Cornelius. *The Educational Philosophy of Herman Bavinck*. Grand Rapids: Eerdmans, 1935.

Jackson, Philip W. "John Dewey." *A Companion to Pragmatism*. Edited by John R. Schook and Joseph Margolis, 54–66. Oxford: Blackwell Publishing, 2006.

Jackson, Roy. *Plato*. Abingdon: Hodder & Stoughton, 2001.

James, William. *Pragmatism in Focus*. Edited by Doris Olin. London: Routledge, 1992.

Johnson, Merwyn, S. "Sin." *The Westminster Handbook to Reformed Theology*. Edited by Donald K. Mckim, 210–211. Louisville: Westminster John Knox Press, 2001.

Joseph, Sister Miriam. *The Trivium: The Liberal Arts of Logic, Grammar and Rhetoric*. Philadelphia: Paul Dry Books, 2002

Kahnis, K. F. A. *Die Lutherische Dogmatik: Historisch Genetisch Dargestellt*. 3 vols. Leipzig: Dorffling & Franke, 1861–1868.

Kallendorf, Craig W. *A Companion to the Classical Tradition*. Oxford: Wiley Blackwell, 2010.

Kittel, Gerhard. *Theological Dictionary of the New Testament*. Vol. 3. Edited by Geoffrey W. Bromiley. Grand Rapids: Eerdmans, 1965.

Kittleson, James M. "Luther the Educational Reformer." *Luther and Learning*. Edited by Marilyn J. Harran, 95–114. London: Associated University Presses, 1985.

Kolb, *Martin Luther: Confessor of the Faith*. Oxford: Oxford University Press, 2009.

Korcok, Thomas. "Forward to the Past: A Study of the Development of the Liberal Arts in the Context of Confessional Lutheran Education with Special Reference to a Contemporary Application of Liberal Education." PhD diss., Free University of Amsterdam, 2009.

———. *Lutheran Education: From Wittenberg to the Future*. Saint Louis: Concordia University Press, 2011.

Kossman, E. H. *The Low Countries, 1780–1840*. Oxford: Claredon, 1978.

Kuyper, Abraham. *Abraham Kuyper's Commentatio (1860) The Young Kuyper about Calvin, a Lasco, and the Church*. 2 vols. Brill Series in Church History. Vol. 24. (Leiden: Brill, 2005).

———. *Calvinism: Six Stone Lectures*. Edinburgh: T&T Clark, 1899.

———. *Encyclopedia of Sacred Theology*. London: Hodder and Stoughton, 1899.

———. *Lectures on Calvinism*. Grand Rapids: Eerdmans, 1943.

———. "Sphere Sovereignty." In *Abraham Kuyper: A Centennial Reader*. Edited by James D. Bratt, 461–490. Grand Rapids: Eerdmans, 1998.

Lampe, G.W.H. *A Patristic Greek Lexicon*. Oxford: Clarendon Press, 1961.

Leith, John. *An Introduction to the Reformed Tradition*. Atlanta: John Knox Press, 1977.

Leff, Michael. "Rhetoric and Dialectic in the Twenty-First Century." *Argumentation* 14 (2000): 241–254.

Lewis, Charlton T. and Charles Short. *A Latin Dictionary*. Oxford: Clarendon Press, 1879.

Lincoln, Andrew T. *Ephesians*. Vol. 42 of Word Biblical Commentary. Dallas: Word Books, 1990.

Littlejohn, Robert and Charles T. Evans. *Wisdom and Eloquence: A Christian Paradigm for Classical Learning*. Wheaton: Crossway, 2006.

Loewenich, Walther von. *Luther's Theology of the Cross*. Translated by Herbert J.A. Bouman. Belfast: Christian Journals Ltd., 1976.

———. *Martin Luther: The Man and His Work*. Translated by W. Denef. Minneapolis: Augsburg Publishing House, 1982.

Luther, Martin. *A Commentary on St. Paul's Epistle to the Galatians*. Edited by Phillip S. Watson. London: T&T Clark, 1953.

———. "Confession Concerning Christ's Supper, 1528." *Luther's Works, Vol. 37: Word and Sacrament III*. Edited by Helmut T. Lehmann, 151–372. Philadelphia: Muhlenberg Press, 1961.

———. "Disputation Against Scholastic Theology." *Luther's Works, Vol. 31: The Career of the Reformer I*. Edited by Helmut T. Lehmann, 3–16. Philadelphia: Muhlenberg Press, 1957.

———. "The Estate of Marriage." *Luther's Works: Volume 45: The Christian in Society II*. Edited by Helmut T. Lehmann. Philadelphia: Muhlenberg Press, 1962.

———. "Exposition of Psalm 127, for the Christians at Riga in Livonia, 1524." *Luther's Works: Volume 45: The Christian in Society II*. Edited by Helmut T. Lehmann. Philadelphia: Muhlenberg Press, 1962.

———. "Lectures on 1 Timothy." *Luther's Works: Vol. 28*. Edited by Hilton C. Oswald, 215-384. Saint Louis: Concordia Publishing House, 1973.

———. "Lectures on Genesis 1–5." *Luther's Works: Vol. 1*. Edited by Jaroslav Pelikan. Saint Louis: Concordia Publishing House, 1958.

———. "Lectures on Genesis 15–20." *Luther's Works: Vol. 3*. Edited by Jaroslav Pelikan. Saint Louis: Concordia Publishing House, 1961.

———. "Lectures on Genesis Chapters 26–30." *Luther's Works: Vol. 5*. Edited by Jaroslav Pelikan. Saint Louis: Concordia Publishing House, 1968.

———. "Lectures on Jonah." *Luther's Works: Vol. 19*. Edited by Hilton C. Oswald, 1–104. Saint Louis: Concordia Publishing House, 1974.

———. "On the Councils and the Church." *Luther's Works: Vol. 41: Church and Ministry III*. Edited by Helmut T. Lehmann, 3–178. Philadelphia: Fortress Press, 1966.

———. "Psalm 111." *Luther's Works: Vol. 13: Selected Psalms II*. Edited by Jaroslav Pelikan, 349–388. Saint Louis: Concordia Publishing House, 1956.

———. "A Sermon on Keeping Children in School." *Luther's Works, Vol. 46: The Christian in Society III*. Edited by Helmut T. Lehmann, 207–258. Philadelphia: Fortress Press, 1967.

———. "Temporal Authority: To What Extent it Should be Obeyed, 1523." *Luther's Works: Volume 45: The Christian in Society II*. Edited by Helmut T. Lehmann. Philadelphia: Muhlenberg Press, 1962.

———. "To the Councilmen of all Cities in Germany that they Establish and Maintain Christian Schools, 1524." *Luther's Works: Volume 45: The Christian in Society II*. Edited by Helmut T. Lehmann. Philadelphia: Muhlenberg Press, 1962.

Maag, Karin. "Education and Literacy." In *The Reformation World*. Edited by Andrew Pettegree, 535–544. London: Routledge, 2000.

Mattson, Brian. *Restored to Our Destiny: Eschatology & the Image of God in Herman Bavinck's Reformed Dogmatics*. Studies in Reformed Theology. Boston: Brill, 2012.

Marius, Richard. *Martin Luther: The Christian between God and Death*. Cambridge, Mass.: The Belknap Press of Harvard University Press, 1999.

McCarter, John. *The Dutch Reformed Church in South Africa*. Edinburgh: T&T Clark, 1869.

McDaniel, Charles and Vance E. Woods. "John Henry Newman and Martin Luther: Balancing Heart and Mind in Higher Education." *Journal of Interdisciplinary Studies* 23:1 (2011): 19–40.

McGowan, A.T.B. *The Divine Authenticity of Scripture: Retrieving an Evangelical Heritage*. Downer's Grove: InterVarsity Press, 2007.

McGrath, Alister. *The Christian Theology Reader*. 3rd ed. Oxford: Blackwell, 2007.

———. *The Intellectual Origins of the European Reformation*. Oxford: Basil Blackwell, 1987.

Mendle, Michael. *Dangerous Positions: Mixed Government, the Estates of the Realm, and the Answer to the xix propositions.* Alabama: University of Alabama Press, 1985.

Menuge, Angus. "Citizens and Disciples." In *Learning at the Foot of the Cross: A Lutheran Vision for Education.* Edited by Joel D. Heck and Angus J. L. Menuge, 51–68. Austin: Concordia University Press, 2011.

Michael, William. "Against the Dorothy Sayers Movement." (January 2011). http://www.classicalliberalarts.com/library/against_sayers.pdf [accessed December 7, 2012].

Mobley, Susan. "Historical Foundations in the Lutheran Reformation." In *Learning at the Foot of the Cross: A Lutheran Vision for Education.* Edited by Joel D. Heck and Angus J. L. Menuge, 3–22. Austin: Concordia University Press, 2011.

Morrison, Karl F. "Incentives for Studying the Liberal Arts." In *The Seven Liberal Arts in the Middle Ages.* Edited by David Wagner, 32–57. Bloomington: Indiana University Press, 1983.

Mulgan, R. G. *Aristotle's Political Theory.* Oxford: Clarendon Press, 1977.

Muller, Richard A. *Dictionary of Latin and Greek Theological Terms.* Grand Rapids: Baker, 1985.

———. *Post-Reformation Reformed Dogmatics.* 2nd ed. Vol. 2. Grand Rapids: Baker Academic, 2003.

Muraoka, T. *A Greek-English Lexicon of the Septuagint.* Leuven: Peeters, 2009.

Murphy, John P. *Pragmatism from Peirce to Davidson.* Boulder: Westview Press, 1990.

Muow, Richard. "Some Reflections on Sphere Sovereignty." In *Religion, Pluralism, and Public Life: Abraham Kuyper's Legacy for the Twenty-First Century.* Edited by Luis E. Lugo, 87–109. Grand Rapids: Eerdmans, 2000.

Niebuhr, Reinhold. *The Nature and Destiny of Man: II Human Destiny* New York: Charles Scribner's Sons, 1941.

Noll, Mark. "The earliest Protestants and the reformation of education." *Westminster Theological Journal* 43:1 (Fall 1980): 97–131.

———. *The Scandal of the Evangelical Mind.* Grand Rapids: Eerdmans, 1994.

Oberman, Heiko A. "Luther and the *Via Moderna*: The Philosophical Backdrop of the Reformation Breakthrough." *Journal of Ecclesiastical History* 54:4 (October 2003): 641–670.

References

Pannenberg, Wolfhart. *Ethics*. Translated by Keith Crim. Philadelphia: The Westminster Press, 1981.

Pappas, Nickolas. *Plato and the Republic*. Routledge Philosophy Guidebook to Plato. London: Routledge, 1995.

Paris, Peter J. "The African and African-American Understanding of Our Common Humanity: A Critique of Abraham Kuyper's Anthropology." In *Religion, Pluralism, and Public Life: Abraham Kuyper's Legacy for the Twenty-First Century*. Edited by Luis E. Lugo, 263–280. Grand Rapids: Eerdmans, 2000.

Plantiga, Cornelius Jr. *Engaging God's World: A Christian Vision of Faith, Learning, and Living*. Grand Rapids: Eerdmans, 2002.

Plato. *Phaedrus*. Translated by Robin Waterfield. Oxford: Oxford University Press, 2002.

———. *The Republic*. Edited by G.R.F. Ferrari. Translated by Tom Griffith. Cambridge Texts in the History of Political Thought. Cambridge: Cambridge University Press, 2000.

Praamsma, L. *Let Christ Be King, Reflections on the Life and Times of Abraham Kuyper*. Ontario: Paideia, 1985.

Price, Timothy Shaun. "Herman Bavinck and Abraham Kuyper on the Subject of Education as Seen in Two Public Addresses." *The Bavinck Review*, 2:1 (2011): 59–70.

Riedel, Volker. "Germany and German-Speaking Europe." In *A Companion to the Classical Tradition*. Edited by Craig W. Kallendorf, 169–191. Oxford: Wiley-Blackwell, 2010.

Reiss, Timothy J. *Knowledge, Discovery and Imagination in Early Modern Europe*. Cambridge Studies in Renaissance Literature and Culture, Vol. 15. Cambridge: Cambridge UP, 1997.

Rodgers, R. E. L. *The Incarnation of the Antithesis*. Edinburgh: Pentland, 1992.

Rombouts, S. *Prof. Dr. H. Bavinck, Gids Bij de Studie van Zijn Paedagogische Werken*. Hertogenbosch –Antwerpen: Malmberg, 1922.

Rosin, Robert. "The Reformation, Humanism, and Education: the Wittenberg Model for Reform." *Concordia Journal* 16:4 (October 1990): 301–318.

Sandnes, Karl Olav. *Challenge of Homer: School, Pagan Poets and Early Christianity*. London: T&T Clark, 2009.

Sayers, Dorothy. *Creed or Chaos*? Bedford, NH: Sophia Institute Press, 1999.

———. *The Man Born to be King*. San Francisco: Ignatius Press, 1990.

———. *The Mind of the Maker*. London: Methuen, 1941.

Schaaf, James L., ed. *Martin Luther: Shaping and Defining the Reformation 1521–1532*. Minneapolis: Fortress Press, 1990.

Schaeffer, Francis. *The Complete Works of Francis Schaeffer: A Christian Worldview*. 5 Vols. Wheaton: Crossway, 1985.

Shea, William M. "John Dewey and the Crisis of Education." *American Journal of Education* 97:3 (May 1989): 289–311.

Simpson, D. P. *Cassell's New Latin Dictionary*. London: Cassell, 1959.

Skillen, James William. "The Development of Calvinistic Political Theory in the Netherlands, with Special Reference to the Thought of Herman Dooyeweerd." PhD diss., Duke University, 1974.

Smith, Leonard S. *Martin Luther's Two Ways of Viewing Life and the Educational Foundation of a Lutheran Ethos*. Eugene, Oregon: Pickwick Publications, 2011.

Spitz, Lewis W. "Luther and Humanism." In *Luther and Learning*. Edited by Marilyn J. Harran, 69–94. London: Associated University Presses, 1983.

———. "Luther's Ecclesiology and His Concept of the Prince as Notbischof." *Church History* 22:2 (June 1953): 113–141.

Splittgerber, Anthony B. "A Research Study: Effects of Classical Education on Achievement in Lutheran Schools." *Classical Lutheran Education Journal* 5 (September 2011): 17–21.

Storkey, Elaine. "Sphere Sovereignty and the Anglo-American Tradition." In *Religion, Pluralism, and Public Life: Abraham Kuyper's Legacy for the Twenty-First Century*. Edited by Luis E. Lugo, 189–204. Grand Rapids: Eerdmans, 2000.

Stump, Eleonore. "Dialectic." In *The Seven Liberal Arts in the Middle Ages*. Edited by David Wagner, 125–146. Bloomington: Indiana University Press, 1983.

Taylor, C. C. W. "Politics." *The Cambridge Companion to Aristotle*. Edited by Jonathan Barnes, 233–258. Cambridge: Cambridge University Press, 1995.

Tertullian, *De Prascriptione Haereticorum Ad Martyras: Ad Scapulam*. Edited by T. Herbert Bindley. Oxford: Clarendon Press, 1893.

Thompson, Mark. *A Sure Ground on Which to Stand: The Relation of Authority and Interpretive Method in Luther's Approach to Scripture*. Carlisle: Paternoster Press, 2004.

Thompson, W.D.J. Cargill. *The Political Thought of Martin Luther*. Sussex: The Harvester Press, 1984.

Torrey, R. A., ed. *The Fundamentals*, 2 vols. Grand Rapids: Baker, 2003.

Vallet, Ronald E. *Stewards of the Gospel: Reforming Theological Education.* Grand Rapids: Eerdmans, 2011.

Van den Belt, Henk. *Authority of Scripture in Reformed Theology: Truth and Trust.* Vol. 17 of Studies in Reformed Theology. Leiden: Brill, 2008.

———. "Herman Bavinck and Benjamin B. Warfield on Apologetics and the *Autopistia* of Scripture." *Calvin Theological Journal.* 45:1 (2010): 32–43.

Van der Kroef, James. "Abraham Kuyper and the Rise of Neo-Calvinism in the Netherlands." Church History 17:4 (December 1943): 316–334.

Van der Zweep, L. *De Paedagogiek van Bavinck.* Kampen: Kok, 1935

Van Klinken, L. *Bavincks Paedagogische Beginselen.* Meppel: Boom, 1937.

Van Til, Kent A. "Abraham Kuyper and Michael Walzer: The Justice of the Spheres." *Calvin Theological Journal* 40:2 (November 2005): 267–289.

VanDrunen, David. "'The Kingship of Christ is Twofold': Natural Law and the Two Kingdoms in the Thought of Herman Bavinck." *Calvin Theological Journal* 45:1 (2010): 165–176.

———. *Natural Law and the Two Kingdoms: A Study in the Development of Reformed Social Thought.* Grand Rapids: Eerdmans, 2010.

Veenhof, Jan. *Revelatie en Inspiratie.* Amsterdam: Buijten & Schipperheign, 1968.

Veith, Gene Edward. *God at Work: Your Christian Vocation in All of Life.* Wheaton: Crossway, 2002.

———. "Vocation in Education: Preparing for Our Callings in the Three Estates." In *Learning at the Foot of the Cross: A Lutheran Vision for Education.* Edited by Joel D. Heck and Angus J. L. Menuge, 97–112. Austin: Concordia University Press, 2011.

Veith, Gene Edward and Andrew Kern. *Classical Education: The Movement Sweeping America.* 2nd ed. Washington, D.C.: Capital Research Center, 2001.

Venema, Cornelius. "Covenant and Election in the Theology of Herman Bavinck." *Mid-America Journal of Theology* 19 (2008): 69–115.

Vincent, Martin R. *Philippians & Philemon.* The International Critical Commentary. Edinburgh: T&T Clark, 1897.

Wagner, David. "The Seven Liberal Arts and Classical Scholarship." In *The Seven Liberal Arts in the Middle Ages*. Edited by David Wagner, 1–31. Bloomington: Indiana University Press, 1983.

Wannenwetsch, Bernd. "Luther's Moral Theology." *The Cambridge Companion to Martin Luther*. Edited by Donald McKim, 120–135. Cambridge: Cambridge University Press, 2003.

Weber, Max. *The Protestant Ethic and the Spirit of Capitalism: and Other Writings*. London: Penguin Classics, 2002.

———. *Political Worship: Ethics for Christian Citizens*. Translated by Margaret Kohl. Oxford Studies in Theological Ethics. Oxford: Oxford University Press, 2004.

Wilson, Douglas. *The Case for Classical Christian Education*. Wheaton: Crossway, 2002.

———. *Recovering the Lost Tools of Learning: An Approach to a Distinctly Christian Education*. Wheaton: Crossway, 1991.

———. *Repairing the Ruins: The Classical and Christian Challenge to Modern Education*. Moscow, ID: Canon Press, 1996.

Witte, John. "The Civic Seminary: Sources of Modern Public Education in the Lutheran Reformation of Germany." *Journal of Law and Religion* 12:1 (1995): 173–223.

Wolters, Albert. "Dutch Neo-Calvinism: Worldview: Philosophy and Rationality." http://www.allofliferedeemed.co.uk/Wolters/AMWNeo_Cal.pdf [Accessed December 7, 2012].

Wolterstorff, Nicholas. "Herman Bavinck—Proto Reformed Epistemologist." *Calvin Theological Journal* 45:1 (2010): 133–146.

Wright, N.T. *Colossians and Philemon*. Tyndale New Testament Commentaries. Leicester: Inter-Varsity Press, 1986.

www.ingramcontent.com/pod-product-compliance
Lightning Source LLC
Chambersburg PA
CBHW061441300426
44114CB00014B/1789